D0677340

THE ENGLISH-SPANISH CONNECTION

Excellence in English for Hispanic Children Through
Spanish Language and Literacy Development

371. 829
T486e

Alverno College
Library Media Center
Milwaukee, Wisconsin

Copyright © 1983 Santillana Publishing Company, Inc.
901 W. Walnut Street, Compton, California 90220

General Manager: Sam Laredo

Design Director: Susan Vander Ploeg
Editorial Coordinator: Teresa Price

All rights reservsed. No part of this book may be reproduced without permission
in writing from the publisher.

ISBN# 0-88272-188-7
FIRST PRINTING 1983
90 91 92 93 94 95 96 97   9 8 7 6 5 4 3 2
Printed and bound in the United States

Acknowledgements

I should like to thank my friends in teaching whose work with Hispanic students is an inspiration to teachers everywhere. From their struggles and successes this book has come.

I am greatly indebted to the scholars and researchers who have validated in rigorous investigations those principles of second language literacy that had previously been only surmised. Among these are beloved and valued colleagues: Jim Cummins, Steve Krashen, Tracy David Terrel, Dorothy Legaretta, and Robert Politzer.

Special thanks also go to Lela Zak for her care and patience in typing the manuscript. Mrs. Zak, a native speaker of Spanish, brought her fluency and biliteracy to a difficult task.

E.W.T.

TABLE OF CONTENTS

Sight Vocabulary
Picture Clues
Configuration Clues
Structural Clues
Root Words
Compound Words
Context Clues
Syllabication
Syllables As Units
Diacritical Marks
Transferability of Word Recognition Skills to English
Sight Vocabulary in English Transfer
Phonics as a Word Recognition Tool in English
Structural Analysis as a Strategy in English Word Recognition
Compound Words in English
Context Clues to Words in English
Syllabication in English
Caveat

CHAPTER IV

Types of Questions
Comprehension Activities in Spanish
The Main Idea
The Details
The Sequence
Inference
Cause and Effect
Other Interpretive Skills
Transferability of Comprehension Skills to Reading in English
Sample Questions
Main Idea Transfer
Finding Details Transfer
Sequence Transfer
Other Comprehension Skill Transfer
Caveat

CHAPTER X

INTRODUCTION

Every Spanish-speaking child who is living and growing in an English-speaking country must develop proficiency in English. Hispanic students must be fluent and literate in English at the highest level of which they may be capable. English is the language of the curriculum; it is the language of the economy; it is the language of social relationships beyond the Hispanic home and neighborhood. Therefore, there is no argument. Excellence in the receptive and expressive skills of English must be the ultimate goal of any educational program designed for Hispanic students. To achieve in the traditional classroom, the students must understand what the teacher is saying and must be able to respond appropriately when called upon. Classroom participation demands that listening comprehension and speaking fluency in English be comparable to that of a native speaker of English assigned to the same grade level. The students must be able to read textbooks, workbooks, study sheets, and examinations. They must write in English to express their thoughts and to demonstrate their knowledge of course content. Throughout their entire lives beyond the school, individuals from Spanish-speaking families will be called upon to speak, read, write, and think using English as the medium of communication. There can be no debate over the need for fluency and literacy in English. Future employment opportunities and personal sense of worth depend upon the acquisition of English language skills which have been developed, not at a minimal, survival level, but rather at the highest level which individual motivation and intelligence may make possible. To be an enlightened citizen in the United States, in England, or in any country where the business of living is carried out in English, the students must expect and must strive for excellence in English. ¡NO CABE DUDA!

To reach the goal of English fluency and literacy, schools have made valiant efforts to offer English language instruction in a variety of ways at many levels of the students' grade placement. The uneven history of second language programs is documented in the literature. English-as-a-second language instruction has been argued from the viewpoint of language theory, methodology, materials, and several other issues. Grammar-based approaches emphasize linguistic forms and expect that after such forms have been acquired they will be used to communicate. Errors must be prevented or corrected so that practice can promote precision and accuracy. Language rules must be studied and internalized, and the teacher is controlling the content ot the language lessons. Communicative-based approaches, on the other hand, stress the creation of situations in which the linguistic forms may emerge. Errors are expected to occur and are not given undue correction. Rules governing language result from the varied opportunities for using language. As the language experiences continue, students and teachers together determine the direction of the lesson. The theorists have tended to support one position or the other, but both groups share the common concern for the development of fluent, literate English speakers. Until recently there was scarce mention of the role of the native language except possibly to caution teachers against its use. Suggestions were made that the students should not speak their own language in the English class or that better second language occurred when first and second languages were learned in separate contexts. Despite differences in theoretical principles, there appeared to be consensus that early introduction to English instruction was the most effective, if not the **only,** road to fluency and literacy in English.

Newer research and carefully formulated hypotheses have resulted in many uncertainties about the abandonment of the children's native language strengths. These studies have raised the question of **early** versus **later** second language learning. The importance of oral language as a requirement for written language has been considered. Language **acquisition** as an entirely different human endeavor than language **learning** has been debated. Such investigations have provided the practitioners in the schools with new knowledge and greater insights into the mysterious realm of children's language, literacy, and thought. The role of the native language as a mediator of meaning and as an instrument of thinking has been examined. The differences between personal language usage and school language usage have been suggested. Educators have been reminded that while the students can readily obtain meaning in social situations where the context offers clues, they may not make much sense of the school situtation which demands more formal, abstract use of language. That linguistic capacity is not specific and dependent upon separate language stimulation, but rather is a global, general capacity independent of specific stimulation has been hypothesized.

From this research,* the central theme of this book has been drawn. There is ample reason to question whether early and exclusive exposure to English is the most effective and efficient route to English for Hispanic students. There is also considerable support for the continued development of the mother tongue, Spanish. The potential for transfer in language, literacy, and thinking skills is astounding when the two speech and print systems are carefully compared. The personal and social benefits of becoming proficient in both languages can scarcely be denied. Given appropriate instruction, patience, and time, Hispanic students can demonstrate strong achievement in subject matter **and** competence in English.

*Schooling and Language Minority Students: A Theoretical Framework. Evaluation, Dissemination and Assessment Center, California State University, Los Angeles, 5151 State University Drive, Los Angeles, CA 90032.

Teachers, like students, bring different perspectives and varied backgrounds to the classrooms. Some teachers who will be working with Spanish-speaking students will have depth of knowledge of the English language and comparable proficiency in the Spanish of their students. At the other extreme, there are teachers who will have excellent language skills in English and very little or no proficiency in Spanish. It is possible, too, that there are teachers who are highly competent in Spanish and who are not so comfortable in English. Some teachers may have studied extensively in English linguistics or in Spanish linguistics or both. For these reasons, among others, it is difficult to write material which will be of interest and value to **all** teachers. Those who are expert in the speech-print correspondences in Spanish may wish to skip that part of the chapter on decoding and move quickly to the transferability of decoding skills to English. A teacher who may not be familiar with the characteristics of the Spanish writing system will need to consider these elements before going on to their transfer in English. This book does not pretend to address fully the many insights from the linguistics of Spanish and of English. Rather, each chapter is an atttempt to suggest practical ways in which classroom teachers can organize reading instruction for Spanish-speaking students to make the most of transfer of learning principles.

Efforts to simplify a complex construct such as the nature of transferability of reading skills from Spanish to English are fraught with theoretical and pragmatic dangers. A book which would include each and every variation of sound, syllable, syntax, vocabulary, and grammatical pattern in both languages would defeat the intent of providing a small, useful reference for classroom teachers. There are omissions of material which may be found in the bibliography for educators whose interests may lead them to more comprehensive comparisons of the English-Spanish connection.

This book has been written for teachers. Its intent is to present in practical terms the implications for teaching that may be derived from the thoughtful and exciting research of the scholars. **The first chapter** describes what may be offered to the Hispanic preliterate children or to the older illiterate students who are at the preparation stage. The contents include concept acquisition, expansion of spoken Spanish, and visual, auditory, and/or kinesthetic skills that must be nurtured at the Spanish pre-reading level. The second part of Chapter One discusses the elements of this developmental stage that are transferable to the reading of English. The new skills and concepts that are specific to English are also presented. The chapter closes with a section of **caveats** for the teacher. These cautions point out the hazards of dual readiness programs in written language.

Chapter Two contains a detailed description of the Spanish writing system. Essentially, the material deals with the decoding skills and suggests how skills may be sequenced. There is a definition of the speech-print connection at the early level. The alphabet, the sounds of the language represented by the letters, the regular and irregular letter-symbol correspondences, the consonant blends, the diphthongs, and the word endings are described. Materials and techniques for classroom activities are suggested. The features of the Spanish writing system that will transfer to English writing are given. Details of the English alphabet, the regular and irregular sound-symbol associations, consonant blends, non-transferable and new learnings are outlined. There are some recommendations concerning criteria for making the transfer into activities in English reading and several words of caution regarding the problems of transfer at this level.

Chapter Three discusses the various techniques and strategies that help students recognize new and unfamiliar words when they are reading Spanish. The use of phonics clues as described in detail in Chapter Two is suggested as one word recognition possibility. Other techniques include the use of word and sentence structures, the obtaining of meaning from context, and the selecting from pictures important clues to recognizing unfamiliar words and text. The system of diacritical marks in Spanish that also provide clues to differentiated meanings is included. Finally, Spanish syllabication, and other transfer possibilities are mentioned. The chapter closes with recommended criteria for expecting word-recognition skills to transfer. There are several **caveats** regarding transfer difficulties.

Chapter Four is an overview on reading comprehension and defines literal and interpretive comprehension. The basic skills of understanding what the author has written include determining the main idea, finding the supportive details, identifying the sequence of events, and making simple inferences. Other necessary comprehension skills are drawing conclusions, recognizing cause and effect relationships, judging relevance, and interpreting the mood or emotional tone of the writing. Suggested classroom materials and methods for promoting these reading skills are given. The second part of this chapter states that these comprehension skills well taught in Spanish are one hundred percent transferable because they are thinking skills. The ability to comprehend what is on a page of print is dependent upon the experiential background of the readers, the extent to which they can decode the written material, and the development of their thinking skills. The emphasis of this chapter is that reading is thinking and that once the students learn to read and to think about what they have read, then the totality of transfer is **general** after the **specific** writing system has been deciphered. Reading is a process that is only learned once.

Chapter Five is a section on helping students develop skill in matching their oral and written forms of Spanish. Such concepts as agreement, formation of plurals, verb inflections, possessives, **apócope**, the pronoun system, punctuation, and capitalization are described. Recommendations for classroom presentations of the relationships between speech and print are offered. The transferability of these learnings to English oral and written language connections is pointed out. Specific transfer of such elements as the formation of plurals, punctuation, and capitalization is given. The non-transfer and the partial transfer problems are also mentioned. The chapter closes with several suggestions for cautious and careful shifts to English while making the most of the speech-print connections that are common to both English and Spanish.

Chapter Six covers the development of a reading vocabulary in Spanish. Homonyms, synonyms, antonyms, inflected forms, derived forms, and subject matter vocabulary are discussed. Materials and recommended techniques are identified. Transfer to English by principle, by Gestalt, by identical elements, and by other applicable transfer of learning principles is described.

Chapter Seven suggests alternatives for organizing a reading program to promote transfer. Grouping activities, order of language learning, pacing instruction, providing practice, and monitoring the progress of students are examined.

Chapter Eight explores the other significant variables, including the qualifications of the teacher or teachers, the time needed for high quality instruction, the criteria for selecting materials, the role of parents, the responsibilities of the administration and community, and the students' interests, motivations, and intelligence.

Chapter Nine is intended to summarize the purpose of the book. This chapter describes the nature of skill transfer and the application of transfer principles in a classroom. The major point concerning transferability is expressed in the need for strength in learnings to be transferred. The dangers or the potential dangers of negative transfer (interference) are summarized. General and specific conditions for teaching for optimum transfer are suggested.

Chapter Ten is an attempt to put everything together for the Hispanic students who move toward the ultimate goal of excellence in English. Such students may have the good fortune to have retained and developed their native Spanish ,which has served them well as a launching pad to success in English. Given these opportunities, Hispanic students are capable of becoming truly bilingual, bicultural, biliterate people. They will have enhanced their personal self-esteem. They will have enriched their own lives and the lives of their families. They will have become any nation's richest resource.

The educational end in view for all Hispanic children and youth in English-speaking milieux must be fluency and literacy in English. There is good evidence to suggest that such second language competency can best be reached through a curriculum with strong Spanish language development, a thoughtful, rigorous program of Spanish literacy, and a careful, sound plan of skill transfer to English.

Eleanor Wall Thonis
Wheatland, California
February, 1983

CHAPTER I

PREPARATION FOR SPANISH PRINT

Every child who enrolls in school expects to learn to read. Under ordinary circumstances, the first reading and writing activities are developed from the written symbol system with which the students are slightly familiar. The writing that they see in their classrooms is similar to the writing they have seen on signs in their neighborhood, at home, or in printed messages on the television set. By school age, children have well established an awareness that written material has a relationship to spoken messages. The assumption that students will read, write, and spell the language that they have heard and can speak is reasonable and logical. Hispanic students in countries where English is the language of instruction, however, may not always have the opportunity of following this rational order. When reading instruction in Spanish is made available to such students, they are fortunate to find represented in **print** the words they have known in **speech**. The preparation period commonly referred to as **El nivel de apresto** is a time when the students will be guided through activities that are essential to learning to read **any** language. The classroom teacher will be extending the background of concepts, training the perceptual skills, providing the spatial orientation, and improving the sensory-motor control. As these lessons are offered, the students will be using Spanish to describe, to label, and to store their knowledge. Much of this information acquired during the readiness period will ultimately be used in reading the second language, English. For this reason, teachers will want to structure the prereading activities carefully and will give the students the time and practice necessary to promote strong skill development. As teachers plan to present the readiness activities in Spanish, they need to appreciate the potential for skill transfer to English.

Concept Acquisition

Although it is well recognized that children begin to acquire simple concepts long before they can express them verbally, the correct naming of a concept is usually considered evidence of its acquisition. Children encounter certain repeated experiences in their environment. They learn to apply a label to that constancy which suggests that other similar experiences may be included in that specific label. Things that are different cannot be included under the same name but must be given a different one. Thus, concepts are formed by the sifting and sorting of experiences and encounters. Young children have very imprecise notions of form, space, time, number, weight, and size. As children mature and have a broader range of experiences, their storehouse of concepts and the words that identify

1

them increase in number and diversity. Early concept formation is highly concrete; later levels of concept formation advance children to an understanding of the use of objects, the materials or substances from which they are made, their color, shape, or size, and/or other attributes held in common. The size of children's listening and speaking vocabularies increases as concepts are given meaningful names. With greater verbal control of the world around them and with improved comprehension of the people, objects, and events in it, children demonstrate clearer pronunciation skills, longer sentence structures, and better grammatical usage. Child development specialists point out that concept formation and language development are difficult to separate from each other, and both of them are difficult to separate from thinking.

Teachers of Hispanic children will want to consider how they may best ensure precision and clarity of concepts. Once the understanding of any particular entity has been established and has been given its proper name in Spanish **all** of the information deposited in the <u>bank of concepts</u> can be made available later when the English labels are learned. The comprehensibility of function, material, size, form, weight, color, or time develops slowly and steadily as examples as well as non-examples of such concepts are presented. Children interacting in a stimulating setting will have many opportunities to acquire concepts. The greater the emphasis on explicit, unambiguous explanations in the Spanish language of the children, the richer the material available for retrieval and use under **any** label. For this reason, new information and ideas should be given both importance and time in the classroom where Spanish is the medium of instruction. Because children have to transform into concepts the words of a speaker or an author, it is absolutely essential that the meanings that are symbolized by the words be made crystal clear.

Some of the important concepts for Hispanic children to acquire during the preparation phase are **los conceptos de forma, de tamaño, de posición, de espacio, de color, de tiempo, y de número.** These basic concepts generally are contained in the readiness materials offered to beginning students. The understanding of size (**tamaño**) is usually limited at this level to small, large, medium-sized. There may be given some opportunity for the children to make simple comparisons of size. Comprehension of size as an attribute of persons, places, and things in these simple learnings can lead to later knowledge of size gradients from **atomic** to **astronomical**. Relativity of size in several categories when developed conceptually has a rich potential for vocabulary growth. Size as a concept can be applied to dimensions of objects, an arrangement of them in order of size, to persons and animals, and to almost anything else in the children's experience. Many different descriptions of size can be learned as these concepts are refined. When Spanish-speaking children learn about **Los Tres Osos** and have developed images of the characters **el oso grande, el oso mediano, y el oso pequeño,** there is no further need for them to change their imagery when they ultimately learn in the English lessons about the big bear, the middle-sized bear, and the little bear.

Stories, pictures, and flannel cut-outs may be used as support for the size concepts as illustrated in the drawing below:

Students may note the sizes of the bears, the plates, the bowls, and the spoons. These concepts may be reinforced through the use of real objects if the teacher wishes to bring such materials to the lesson for a hands-on experience.

Other needed concepts may be developed using the real experiences and objects in the classroom. When it is not practical for children to have first-hand encounters with a reality for the purpose of acquiring specific concepts, they may make discoveries through film, pictures, television, and other media. As students learn to make distinctions in position, form, color, number, and time, they will be adding to their receptive and expressive vocabularies such words as **arriba, abajo, adentro, en medio de; al lado derecho, al lado izquierdo; el triángulo, el círculo, el cuadrado,** and other necessary terms for their daily work. Each spatial, temporal, or number concept can be expanded as fully as the children's capabilities allow. As these concepts grow in clarity and in number, students will be adding new words to describe them.

A few lessons designed to develop concepts and to present the vocabulary that accompanies such development will serve as examples of appropriate preparatory activities. Using large pictures of animals, the teacher can encourage students to give the animals their names, to talk about where the different animals live, what they eat, how they help or hurt man, what the names of their young are, how their bodies are covered, what sounds they make, and any other information that may be of interest and relevance.

Conversations about animals have the potential for developing these concepts:

Conceptos de tamaño
pequeño — grande
largo   — corto

Conceptos de color
blanco
pardo, castaño
negro
gris

Conceptos de los sonidos de los animales
pato   — graznido
vaca   — mugido
burro — rebuzno
gallo — canto del gallo

Conceptos de piel
plumas
pelo

Conceptos de habitaciones (hogares)
cueva
granero
casa
nido
pastura
agua

Conceptos de movimiento
correr
andar
nadar
volar

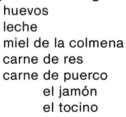

Conceptos de los regalos para los humanos
huevos
leche
miel de la colmena
carne de res
carne de puerco
    el jamón
    el tocino

Perception — Visual and Auditory Awareness

In part, reading is a perceptual process. Readers must make a response to written material that is comprehensible. The students must go beyond the mere sensory act of **seeing** what is on a page of print. The letters, the words, and their arrangement into sentences or paragraphs must stand for something that makes sense to them. The written symbols must evoke something of significance in the minds of the readers. The print on the page is the stimulus; perception is the search for meaning; and comprehension is the response. Perceptions are drawn from the readers' own experiences and are highly personal. Hispanic students have stored their experiences in Spanish labels. Their perceptual searching makes comprehension possible when the written stimulus is also Spanish. Visual and auditory language connections that have been learned or that are in the process of being learned then may be associated with their meaningful referents.

When pre-literate or illiterate Hispanic students are acquiring and refining their perceptual skills, they need opportunities to see and to interact with materials that represent the **real**, authentic writing system. They may have fun and find success in seeing and perceiving pictorially presented dogs, flowers, cats, houses or other objects from their experiences, but perceptual training must move quickly beyond this stage. Speed and accuracy in learning to read will be promoted through responses to the salient features of the Spanish writing system. Students need practice in matching and sorting like and unlike letters, syllables, and words that are different from one another in only minor detail. Teachers must remember that students are not expected to know how to read such material but only to make accurate visual perceptual responses. Specific to the Spanish writing system are the details of the accent mark ´, the tilde ~, and the dieresis ¨ ; the small diacritical marks make large differences in meaning. Besides the diacritical marks, there are many letters and words that may cause confusion because of their position in space or in a line of print. These perceptual problems are **b, d, p, q, u, n, m, w.** Interestingly enough, they are the same troublemakers that confuse children learning to read English. If during the Spanish reading readiness lessons, teachers have given enough practice and attention to these letters, the students will not need to worry about them again.

All students from any language group can improve their visual perceptual abilities by becoming better observers of their immediate environment. Teachers can encourage students to develop greater attention to frequently overlooked or taken for granted everyday details. Suggestions to notice, to count, to observe, and to remember what the students see as they travel to school will create an awareness of larger details that may transfer to the small, fine details of printed material. Games that demand skills in remembering, in matching, and in sorting are useful for additional practice. The key factor in the presentation of lessons that enhance figure-ground discrimination and attention to visual detail is the instruction in Spanish.

To introduce the need for careful observation of visual materials, teachers may at first use incomplete pictures with obvious missing details. These activities are success-oriented for almost all students. They will note with satisfaction the missing sleeves or handles and learn to compare and observe differences immediately. Then they may be advanced to materials that demand greater attention to finer detail — the **n** and **ñ,** the **cl** and **ch,** the shapes of the vowels, and the words written with diacritical marks. The goal of these lessons is accurate visual responses given rapidly. A few examples of visual perceptual lessons follow.

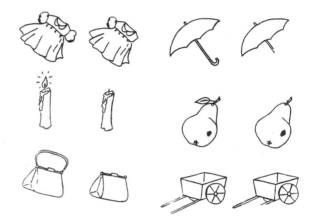

For visual attention.
**Completa las partes que
le faltan.**

For figure-ground practice.
   **¿Dónde están los otros
   cochinitos?**

For matching the shapes and directions of letters.

Rodeen con un círculo la letra que es igual a la letra al lado izquierdo.

a	o	a	e	u
u	u	n	a	e
o	e	u	a	o
e	o	e	a	u
b	b	d	p	q
q	d	p	q	b
f	j	f	l	t
ñ	n	m	ñ	u

For noting likenesses and differences in groups of letters.

Rodeen con un círculo las letras que son iguales a las del lado izquierdo.

ch	cl	ch	cr	ca
ll	lr	fl	ll	tl
ce	co	ce	ca	cu
pr	pe	pu	pr	pa

For recognizing the letters in a variety of environments among other letters.

Rodeen con un círculo las letras parecidas a las que están dentro del cuadro.

Cc cc	cola cara	dedo casa	gato coro
Mm **Mm**	mamá mono	fuma mano	mira dama
Pp **Pp**	pera puro	mayo pita	vaca arpa
Tt **Tt**	toro faro	tinta topo	dado tela
Aa **Aa**	abril arroz	niña avión	misa ala
Ff **Ff**	fama foca	luna foto	fusil faro
Rr **Rr**	niño rama	nada roja	rana rabo

Bb **Bb**	beso burro	buho pavo	nido pita
Dd **Dd**	dedo dice	dulce caldo	dado pedí
Oo **Oo**	ojo oso	asno loco	oro oye

For recognizing the letters in a variety of environments among other letters.

Rodeen con un círculo las letras parecidas a la que está dentro del cuadro.

a	**beso**	**casa**	**beta**	**bola**	**cara**
l	**pastel**	**baúl**	**lira**	**ángel**	**loro**
n	**violín**	**pavón**	**nido**	**balcón**	**volcán**

For matching words.

mamá	mama	mamá
niño	niño	nino
gato	cato	gato
sol	sal	sol
lana	lana	luna
llora	lloro	llora

perro

perro	perla	perro
pero	perro	pedro

gato

gano	gato	gato
gato	garo	toga

tortuga

tortura	tortuga	tortilla
tortuga	tortuga	toronja

conejo

conejo	consejo	conejo
conejo	coneja	corona

11

For matching words and for selecting the word that does not match.

Rodeen con un círculo las palabras que no pertenecen en el grupo.

gato	gato	gato	faro	gato	gato
perro	perro	pedro	perro	perro	perro
tomate	tomate	tomate	tomate	tomate	tomaré
caballo	caballo	cabello	caballo	caballo	caballo

For recognizing the initial letter in the environment* of a word.

Rodeen con un círculo la letra que es igual a la letra inicial en la palabra al lado izquierdo.

toro	t	d	f	p	l
diente	f	t	b	l	d
pared	p	d	b	r	h
oído	a	u	i	o	e
ratón	p	d	r	k	b

*In reading, the word environment is used to indicate that letters look different in and among other letters.

Auditory perception and discrimination are correlates of reading achievement. At the prereading level, activities are generally designed to improve attention and listening skills. Teachers are especially concerned that their students hear fine distinctions among speech sounds because such abilities will enable students to deal successfully later with phonics. Some ear training lessons focus on gross sounds in the environment — horns, bells, lawn mowers, animal noises, and so on. These early efforts are fun and very enjoyable. The refinement of auditory skills that promote reading, however, must be practiced in the material drawn from human speech. For Hispanic children, the task is one of hearing, perceiving, and discriminating among the twenty-five phonemes of their language. They need to be able to recognize them in initial, final, and medial positions in words. They need to develop a sense of rhyming, of how words begin or end with the same sound, and of the alliterative effect of tongue twisters. As children play with these elements orally, they are building the background for the skills needed in written word recognition. As teachers provide opportunities for students to pay attention to the sounds in words, they may wish to organize the lessons for practice in careful listening. Pictures can be an excellent means of helping children hear sounds, note how sounds are made, imitate sounds, match sounds, and group sounds into categories of likenesses and differences. A large picture of something familiar to the students may be presented. The teacher should identify the word that is serving as the model and should use the word in context. The students may listen for the beginning sounds of the stimulus word. They may be encouraged to suggest other words with the same beginning sound from their own experiences. They may then look at other pictorial material and select those pictures that match the beginning sound.

Teachers should first emphasize activities that require their students to find pictures that are **like** the sounds. Later, they may be given activities that ask them to find pictures that are **different** from the given sounds. It is important for teachers to remember that auditory training does not involve the written symbols. For this reason, the pictures can be grouped by sounds, for example, **b**urro, **b**olsa, **b**oca, **v**ela, **v**entana, and the like, represent **one** sound.

Another group can be **s**apo, **s**ol, **z**apato, **s**andía, **c**isne for certain Hispanic speakers.

Another group can be **c**ampana, **c**aballo, **q**ueso, **c**abeza, **q**uitasol.

Another group can be **g**allo, **g**uitarra, **g**allina, **g**anso, **g**ato.

Another group can be **j**inete, **j**abón, **g**elatina, **g**irasol, **j**amón.

Another group can be **ll**ave, **ll**uvia, **h**ielo, **y**arda, **y**ema.

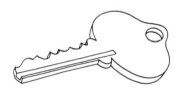

Initial sounds of words may be introduced by pictures and then may be recognized in other words that the students may suggest. These exercises serve several purposes in helping students to listen carefully, to hear the sounds that are the same, and to discriminate among sounds that are not the same. After the students have been successful in these activities, they may listen for distractors, and pictures may be used in the same manner. For example, while listening for the initial sound of **M m** in words, students may be asked to cross out the pictures whose names do not begin with the **M m** sound.

The **Mm** in initial position with distractors.

The initial sound of **Bb, V,v.**

The **Bb, Vv** in initial position with distractors.

The students need to hear and practice the ending sounds and the medial sounds in much the same manner of presentation. Some pictorial examples follow.

Sensory-Motor Skills

Young children in the realm of play outside the school have little reason to be concerned about fine motor skills. Children are well able to run, to swing, to climb, and to engage in other **gross** motor activities. They do not need to worry about the control of small muscle movement, the dexterity of their fingers, the strength of their wrists, or other **fine** motor activities. When seated in the classroom, however, they are expected to perform tasks with pencils, crayons, and scissors. Such demands of sensory-motor control assume that the children will organize their movements in a smooth and coordinated manner. To read and write the students have to track their eyes and hands in the direction consistent with the writing system. Spanish reading requires the readers to move their eyes from left to right to the end of the line and sweep back to continue from left to right again, moving from the top to the bottom of the page. The more automatic and effortless these eye movements are, the easier are the fixations or stops the eye can make to take in the visual stimuli. During the preparation period, young students need to learn how to coordinate the way the dominant eye and the preferred hand move together in this left-to-right direction and to practice following the written material from top to bottom. As they engage in the many activities and use the variety of classroom instruments, they acquire spatial and directional concepts. They also have opportunities to organize themselves and their materials in a manner consistent with the arbitrary conventions of written Spanish. When the teacher describes the lessons or gives specific instructions, the students are adding many essential words to their vocabularies. These expressions are to be used by them over and over again during their entire school experiences. Among the several classroom activities that will provide sensory-motor skill development are the ones that **any** primary teacher in **any** language setting would offer. Such opportunities may include, but are not limited to, tracing and drawing as illustrated in the following examples.

Tracen una línea desde el lado izquierdo hasta el lado derecho.

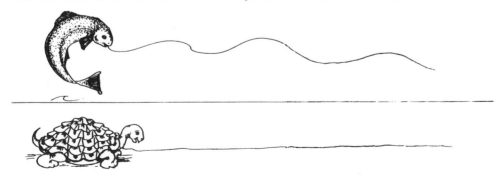

Tracen una línea de la izquierda a la derecha.

Tracen un círculo.   Tracen un cuadrado.   Tracen un triángulo.

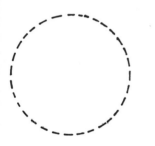 

Tracen los cuadrados, triángulos, y los círculos.

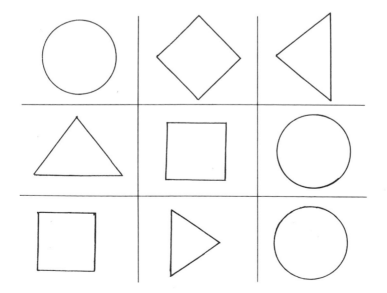

19

Sigan los números.

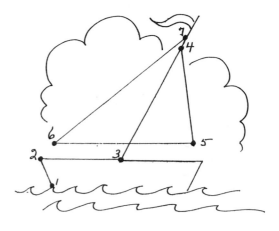

Sigan los números.

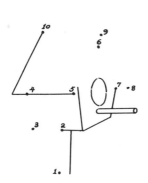

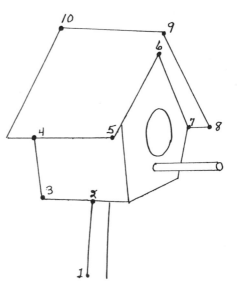

20

Early concepts related to the students' understanding of their own bodies and the variety of actions that human beings can perform are basic to prereading. Most of the students will already have an awareness of the location, function, and names of parts of their bodies. They should, for example, know the terms: **el cuerpo, la cabeza, el pelo, los ojos, la naríz, la boca, los oídos, las manos, los pies, los dedos y los brazos.** They may **not** have some of the other words and concepts that are also important. A few of these include **el cuello, los hombros, el pecho, la cintura, las piernas, las rodillas, el codo, la quijada, la palma, los nudillos.** These concepts may be presented through games such as **Simón dice,** or by incomplete drawings. Actions may also be pantomimed, or pictured while the teacher supplies the necessary vocabulary. When such activities are promoted for the additional purpose of introducing spatial and directional concepts, teachers should be especially careful about the position of the students in relation to the position of the teacher who is demonstrating. Concepts of **el lado izquierdo, el lado derecho, la mano izquierda, la mano derecha, el pie izquierdo, el pie derecho, el ojo izquierdo, el ojo derecho,** are vital to the reading, writing, and spelling lessons that follow after **el nivel apresto.** Students will have to follow many instructions regarding the placement of the material on this page — on the left side or on the right, at the top or at the bottom. Practice with these concepts and vocabulary gives them the understanding and the language to follow directions and to get themselves organized. They are then much better equipped to accommodate the arbitrary directionality of the Spanish writing system.

The students can really become involved in many of the actions that can be named as they are performed. Students may demonstrate the act of **sentarse, estar en pie, barrer, chapotear, ooser, cooinar, bailar, dibujar, trazar, andar, callarse, jugar, comer, and** any other movements that students and teacher can create. For example, they may perform the action and have others guess; they may have imitations of actions; they may play games or use pictures to add to the experiences and the language that describes them.

barrer

chapotear

lavarse

lavar

dar el azucar

jugar

22

ORAL SPANISH

Spanish-speaking students who are not reading in their own language may be described as follows:

- young pupils at the pre-literate stage of their development
- older students who are illiterate
- students struggling for literacy in a language that is insufficiently developed

Although the activities may differ for these three groups of students in terms of content and interest level, the materials must offer opportunities for practice in the same skills. At the pre-reading level, all students may benefit from extended oral language to increase their listening and speaking vocabularies. Memory skills may be enhanced through the presentation of authentic materials that represent the auditory patterns of Spanish. When students are ready to read Spanish, the knowledge and understanding of the world around them, which they bring to reading, will predict to a great extent their success in understanding what reading is all about. For this reason, students should hear and understand the Spanish language in a variety of activities.

Students from Hispanic homes are accustomed to hearing the sounds and melodies of their native language. Like the students of any language in any country, the home language may only approximate the speech patterns of the teacher in a classroom. Children of school age have the basic control of sounds and structures of their language, but they continue throughout their lifetimes to acquire additional vocabulary and richer meanings for language. Classroom teachers are engaged in the important business of helping their students improve diction and grammar. They work diligently to extend the background of concepts and the words, which may then become available to explain, store, and retrieve concepts. Children are naturally curious about their environment and enjoy talking. They may not be such good listeners because listening demands certain behaviors that young and not-so-young children find it difficult to sustain. The teacher must encourage good listening habits early through the provision of such lessons as will be engaging and stimulating. Storytelling, poetry, tongue twisters, rhymes, jingles, riddles, discussions, pictures, films, and real objects offer opportunities for active listening. Though the students' Spanish may differ somewhat from the teacher's Spanish, because regional and geographical influences contribute to the flavor of these variations, it seems prudent to suggest that classroom teachers make an effort to follow the sound system and the lexical system most familiar to the students. The situation is in reality no different from the children in classrooms in Mississippi trying to listen to a teacher from Massachusetts; or a group of students in New York listening to the language of a teacher from Birmingham, England. Though in both instances the teacher speaks English, the students will have to listen carefully to what is said. When children from Puerto Rico hear Spanish as spoken in Argentina or in Cuba, there may be both vocabulary items and pronunciations with which they may be unfamiliar. There has been considerable debate over this issue of differences among the Hispanic speakers. It is quite likely that the arguments will continue and that there will be little agreement over whose phonology, or which vocabulary, is **the** correct or **the** approved one to teach. For the purposes of classroom teachers, however, the best principle to guide practice is one that accepts the students' language as the starting point, and brings them along sensitively to a reasonable standard. Oral expression is highly personal, and criteria for quality speech production are idiosyncratic. Songs have been written about tomato (tomayto), versus tomato (tomahto) and either (eether) versus either (aiyther). Should secretary receive a stress on the third syllable as in American English, or should the third syllable be swallowed up as in the English of Great Britain? The classroom teacher should be aware of the major sound differences and the important lexical variations, but such concerns should not in any way prevent the teacher from going ahead with oral language development in Spanish that is reasonably familiar to the students. A classroom that is attractive and enticing and a teacher who is excited about the wonder of language will elicit the important ingredient of enthusiasm for language among the students.

An effective vehicle for improving oral language skills is storytelling. Every day at every grade level, teachers can bring the delight of words through the magic of stories. Younger students will especially enjoy the traditional offerings from the universal literature of childhood. Among the many stories in children's collections are **La Semilla Prodigiosa, Blanca Nieves y Rojaflor, El Enano Saltarin, Los Músicos Viajeros, La Mesa, El Asno y El Palo, El Zapatero y Los Duendes, Los Ratoncillos Traviesos, Los Cuatro Sirvientes, La Bella Durmiente del Bosque, Caperucita Roja, Blanca Nieves y Los Siete Enanos, El Soldadito de Plomo, El Sastrecillo Valiente, El Flautista de Hamelín, Alí Babá y Los Cuarenta Ladrones, Aladino y La Lámpara Maravillosa, Pulgarcito,** and **La Cenicienta.** Older students will enjoy the myths, legends, and adventures of **Los Mayas, Aztecas, Incas, Los Tres Mosqueteros, Don Quijote, Martin Fierro, Mujercitas,** and **Viajes de Gulliver.** The libraries and resource centers of schools and communities where Hispanic groups live should be fruitful sources of stories that may be read or told for students at many levels of interest. The histories of famous men and women who are honored in Hispanic countries can be offered in the original form or edited to suit the interest spans of students. Stories are a never-ending source of language development. The teacher may use them as means for developing concepts, for increasing vocabulary, for improving memory, for creating an awareness of sequence and order, for bringing relationships into focus, for making contrasts and comparisons, and for encouraging thinking skills.

One of the questions that often arises is the modern Spanish-speaker's lack of familiarity with more formal language or literary forms that may be found in many of the traditional materials. Teachers may best work through this small stumbling block by introducing such words that may be in a story as **new** vocabulary and by telling the students about whatever part of the Hispanic world the words came from or whatever time period they emerged. Students may find expressions such as **en vos** and recognize the meaning **en ti.** This form represents in Spanish the familiar singular form of the pronoun of address as a survival from older Spanish. **Vuestro, vuestra,** forms used by a subject addressing a sovereign or by persons saying their prayers, are likely to be new words in Spanish for many students. Older forms of address in English — thee, thou, ye — have to be taught to English-speaking students who meet them in English literature for the first time. Vocabulary items that are preferred in different Hispanic settings can be discussed and presented. Mexican children use **elote** for the **maíz** of other places. Sometimes, they even spell it **helote!** There are several words for the kite that children enjoy — **cometa, papalote, chiringa.** The choice can be elicited from the students when a picture or the real object is presented as the stimulus. While Argentinian and Uruguayan students may be familiar with the word **ñandú,** other children from Hispanic countries may know the word **avestruz.** The important information that they both must possess is that the label refers to that particular bird. English-speaking children may call this bird the **ostrich.** If students have no concept of the characteristics of this member of the bird category, then the label by which the bird is called will not evoke meaning. Students grow in language as they acquire concepts, and concepts accrue as a result of encounters with specific environments. Rural children know a lot of words that urban children do not know. The vocabulary of the city streets is vastly different from that of the seashore, the country, or the mountains. Children in every setting learn to name the objects, people, and events with which they have had personal or vicarious contact.

Oral language can be stimulated through pictures of interest to children. Pictures of people, places, animals, events, and actions may serve as sources of information and discussion. Attractive pictures from popular magazines are effective for this purpose. The teacher may collect and mount pictures on sturdy paper or tagboard. Pictures may be filed according to the various categories. Then, they are available to illustrate a concept or to use for classroom practice in language. Drawings taken from old workbooks and other discarded material can be used not only for conversational purposes but also for sensory-motor practice in tracing or coloring. Many commercial materials are available to stimulate students' talking and listening skills. These study prints are generally accompanied by valuable teachers' guides that offer strategies for questioning and eliciting language from the students. Teachers should be certain that their discussions lead the students to more than factual responses. They need to encourage imagination, creativity, and divergent thinking through various questions that have no specific correct response.

Real objects may be used in a similar manner to interest students in talking. Coins, rocks, shells, leaves, and other common objects in the environment can be passed around the classroom for a good, close look. Students may talk about their size, shape, color, function, and texture. They may discuss where they are found and why they are of interest or use. Often, teachers think that the objects they bring to class have to be unusual or exotic to generate excitement. Though special items will create curiosity, students can also acquire new information and extend their vocabularies by examining the more ordinary objects around them. Teachers will find that luggage receipts, airline ticket jackets, menus, kitchen utensils, lumber scraps, or any number of the commonplace things are useful for language acquisition.

Poetry has enchanted children everywhere. Young children, especially, enjoy the rhythm, rhyme, and melody of words that seem like music to them. They are eager imitators and find it easy to memorize at this age. Teachers will want to build collections of verse from the many authors of **poesia infantil.** They will want to use poetry to develop sensitive listening, to increase vocabularies, to discriminate among sounds, and to extend auditory memory spans. Older students may engage in practice of these same skills using poetry with more relevant content and more sophisticated language. Teachers have a true gold mine in the writing of Hispanic poets. A few examples follow.

LOS RATONES Y EL GATO

Lope de Vega

Juntáronse los ratones
para librarse del gato;
y después de largo rato
de disputas y opiniones
dijeron que acertarían
en ponerle un cascabel
que andando el gato con él
librarse mejor podían.

Salió un ratón barbicano,
colilargo, hociquirromo,
y encrespando el grueso lomo
dijo al senado romano
después de hablar culto un rato:

—¿Quién de todos ha de ser
el que se atreva a poner
ese cascabel al gato?

PIRINEOS

Juan Ramón Jimenez

En la quietud de los valles,
llenos de dulce añoranza,
tiemblan bajo el cielo azul,
las esquilas de las vacas.

Se duerme el sol en la yerba,
y, en la ribera dorada,
sueñan los árboles verdes,
al ir lloroso del agua.

El pastor descansa, mudo,
sobre su larga cayada,
mirando al sol de la tarde
de primavera, y las mansas

vacas van, de prado a prado,
subiendo hacia la montaña,
al sol lejano y dormido
de sus esquilas con lágrimas.

. . . Pastor, toca un aire viejo
y que jumbroso en tu flauta;
llora en estos grandes valles
de languidez y nostalgia;

llora la yerba del suelo,
llora el diamante del agua,
llora el ensueño del alma.

¡Que todo, pastor, se inunde
con el llanto de tu flauta:
al otro lado del monte
están los campos de España!

PRIMAVERA

Lope de Vega

En las mañanitas
del mes de mayo
cantan los ruiseñores,
retumba el campo.
En las mañanitas
como son frescas,
cubren los ruiseñores
las alamedas.

Ríense las fuentes
tirando perlas
a las florecillas
que están más cerca,
Vístense las plantas
de varias sedas,
que sacar colores
poco les cuesta.

Los campos alegran
tapetes varios,
cantan los ruiseñores
retumba el campo.

FRENTE A MI VENTANA

Antonio Machado

Abril florecía
frente a mi ventana.

Entre los jasmines
y las rosas blancas
de un balcón florido
vi a las dos hermanas.

La menor cosía,
la mayor hilaba.

Entre los jasmines
y las rosas blancas,
la más pequeñita,

risueña y dorada
—su aguja en el aire—,
miré a la ventana.

La mayor seguía
silenciosa y pálida,
el huso en su rueca
que el lino enroscaba.

Abril florecía
frente a mi ventana.

QUIERO PREGUNTAR

Quiero preguntar
¿qué palabras dice un animal?

—¿Qué hace el perro?— LADRA.
—¿Que hace el gallo?— CANTA.
—¿Quién BALA?— El cordero.
—¿Quién MUGE?— El ternero.
—¿Quién PIA?— El pollito.
—¿El pájaro?— CANTA.
—¿Y la rana?— CROA.
—¿RELINCHA?— El caballo.
—¿Quién RUGE?— El león.
—¿La serpiente?— SILBA.
—¿Y los cuervos?— GRAZNAN.
—¿Y el burro?— REBUZNA.
—¿Y los toros?— BRAMAN.
—¿Quién habla?— El lorito.

Y, entonces, ¿qué hace
el niño bonito?
¿Hablar?
El niño habla y reza
y a la escuela va.

LOS SENTIDOS

Amado Nervo

—Niño, vamos a cantar
una bonita canción
yo te voy a preguntar,
tú me vas a responder.

—Los ojos, ¿para qué son?
—Los ojos son para ver,
—¿Y el tacto?— Para tocar.
—¿Y el oído?— Para oír.

—¿Y el gusto?— Para gustar.
—¿Y el olfato?— Para oler.
—¿Y el alma?— Para sentir,
para querer y pensar.

Trabalenguas are fun and are great practice for experimenting with the sounds of language. Teachers may select tongue twisters that illustrate specific sounds that may be creating some difficulties. Usually, the students are encouraged to begin slowly and carefully and then to speed up the expressions as the production of sounds becomes more fluent. A few examples of old favorites follow.

PABLO

Pablo clavó un clavito
Un clavito clavó a Pablito.

R con R

R con R cigarro,
R con R barril,
Rápido corren los carros,
Allí en el ferrocarril.

TRES TIGRES

Tres tristes tigres tomaban trigo
en tres tristes platos;
en tres tristes platos tomaban trigo
tres tristes tigres.

JUAN CUINTO

Juan Cuinto contó un cuento;
Contó de cuentos un ciento;
Y un chico dejó contento;
¿Cuántos cuentos cuenta Cuinto?

Riddles and word games are also a source of language. They are especially good for developing figurative language and for finding new meanings in old expressions. Students in the late primary or middle grades are particularly interested in riddles and word games. The dog-eared volumes checked out of school libraries document the enthusiasm that students in middle childhood seem to have for these activities. Solving riddles and figuring out a play on words involve literal and creative skills of language. Ever-popular riddles include those given as follows:

¿Qué es aquello
prendido en la pared?
Tiene dos manos
y anda sin tener pies.
(reloj)

Una vieja larga y seca
que le escurre la manteca.
¿Qué es?
(una vela)

En alto vive,
en alto mora,
en alto teje
la tejedora.
(la araña)

Vuela sin alas,
silba sin boca,
y no se ve
ni se toca.
¿Qué es?
(el viento)

Finger plays are another activlty for young children who use their hands and fingers to illustrate the action of the rhymes. These **Jueguecillos Meñiques** have universal appeal for children everywhere. Examples of well-loved plays are these:

¿Quiénes son?

Este, el Gordito;
¡su fuerza es mucha!

Este, el Curioso,
que dice: "¡escucha!"

Este, el Mayor,
lleva sombrero

y éste, el Pequeño
baila ligero . . .

Y éste . . . el Huraño
nunca saluda
sin un hermanito
no presta ayuda.

La Iglesita

Esta es la iglesita
con su campanario.
Dentro hay mucha gente
rezando el rosario.

Ya se abre la puerta;
ya sale la gente*
que rezó en la iglesia
muy devotamente.

*Los dedos se agitan.

Pre-reading activities that nurture oral language include constructing, building models, using a variety of art media, memorizing poetry, retelling stories, dramatizing, role playing, singing, conversing, and reporting. As students engage in these activities, the teacher can guide the oral language production through questions: **¿Cuál es? ¿Cómo se llama? ¿Qué hay primero? ¿Qué pasó? ¿Quién hace?** by explanations: **El cepillo sirve para limpiar. Las dos mesas son iguales. Juan es más alto,** and with suggestions: **Ahora, miren al otro. Repitan las palabras. Miren el que está debajo.** These opportunities build the necessary skills of comprehending connected discourse in speech prior to the challenge of comprehending written discourse. The pre-reading activities are limited only by the imagination of the teachers and the attention spans of the students. Questioning and discussing should be planned to go beyond the literal facts. Teachers will want to encourage the interpretation of materials in terms of the students' personal experiences and ideas.

Transferability of Readiness Skills to English

The preparation for entrance into Spanish reading may have required several months. The time of the readiness period will depend upon the age, the developmental maturity, and the experiences of the beginning students. Readiness to read English, however, for students who are already reading Spanish, should take only a short preparation time. There is an array of habits, skills, and concepts that the students will bring to the reading of English from their previous positive encounters with Spanish print. For instance, they may be expected to use these concepts, habits, and skills:

- their auditory and visual perceptual skills
- their understanding of classroom routine
- their awareness of the teacher's expectations
- their abilities to pay attention, to listen, and to respond when called upon
- their knowledge of the function of the classroom tools — pencils, lined paper, rulers, scissors, easels, crayons, books, and other classroom equipment
- their information about the school schedule — lunchtime, recess, arrival, dismissal, and other details of the school day.

Teachers responsible for the preparatory activities in English will have to provide **only** English names for all the size, number, spatial, form, and color information. Names are easier to learn than concepts. Perceptual training for visual forms in English will most likely be unnecessary for normal students. All the sensory-motor activities may be skipped. Children who can draw, trace, follow dotted lines, or otherwise demonstrate their eye-hand coordination and fine muscle control as a result of the carefully planned activities of **El nivel de apresto,** are ready for English. Students who have been taught to observe the direction and details of letters and words in Spanish will have developed good attention to visual detail. Further training is not required.

Perhaps the single most important characteristic of the English readiness program is its emphasis on oral English. The new sounds, new arrangement of them into words, different syntactical patterns and additional vocabulary should be the heart of the prereading plan. Just as the children were presented with rhymes, riddles, tongue twisters, poetry, stories, songs, puppetry, dramatization, and sharing time in Spanish, they should now have the same opportunities to enjoy rich, authentic children's literature in English. It is often possible to select a particular song, story, or poem to provide practice in specific sounds or structures that frequently cause difficulties for Spanish speakers. With the help of a simple comparison of both Spanish and English, sounds that are entirely **new** may be introduced and sounds that are slightly different can be pointed out. There are a few Spanish sounds that will not be used in English at all, and the children may be helped to hold them in reserve for use only in Spanish.

Earlier it was necessary to offer ear training in Spanish; now the teacher will need to address carefully those sounds that up to this point have had no phonological reality in the Hispanic child's home or neighborhood.

The readiness to read English should be swift and comfortable for both the children and their teachers. The good background of information about themselves and the world they are in need be labeled only in English. Their awareness of themselves and their bodies in space need only the English names. The attention to fine details of written material needs only a reassurance and a reminder of the perceptual process involved. The left-to-right direction and the top to bottom flow of Spanish print is happily the same as English print. The eye fixations and movements needed to read English are identical.

Concept Acquisition and Transfer

Clear concepts that have been acquired and stored in Spanish provide a rich, deep background for reading readiness in English. All of the information and understanding about the world in which the students have been living and growing need be labeled only in English at this time. Good experiences made meaningful through the Spanish language are now made comprehensible in English. Teachers will want to use real objects, pictures, film, study prints, and other materials that have proven to be of interest to students. Lessons in English may be presented in the same manner as those offered earlier in Spanish. Discussions and questions will serve to attach the new language to the old information. Teachers should be careful to use natural speech patterns and to create activities that are stimulating as well as comprehensible.

Some of the major prereading concepts that transfer are these:

- people, events, objects have names
- people, events, objects can be grouped
- some people, events, objects cannot be grouped together
- speech sounds can be recognized in certain positions
- objects have recognizable shape and form
- events can be ordered in a specific sequence
- people and objects occupy certain positions and directions in space
- people, objects, and events can be compared for size, shape, and other attributes
- tools of learning have names and functions.

In addition, many of the essential understandings for following directions and taking instructions are known.

Such concepts as where to begin when writing or drawing, how to respond or to ask a question, when to be quiet and listen, and how to follow the classroom routine are valuable concepts that **all** transfer in a **general** sense and require only the **specific** English words to carry them out on demand as needed.

Perception and Transfer

Visual perception, well trained and practiced during readiness activities in Spanish, will transfer fully. Since attention to visual detail can be promoted as a good study habit in the general sense, only the **specific** detalls of the writing system need be provided. The auditory perceptual skills in English, however, will need careful consideration. Ear training for the forty-four phonemes of English can be offered through pictures, poetry, word games, and songs. English and Spanish have many sounds in common. A comparison of Spanish sounds that students can use in listening for English sounds are these:

Vowels

English	Spanish
a — play	ley
e — feet	isla
i — five	¡ay!
o — home	rosa
u — rule	uvas

The short vowels in English are **new** sounds to be learned and practiced.

a — hat
i — hit
o — hot
u — up

The **r**-controlled vowels in English are almost all new to the Spanish speaker because with or without a vowel next to an **r**, the **r** is a different phoneme in each language. The closest comparisons may be found in **ar - carne** and **ar - cart; or - horno** and **or - horn**. Other r-controlled vowels are **ir, er, ur (bird, herd, hurt)**. For most English speakers these are the same sound. This is a **new** sound for Spanish speakers. They will need to hear it, to say it, and to use it in planned listening and speaking activities. The teacher should not be too insistent upon the so-called mastery of these **r**-controlled vowel sounds because they are frequently pronounced differently among native speakers of English and are highly influenced by regional variations of speech. The purpose of ear training exercises should be to help Spanish speakers recognize the sounds when used by others, to approximate the sound with a reasonable degree of accuracy when they need to use them, and to to use the phonic clue as a word recognition strategy in reading later.

The Consonants of English

English consonant sounds may be heard in initial, medial, and final positions in words as illustrated by the following list:

not in Spanish	Initial Position	Medial Position	Final Position
Bb	bat	baby	cab
Cc /k/	cat kite	walking	take
Dd	dog	Daddy	bed
Ff	fence	puffy	if
G/g/	goat	buggy	dog
Hh	hop	aha	- - -
Jj	just	gadget	edge
Ll	like	yellow	ball
Mm	man	mama	Mom*
Nn	no	money	run
Pp	pin	puppy	up
Rr	rose	carry	far
Ss	soup	faster	chase
Tt	ten	butter	not
Vv	very	even	five
Ww	wagon	away	- - -
Xx	- - -	exit	fix
Yy	yard	beyond	- - -

*except álbum

36

not in Spanish	Initial Position	Medial Position	Final Position
Zz	zero	puzzle	fuzz
ng	- - -	singing	king
th	the	other	bath
th	think	bathtub	tooth
zh	---	measure	mirage
sh	sheep (chef)	dishes	fish
ch	church	matches	touch

The receptive and expressive control of the new sounds of English may have already been developed. Many oral language opportunities in school and in the neighborhood may have provided structured and unstructured practice in English sounds. These are demons for Spanish speakers learning to read English:

- all the short vowels — hat, bed, hit, top, up
- the sh of shoes; mission, nation, ocean, chef, special, sugar
  one sound — six spellings!
- the th of this and the th of thank
- the j of jello, edge
- the z of zero, has
- the v of voice, very
- the r-controlled vowels — especially the one sound (ir, er, ur)
- the zh of measure, mirage
- the d of day, ladder, bad
- the h of home, house, hare

Sensory-Motor Transfer to English

There is a total transfer of all the sensory-motor skills. This area is one of the most rewarding for both students and teachers. The same sensory-motor integration skills practiced in the Spanish prereading activities will be applied without change in the preparatory lessons in English. The students' awareness of their position in space, their gross motor skills, their fine muscle control, their eye-hand coordination, their directional orientation from left to right are all skills that are needed for English reading readiness. Both writing systems are arranged from left to right and from top to bottom. Lines and spaces are organized in the same manner. Sizes of letters and distances between words are identical for both languages. All of the earlier opportunities with puzzles, pegboards, scissors, clay, tools, and manipulative materials have most probably nurtured the essential sensory-motor skills in students of normal development. The students will have the terminology to acquire, but the activities to be carried out will be well known and well developed by students who have enjoyed appropriate activities, sufficient practice, and successful habits. Teachers will want to skip or to pass over very quickly these readiness lessons in the English workbooks and seatwork. For the students' sense of self-esteem, it is important to remind them of how much **they know** and how much they **know how to do.**

Oral English

The second language instruction of Spanish-speaking students will have been in process informally in the unstructured settings of play, in the classroom, and in other places where Spanish and English may have been in contact. Classroom lessons in the formal sense will vary according to the second language rationale and the materials selected for this purpose. The preparation for the print of English must consist of substantial and serious efforts in listening to and in speaking English. The activities that were productive for oral Spanish can be offered for oral English. The students can be given pictures for discussion. As teachers provide these stimuli, they must remember that the new words and expressions to describe the pictures need to be presented and modeled. They need to allow time for silent listening, for gestural responses, for one-word answers, and for shorter comments. Teachers will find storytelling a useful strategy. If the traditional stories loved in Spanish can be told now in English, then comprehension is assured while new English expressions are being acquired. Stories with refrains are excellent for learning not only the words but the rhythm and melody of phrases. The magic of poetry that delighted students in their own language can be carried forward in the second language. The natural interest in playing with words contributes to comprehension and fluency. For second language learners rhymes and poems that have difficult features of the language offer informal relaxed practice. Nursery rhymes for young children can give opportunities to try out some of the unpredictable and unfamiliar vowel sounds. For example:

Hey Diddle Diddle

Hey diddle diddle, the cat and the fiddle,
The cow jumped over the moon.
The little dog laughed to see such sport,
And the dish ran away with the spoon.

Baa, Baa, Black Sheep

Baa, baa, black sheep, have you any wool?
Yes sir, yes sir, three bags full.
One for my master and one for my dame,
But none for the little boy who lives in the lane.

Verse and doggerel are useful, too, and may be more appropriate for older students.

As I Was Going to St. Ives

As I was going to St. Ives,
I met a man with seven wives;
Each wife had seven sacks,
Each sack had seven cats,
Each cat had seven kits.
Kits, cats, sacks, and wives,
How many were going to St. Ives?
(One)

Thirty White Horses

Thirty white horses
On a red hill;
Now they tramp,
Now they champ,
Now they stand still.
(The teeth and gums)

Riddles, tongue twisters, word games, real objects, room environment, and food are the same source of English language development as when used for first language stimulation. Teachers should be careful to keep the pace comfortable to accommodate meaning and should be alert for indicators of any misunderstanding. If a structured program of English as a second language is in place, the plan may always be supplemented and complemented by a variety of other activities that create interest, enthusiasm and fluency.

Caveats in Transfer to English

At the readiness level, teachers should be very cautious about the sequence of instruction. There is little to be gained by rushing through a token set of Spanish prereading activities to get to English. So important are these early learnings — the acquisition of concepts, the habits of listening, the sensory-motor opportunities, the ear training, the perceptual activities, and the language fluency — that **strength** in these skills and in this knowledge should be the primary goal. Simultaneous readiness programs and two sets of materials in use at the same time are very likely to cause confusion, and may even result in poor progress at this level. The unfortunate outcome may be a weak background in prereading skills in **two** languages. Teachers may feel confident that strong readiness skills from the Spanish lessons will be available for use and for transfer in English. In the long run, students who have been taught carefully and have learned well at this introductory phase of reading will be the winners in English as well.

In summary, readiness to read English will transfer from Spanish as **general** language development and as **specific** skill in the visual skills of sequencing, attention to detail, awareness of figure-ground, and memory. The auditory skills of figure-ground, sequencing, discrimination of likeness and differences among sounds will have potential for use as well. The spatial skills of directional organization, lateral orientation, and integration are identical in both languages; thus, no transfer is needed. The kinesthetic abilities needed to manipulate the classroom instruments of learning are the same, and good skills should serve the students well in any language. The habits of listening, paying attention, concentrating, persisting, and completing assigned tasks will put the students on the royal road to literacy in English.

References

1. Jáurequi, A.L. **Jardín de niños.** Mexico: Editorial Avante S. de R.L., 1967.

2. **Lectura en dos idiomas.** Northvale, N.J: Santillana Publishing Company, Inc., 1977.

3. **Schooling and Language Minority Students: A Theoretical Framework.** Sacramento, California: California State Department of Education, Office of Bilingual Bicultural Education, 1981.

4. Smith, Henry P. and Dechant, Emerald V. **Psychology in Teaching Reading.** Englewood Cliffs, N.J: 1961.

5. Stockwell, Robert P. and Bowen, J. Donald. **The Sounds of English and Spanish.** Chicago: University of Chicago Press, 1965.

6. Thonis, Eleanor W. **Literacy for America's Spanish Speaking Children.** Newark, Delaware: International Reading Association, 1976.

7. Thonis, Eleanor W. **Aprendamos a leer.** Arlington, Virginia: Media Marketing, Inc., 1975.

8. Wills, C.D. and Stegemen, W.H. **La vida en el jardín de infantes.** Argentina: Editorial Troquel, 1965.

CHAPTER II

THE SPANISH WRITING SYSTEM

The Spanish language is elegant in its simplicity. In its spoken form, there are approximately twenty-five sounds (some linguists suggest twenty-seven phonemes in Spanish), that are combined or recombined to form the words, phrases, and sentences that carry meaning. These twenty-five phonemes are represented graphically by symbols from a twenty-eight letter alphabet (or thirty letters if **K** and **W** are included). The luxury of such choice in letter-sound (phoneme-grapheme) correspondence has resulted in one of the most nearly perfect writing systems in the world. A perfect writing system would specify that only **one** sound be represented by **one** symbol, and that **one** symbol represent only **one** sound. Thus, there would be strict and regular correspondence between sound and symbol, as between the auditory and visual stimulus. Artificial alphabets at times have been created for accomplishing this purpose. In English, the Initial Teaching Alphabet (ITA) has forty-four symbols that serve to represent the forty-four speech sounds. The International Phonetic Alphabet is another such system that attempts to offer a one-to-one correspondence for sound and symbol. Spanish has few discrepancies between auditory and visual symbols. For this reason, many primary teachers believe it is effective to use a synthetic (a part-whole) approach, and introduce beginning readers to the written conventions immediately. After the readiness level stressing oral language, ear training, and other preparatory activities, the students learn the letter names (alphabet), the sounds represented by the letters, and other important features of speech-print associations. These lessons are intended to guide the students safely through the written forms of Spanish and to help them recognize in the visual appearance what the students already know in the auditory form. Usually, the method results in establishing good decoding skills of students who are prepared and who are able to benefit from such instruction.

The Letter Names
The importance of teaching the alphabet has been debated for many years. When the writing system is based upon an alphabetic principle as in Spanish, the knowledge of that alphabet, the recognition of its various forms, and its order have been considered legitimate learnings. Some teachers feel that the alphabet should be the starting point of all reading or pre-reading instruction. Others may be of the opinion that the alphabet is needed only as a study skill after the student begins to use reading and writing and to encounter indices, glossaries, tables of contents, and reference materials that are sequenced in alphabetical order. Some

of the controversy centers around the tendency to teach the alphabet by rote in songs, jingles, or rhymes, and to have such activities carried out with very little or no awareness of what an alphabet is or what purpose it may serve. Regardless of the varied opinions, children in many parts of the school world have historically learned to read by learning the alphabet of their language. The child was expected to memorize the letter names and to recognize the forms; the sounds that the letters represent; the pronunciation of syllables formed by letter combinations; the combinations of letters and syllables into words; and finally the arrangement of words in short sentences. Following the act of learning the alphabet itself, students would engage in other activities that would then promote learning to read, to write, and to spell. One apparent advantage of learning the letter names lies in the fact that in letter names may be found the sounds represented by the letters. For reading, the letters themselves are not the most important, but rather the sounds that the letters represent. The need for the alphabet has not been considered that critical at the early learning stage and has not been a major concern to reading teachers. The fact is that children like learning the letters. They generally have a real interest in finding out which are the letters in their own names, and which are the letters in the signs around them. One basic learning from the alphabet is not necessarily the **name,** but rather the speech **sound** represented by the letter or letters. At the pre-reading stage, the children may have a wonderful time learning the names of the letters. They may begin with the letters in their own names, their initials, their first names, the names of their family members, or the names of their favorite television channels, KCRA, KTVR, WBS. Ordinarily, students are introduced to the names of the letters through pictures or objects that are to be found in their immediate environment. Since the majority of learners first meet letter names before school age, most of the alphabet books draw upon the familiar places, persons, or things of early childhood. The **ABECEDARIO** is a colorful and welcome sight to kindergarten and first grade children. In Spanish, unlike many other languages, the picture-symbol cards of the alphabet with which the teacher adorns the classroom may provide steady and reliable associations with few irregularities. There is little need to unlearn sound-symbol relationships or to introduce exceptions where the rule does not apply. The **A** is for **Apple** of English has to be explained and explained; **A** is also for **Apron, A** is for **Awful, A** is for **Armadillo,** and so on. It is possible that the introduction of the letter **A** in English could be pictured in at least seven different ways. In Spanish, however, no matter what object is pictured to suggest the **A** in its initial position, the **A** always represents the same sound. The **A** de **A**nillo, de **A**gua, de **A**brigo, or of any selected pictures to suggest the **A** sound-symbol connection remains constant. When only the names of the letters are to be taught, the teacher does not attempt to teach the sounds, but the pictures arrayed around a classroom can be used for this purpose later if the choice of pictures has been a careful one. Ordinarily the letters of the alphabet in Spanish may have **one** picture for each letter, and sound, except as follows:

c followed by **a e u**	**h** silent	**r** and **rr**
c followed by **e i**	***ll, y, hie**	**j** and **ge, gi**
g followed by **a e u**	***s, z, ci, ce (x)**	and at times **x.**
g followed by **e i**	**gü** and **güe**	
	*May vary from region to region	

A a
árbol

B b
bota

C c
casa

Ch ch
chango

D d
dulce

E e
elefante

F f
foca

G g
gato

H h
helado

I i
iglesia

J j
jarro

K k
kiosco

L l
luna

45

Ll ll
llave

M m
mariposa

N n
nido

Ñ ñ
ñandú

O o
oso

P p
pato

Q q
queso

R r
rata

S s
sapo

T t
tortuga

U u
uvas

V v
vaca

W w
W

X x
xilófono

Y y
yema

Z z
zorro

In the beginning, the purpose of surrounding the child with a pictorial alphabet is to develop the rudimentary letter recognition skills. Letters in their **mayúscula** forms must then be associated with their **minúscula** mates. Visual, perceptual, and discrimination responses are practiced as students are gradually taught names, forms, and sizes of letters. Some teachers like to offer the letters in random order using a letter or letters of importance to the students. After all the letters are known by their names and can be recognized in several forms, then the proper sequence of the letters is presented. Other teachers prefer to begin at the beginning with **A** and move along in proper order until the **Z** is learned. At critical points along the way, teachers find it wise to check students' learning. **Rote** recitation without the recognition of randomly given letters is not very useful.

When an alphabet chart is arranged around the room at eye level convenient for the students, they may refer to the letters when needed for their written work. When each card illustrative of letter-sound correspondence also has a representative word, students may begin to develop a small sight vocabulary of these stimulus words.

Activities that encourage students to match and sort letters, to select a certain letter from several, to pair upper and lower case letters, to recognize a stimulus letter in a line of other letters of similar configuration, to differentiate among the directionality of certain letters **(b-d, u-n, M-W)** are prerequisites to writing the letters. Copying letters, writing them on the blackboard, tracing them in the air, taking them from dictation, writing them on lined paper are appropriate activities for five and six-year old students.

The Sounds Represented by Letters
Knowledge of the alphabet alone is no guarantee of safe conduct into reading. Although many children in Hispanic countries have begun **en un método alfabético**, they soon may have to learn the sounds represented by the letters in order to blend sounds and syllables into words or to learn by some other method. If the teachers have decided on a code-emphasis approach and have moved on from the names of letters to their representative sounds, they will have to decide further on the sequence of sound-symbol relationships and the forms of written material. In some countries, cursive writing is introduced first; in other places, the manuscript forms come first; and in some few countries both manuscript and cursive writing systems are taught within the same lesson. Sometimes the choice is determined by the materials that have been selected, and at other times, dictates of the administration or community are followed. Few theorists agree on a fixed order of presentation of sound-symbol correspondences. The students

ultimately have to learn all twenty-five phonemes as written by means of a thirty-letter graphic system. The materials available to provide practice in these phoneme-grapheme relationships appear to order them in slightly different ways, but eventually all of them are included. Lessons should include the following teaching and learning:

- the name of the letter;
- the sound represented by the letter or letters;
- the association between sound and symbol(s);
- the correct formation of the letter in manuscript writing (and cursive writing for older students);
- the correct formation and matching of both upper case (**mayúscula**) and lower case (**minúscula**) forms;
- the blending of vowels and consonants into syllables;
- the combining of syllables into words;
- the constructing of sentences from groups of words;
- The function of diacritical marks and their names;
- The writing, reading, and spelling **practice** of each feature of the writing systems as presented for overlearning.

One suggestion is to introduce the **O** first since it is the easiest letter to write and is the most familiar shape. Infants first observe the round face of their mothers; toddlers' first attempts at scribbling are circular; and primary pupils' drawings almost always have a round sun or moon. Another suggestion is to reorder the lessons to leave the **A** until last because it has two forms — **la forma manuscrita** and **la forma imprenta**. Stimulating pictures of recognizable places, people or objects are useful to help students hear and see the speech-print connection. The teaching must emphasize the initial sound-symbol correspondence and should avoid giving excess attention to ending sounds during this early stage. Later, when students are working with words instead of pictures, they will need to be careful to track their eyes in a left-right direction. If the teachers have made the focus of attention the initial sound, the habit of beginning at the left of words will have been established for most students. As has been mentioned, there is nothing magic about a sequence of sound-symbol associations. One order is presented in the following pages. It is based upon consistent speech-to-print patterns and treats the few irregularities of the Spanish writing system by grouping all orthographic (spelling) variations of the same **sound** together. These differences in written forms then become spelling concerns for later attention and do not interfere with the introductory reading skills at a decoding level.

Las Vocales

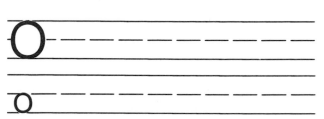

O — — — — — — — — — —

o

E — — — — — — — — — —

e

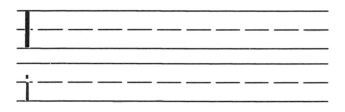

I — — — — — — — — — —

i

U — — — — — — — — — —

u

A — — — — — — — — — —

a

After working through the sound-symbol relationships of the vowels and learning letter names and letter sounds, teachers may wish to check the extent to which their students are indeed making an accurate connection between them. A simple teacher-made test will provide the information so that decisions can be made about individual students. Teachers will want to know if most of the class has mastered this phase of the program, and/or if there are a few students whose auditory skills are insufficient for benefiting from this method of teaching. If students are able to write the letters that represent the sounds in the initial position of words dictated; if they are able to match the upper and lower case forms of the letters; if they can write letters to show the initial letter-sound of stimulus pictures; and if they can draw something from their own experiences to illustrate sound-symbol relationships, then they will demonstrate knowledge and skill at this very beginning of the decoding process.

During the lessons on the sound-symbol correspondences in the system of vowels in Spanish, the students should also have learned how to pay close attention, how to listen, and how to put together picture, speech, sound, and letter. They should have little difficulty following the same behavior in activities designed to teach the consonant system. The pictures ideally should be selected as fairly representative of the vocabulary development of the students. The teacher should identify the picture first so that there is no doubt as to what the picture conveys. Students' perceptions are not always the same as teachers' intentions. If a beribboned package is supposed to elicit the **c/k/** for **caja,** then a student response **r/rr/** for **regalo** can only cause confusion for the student and defeat for both of them. Teachers also may be helping students sharpen their auditory discrimination and pronunciation skills by having them repeat the word after the teacher has given the word illustrated by the picture.

One suggested order for the consonants is offered with the reminder that didactic materials for this purpose vary enormously. There is probably no special virtue in one order or another. An easy beginning is one with the **bilabials** because these emerge very early in human development. **M, P, B,** and **V** may be considered as the first group. **M** and **P** have one-to-one connections between sound and symbol in initial positions. **B** and **V** are together in this grouping because they represent **one** sound but have **two** spelling variations. Pictures to illustrate **La M, m** including **manzana, mano, mariposa, muñeca, mamá, mono, maracas, martillo,** and **montañas.** If teachers wish to avoid the lexical variations of **mono (chango)** at this point, other stimulus pictures are plentiful to represent **M, m.**

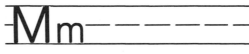

Mm

Pp

Bb

Vv

51

Syllables

According to many theorists, the syllable in Spanish is a most important concept for beginning readers because so many words may be constructed from the combination of simple syllables. In addition, the recognition of syllables allows for a useful tool in recognizing words that may be familiar in speech but not in written form.

To move the students toward meaning as rapidly as possible and to help them realize that merely knowing letter and sound combinations is only an activity on the way to reading, but not really reading, teachers may wish to put the consonant **M, m** together with the vowels previously learned. This activity should include the teaching of the concept of the syllable. At this level, the simplest definition of a syllable as the joining of a consonant and a vowel will probably suffice. Later, the concepts of **silabas directas, inversas, y mixtas** may be taught. The practice in blending consonants and vowels together should be oral and accompanied by guided instruction on the blackboard and on worksheets. Students should be encouraged to experiment with putting **M, m** and the **a, e, i, o, u** together so that they can **hear** how syllables are formed. After recognizing and perceiving syllables in speech, they are ready to **see** the written forms. Students may be given the opportunity to create words at this point if the teachers wish to point out that many words can be made simply by putting syllables together.

Sound Blending

Sound blending can be described as the act of putting the sound together naturally and smoothly to create a normal pronunciation of the syllables or words. Sound blending requires a lot of practice and must be carefully presented in order to preserve natural pronunciation, and to move quickly to meaning. Examples of blending consonant and vowel sounds:

Ma	**Me**	**Mi**	**Mo**	**Mu**
ma	**me**	**mi**	**mo**	**mu**
Pa	**Pe**	**Pi**	**Po**	**Pu**
pa	**pe**	**pi**	**po**	**pu**
Ba	**Be**	**Bi**	**Bo**	**Bu**
ba	**be**	**bi**	**bo**	**bu**
Va	**Ve**	**Vi**	**Vo**	**Vu**
va	**ve**	**vi**	**vo**	**vu**

Examples of blending syllables into words.

mamá	**papá**	**papa**	**vivo**
mapa	**puma**	**mi**	**bebe**

Examples of arranging words into meaningful sentences.

Amo a mi mamá. Mi papá me ama.

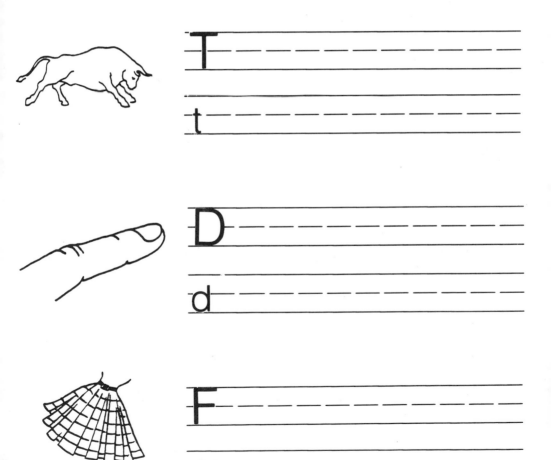

T

t

D

d

F

f

Examples of blending consonants and vowels.

ta	**te**	**ti**	**to**	**tu**
da	**de**	**di**	**do**	**du**
fa	**fe**	**fi**	**fo**	**fu**

Examples of blending syllables into words.

dedo **foto** **tía** **dado**

Examples of arranging words into meaningful sentences.

Tito toma té. ¿Dónde vive tu tío?

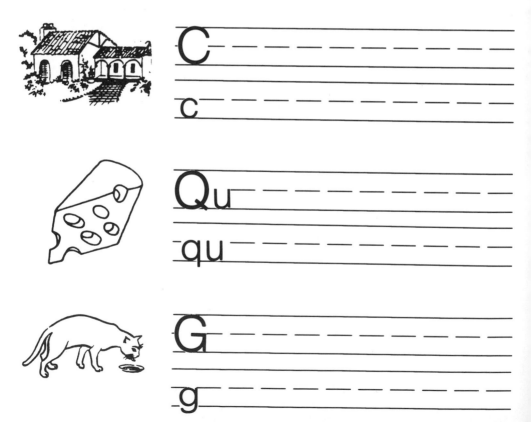

C

c

Qu

qu

G

g

Gu

gu

Consistent with the speech-to-print direction students will learn one sound and two spellings for the /**c**/ and the /**g**/. When they practice blending sounds and creating syllables, they may be assisted visually by these charts:

ca	_____	_____	co	cu
_____	que	qui	_____	_____
ga	_____	_____	go	gu
_____	gue	gui	_____	_____

Examples of blending syllables into words.

cama	goma	boca
quema	poco	pico

Examples of arranging words into meaningful sentences.

Vi a mi gato. Pepe vió a mi mamá.

Ch

ch

N

n

Examples of blending consonants and vowels into syllables.

la	le	li	lo	lu
ra	re	ri	ro	ru
cha	che	chi	cho	chu
na	ne	ni	no	nu

Examples of blending syllables into words.

lava	coche	ratón
rana	nido	nudo

Examples of arranging words into meaningful sentences.

Chico come chile.   **¿Van con Paco?**

S

s

Z

z

Ce

ce

Ci

ci

Examples of blending consonants and vowels into syllables.

sa	se	si	so	su
za	ze	zi	zo	zu
____	ce	ci	____	____

Examples of blending syllables into words.

zerape	círculo	azúcar
oso	cereza	mesas

Examples of arranging words into meaningful sentences.

Sara quiso almorzar. Es fácil hacer dulces.

J

j

Ge

ge

Gi

gi

Examples of blending consonants and vowels into syllables.

ja   **je**   **ji**   **jo**   **ju**

_____   **ge**   **gi**   _____   _____

Examples of blending syllables into words.

jabón   **girasol**   **naranja**

gelatina   **jefe**   **jota**

Examples of arranging words into meaningful sentences.

El general es el jefe. José trajo el girasol.

Ll

ll

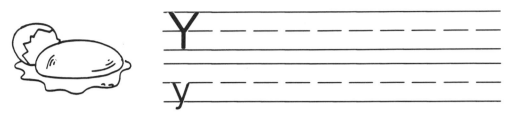

Examples of blending consonants and vowels into syllables.

lla	**lle**	**lli**	**llo**	**llu**
ya	**ye**	**yi**	**yo**	**yu**

Examples of blending syllables into words.

llave	**cepillo**	**silla**
yema	**yelmo**	**suyo**

Examples of arranging words into meaningful sentences.

La llave es suya. El cepillo está en la silla.

H is always considered silent in Spanish, but when **h** is followed by the diphthong **ue** it creates the sound heard in such words as **hue**vos, **hue**llas, **hue**rta. When **h** is followed by the diphthong **ie,** it creates the sound heard in such words as **hie**lo, **hie**na, **hie**rba. Students should recognize this sound as the same one found in **yarda, lluvia.** These sound-symbol connections must be differentiated from the customary silent **h.** Thus, they will have **one** sound and three spellings as they make their connections — **hie, y, ll.**

huellas   hueso

Hie

hie

hielo

hierba

hiedra

H

h

hacha

hebilla

hilo

Students will also need to recognize and respond to the **ñ** in initial and medial positions.

ñandú

Ñ

ñ

They will also need to learn the written symbol **rr** found only in medial positions although the **/r/** in initial positions represents the same sound.

burro

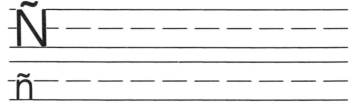

rr

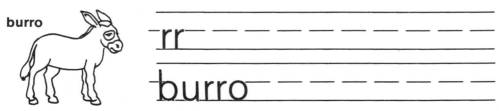

burro

The **x** with its variations may be among the last sound-symbol associations to be acquired because of the many differences influenced by regional speech.

Mexico	X X

Como la jota.

Xochimilco	X X

Como la ese.

texto	X X

Como la k y la ese — ks.

examen	X X

Como la g fuerte y la ese — gs.

jamón
y huevos

Yy

Como la i.

W

Ww

Letras prestadas de otros idiomas.

K

Kk

pingüino

güi

cigüeña

güe

Once direct speech-print correspondences and syllables have been introduced and practiced, the students may acquire the **inverse** and mixed syllables. Inverse syllables simply reverse the consonant-vowel pattern and appear as vowel-consonant syllables. Almost all of the previous syllables as learned can be recognized in this vowel-consonant pattern. Mixed syllables are those with consonant-vowel-consonant patterns — for example, **car/ne, des/can/san, tam/bién.** There are many excellent activities in **Lectura en dos idiomas** that provide practice in these features of the writing system.

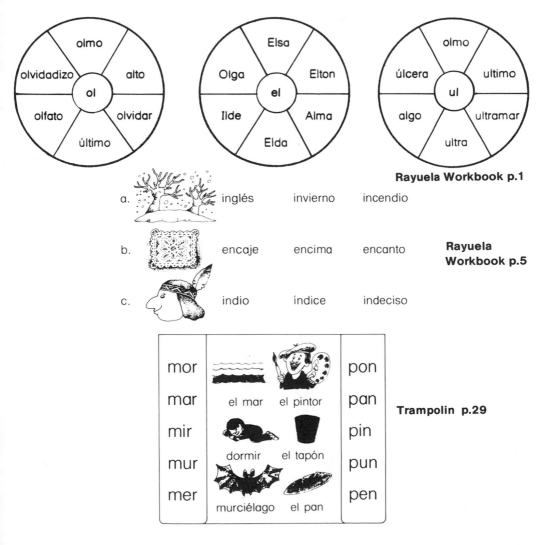

Rayuela Workbook p.1

a. inglés   invierno   incendio

b. encaje   encima   encanto   **Rayuela Workbook p.5**

c. indio   índice   indeciso

Trampolin p.29

Consonant Combinations

The combining of two or more consonants together into a single blend in which **both** consonants retain their identity provides for more fluent reading. Consonant clusters may be found in the initial and medial positions in words. A few may be found in the final position — for example, **Quetzalcóatl.**

blusa

clavo

flores

plaza

iglesia

abril

cidra

 cruz

 frijoles

 grúa

 princesa

 rastrillo

Word Endings

Spanish has only a few ways in which words may end. They may end in the five vowels **a, e, i, o, u.** They may also end in **d, l, n, r, s (z).** Students may need opportunities to **hear** these word endings before they **see** them in print. At best, students are casual in their speech habits and may benefit from practice that is lively and varied. An essential factor for teachers to keep in mind is that oral pronunciation may obscure the places where one word ends and another begins. Fluent Spanish speakers observe automatically the enlacing of the final sound of one word with the beginning sound of the next. Expressions such as **el loro — el oro** or **un ovillo — un novillo** may challenge spelling skills but their comprehensibility is to be found within the context of specific usage, not in their pronunciation, which is the same, nor in their written forms, which are different.

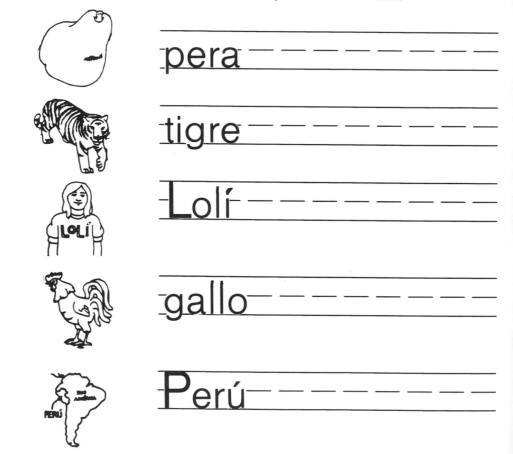

pera

tigre

Lolí

gallo

Perú

tempestad

árbol

león

flor

tos

lápiz

Diphthongs

Although students may have developed well their skills in responding to the single vowels, the vowels in combinations may not be so easily mastered by beginning readers. The Spanish diphthong system should be introduced, and the sensible rules governing diphthongs may be taught directly. Students may be provided with these basic understandings to assist them in making an association between **one** sound and **two** symbols:

- a definition of a diphthong;
- a list of the diphthongs with examples of each;
- the three diphthongs that have two spellings;
- the three simple rules governing diphthongs.

A diphthong is defined as a combination of **two** vowels pronounced as **one** sound. Unlike consonant clusters that students may have already learned and that retain the identity of each consonant, a diphthong combines the two vowels to create a single new sound. The diphthongs may be listed and illustrated as follows:

ia as in igles**ia**

ue as in p**ue**rta

ie as in f**ie**sta

uo as in antig**uo**

io as in rad**io**

ui as in r**ui**do

ua as in parag**ua**s

au as in fl**au**ta

iu as in c**iu**dad

eu as in d**eu**da

There are **three** diphthongs that have **two** written forms for the same speech sound.

ai — oy as in **ai**re, h**ay**
ei — ey as in s**ei**s, r**ey**
oi — oy as in **oi**ga, h**oy**

Like most other features of the Spanish writing system, the diphthongs are governed by simple rules that apply without exception. These rules may be summarized and presented to the students. They may be written on a chart and placed in a convenient location for the students to refer to as needed in written work. The rules for diphthongs are these:

- A **weak** vowel and a **strong** vowel or two weak vowels may combine to form a diphthong

  a, e, o are strong
  i, u   are weak

- A written accent on a weak vowel prevents the vowels from forming a diphthong.

  río, maíz, frío

- All other vowels in combination are pronounced separately and each one has its own identity.

  mus**eo**, **oe**ste, **ae**rodinámico

Four other vowel combinations of **three** vowels exist in Spanish to form triphthongs

—**iai** as in estudi**ái**s
—**iei** as in estudi**éi**s
—**uai** as in contin**uái**s
—**uei** as in conti**uéi**s

Two of these forms have **two** spellings

uay — Urug**uay**
uey — b**uey**

When teaching students about the diphthongs or triphthongs, you should keep in mind that these learnings merely support the awareness of how the writing system works. Such skills may be of great assistance in improving spelling but do not necessarily improve reading. Meaning in either spoken or written discourse comes from phrases, sentences, and larger units of speech or print.

Transferability of Decoding Skills to English

A code-emphasis approach that presents parts of the written conventions in small increments of letters, sounds, syllables, words, phrases, and sentences may be deceptively simple. Teachers will need to check continually to ensure that students are really getting their skills all together and are truly comprehending as they decode the speech-print relationships. Learning to read by this method requires the combining of visual attention to detail, auditory discrimination, sound blending, and integration of these three elements. Further, unless the phonic abilities are applied to words and phrases in connected discourse where meaning can be obtained from context, there is little value or great virtue in learning the code as an intellectual exercise. For these reasons, teachers will want to consider the extent to which students are skillful in integrating and applying phonic elements to find meaning in written material. Teachers will also want to be mindful of the fact that there are other effective approaches for students who do not seem to be successful in grasping the intent of phonics instruction.

If it has been determined that the students have developed the skills needed to decode Spanish, then the useful composite of phonic skills that may be available for decoding English are minimally these:

- visual attention to detail and auditory discrimination;
- auditory attention to detail and auditory discrimination;
- sound blending of elements combined smoothly to create natural words;
- application of phonic skills to words in the context of connected discourse.

Writing systems both in Spanish and English are alphabetic systems, arrangements of graphic symbols representative of auditory-vocal ones. This basic understanding has already been reached by the students who have worked through the kinds of activities described for learning the system in Spanish. An awareness of reading English as substantially the same act as reading Spanish has certainly been established. The students do know, however, that English does sound different from their own native speech and that, though most of the letters of the alphabet look the same, the arrangement of them into words and sentences as well as their rhythm and melody are most often different. If the teachers have used a code-emphasis approach and students have demonstrated skill in organizing the written conventions of Spanish into a manageable system for their introductory reading and spelling needs, then they should be able to master the second writing system with confidence. To avoid boredom in a review of the sound-symbol relationships that are the same and to keep students moving along at a challenging pace, it should be valuable to remind students of how much they already know that can be applied **now** to English reading. The questionable practice of placing older students in the pre-primer or of offering them unsuitable materials can be eliminated if teachers begin with an inventory of skills that transfer immediately. Students need to know what skills they have and need to be reassured that they do indeed have them available for the additional responsibility of reading English. A classroom strategy that should be most effective is to prepare several charts and place them around the classroom to serve as reminders. These charts may be developed as the English lessons proceed and may be put in a place of prominence for the students to refer to whenever they are dealing with reading and spelling in English.

Good transfer may be expected from such speech-print connections as the **M, m. Mamá, miel, moneda, mono** have initial sounds and written symbols identical to those found in English words **maybe, mother, money, mountain, more.** The same transfer applies to **papá, pipa, pan, patata** for **paper, papa, pal.** Transfer may also be expected from **boca, bolsa, barco, barril** to English words **boy, bacon, boat**, but the spelling variation of **V, v** will not be useful and for pronunciation purposes may even create problems. Teachers are familiar with their Spanish-speakers saying **B**erry, for **very** and **B**oice for **voice** as they apply the **B, V** sound-symbol learnings to English. These difficulties are spelling and pronunciation problems **only** and may not at all interfere with effective reading and comprehension of these words if they are in the listening and speaking vocabularies of the students who are reading them. The **D, d** words will not offer great transfer possibilities because the **D** phoneme is influenced by its position in the words **dulce, cada, verdad** and at best bears little resemblance to the phoneme /d/ in English. The **J, j, GE, ge, GI, gi** are unlikely to help much and will require special teaching. The **LL, Y** is similar to the **B, V** in that part of the connection can be used, as **yarda, yelmo,** and **yuca** represent useful connections in English for **yard, yucca,** but the **Y** phoneme cannot in English be represented by the **LL.** For the purposes of making the most of the sound-symbol correspondences that will transfer, the teacher may contrast the Spanish and English consonant systems and may discover words illustrative of the sound-symbol relationships for transfer.

Speech-Print Connections for English
A general comparison of the sound-symbol likenesses and differences in Spanish and English can lead the teacher and students to these steps in taking a quantum leap from their known language and literacy skills in Spanish to the uncertainties of the capricious unknown writing system of English. First, the students need some dramatic reassurance that they already **know** nearly half the phonics

(decoding) content in the second language. An old, used workbook could be used to demonstrate this fact with great flair. Tear out the pages that deal with the practice lessons on the abundance of sound-symbol associations that transfer. If each one has two or three pages of practice, the teachers will have an impressive stack to show the class. Students will enjoy being told that they know this material already and can skip it!

One of the major difficulties in using a phonics approach in English is the reality that **one** sound may be represented by **several** symbols and **one** symbol may represent **several** sounds. For example, the **ch** of Spanish exists as an identical element in English but also may be a **sh** as in ma**ch**ine or **ch**ef and may be a **K** as in **ch**emistry. The irregularity or lack of exact correspondence between speech and print presents problems for native speakers of English. Imagine, then, the difficulties compounded for students who are not native to English. The transferability of phonic skills from Spanish to English can, however, be effective if the **general** phonics skills can be used in the **specific** sound-symbol connections of English. Teachers of reading in English need to know the following:

- sounds that are **identical** or close in both Spanish and English are represented by the **same** written symbol;
- sounds that are **identical** in both languages but are represented by **different** written symbols;
- sounds that are **different** in both languages but are represented by the **same** symbols;
- sounds that exist **only** in English but are represented by the same symbols in combination;
- sounds that exist **only** in Spanish but are represented by the same symbols;
- written symbols — **no sounds.**

The English phonics skills as compared to the Spanish skills may be viewed in the following charts:

	INITIAL		**MEDIAL**	
	English	**Spanish**	**English**	**Spanish**
b	boot	boca	baby	abeja
c + o (K)	cat	casa	account	acostar
a				
u	kite	kiosco	akin	- - -
f	fence	falda	after	afuera
g + o	gate	gato	ago	aguja
a				
u				
l	look	luna	alike	alta
m	me	mi	mama	mamá
n	nest	nido	annoy	Ana
p	post	puma	apple	apagado
s	soup	sopa	ascend	asado
t	tomato	tomate	atone	atender
w	wagon	*Wolfgang	away	- - -
y	yellow	yarda	beyond	ayudar
ch	cheese	chocolate	matches	fecha

	FINAL	
	English	**Spanish**
b	cab	- - -
c + o (K)	bric-a-brac	frac
a		
u	tick	
f	off	- - -
g + o	tag	- -
a		
u		
l	ball	col
m	beam	- - -**
n	ruin	jamón
p	tap	- - -
s	mass	tos
t	mat	- - -
w	- - -	- - -
y	- - -	- - -
ch	church	- - -

*Used principally in spelling proper names.
**album (only one word in common usage)

For the gaps that may be found in these sound-symbol connections represented in the two languages, teachers will want to provide listening and speaking opportunities and to present many examples of needed words. Good teaching according to sound phonics principles requires the accumulation of several words known to the students, words from which they may generalize the phonic elements needed. For the sound-symbol associations that exist in **both** languages in initial, medial, or final positions, teachers will want to reassure students that these skills transfer as identical phonic elements. It will help language minority students' confidence and their sense of self-esteem to be reminded that they **know** these **thirty** connections and already possess many of the phonic skills **needed** for English.

1. Same sounds — different written symbols

English	Spanish
fate	elote
five	ay aire
feet	isla Ysidro

2. Same written symbols — different sounds

ph	phone	a — hat	herd
gh	rough	e — met	hurt
ph	Stephen	i — hit	bird
ch	chorus	o — rot	
		u — run	

3. Sounds **only** in English

sh	shell	delicious	ng	sang
		nation		
		chef		
		sugar		
th	thank		nk	bank
th	this		h	hope (h is silent in Spanish)
wh	white		s(zh)	measure

4. Sounds **only** in Spanish — same written symbols

jinete	geranio	zero	amistad
girasol	llama	dedo	

5. Silent written symbols — no sounds
   In Spanish, all consonants represent their own sounds except for **H,** which
   is always **silent.** In English the writing system contains many combinations
   of silent letters that the students must learn. These are listed as follows:

silent letters		
	—gh	ghost
	—gn	gnat
	—kn	know
	—pn	pneumonia
	—ps	psychic
	—rh	rhythm
	—wr	write
	—sc	scene

   These variations in sound-symbol associations are likely to be the cause of
   spelling and pronunciation difficulties rather than reading problems.

6. Consonant clusters of **l** and **r** are identical.

Spanish	English	Spanish	English
blusa	blouse	bruja	broom
clavo	clarinet	cruz	crest
flor	flour	frío	free
globo	glory	grillo	grid
pluma	play	prisa	pray
Tlasca	- - -	tren	train

   But **S** clusters may present problems for Spanish speakers because they
   do not exist in Spanish..

scour	small	star
skein	snail	swing
sleep	spoon	

   Other consonant blends are these:

twin	strike	splash
scream	phrenology	
spring	school	
squeak	three	

English vowels in combinations may create **one new** sound, may represent the **first** vowel and keep the second silent, or may keep the first silent and represent the second vowel. These lists are as follows:

au	maul	**ea**	head	**ai**	captain
aw	law	**ou**	bought	**eu**	eulogy
ou	out	**ai**	rain	**ey**	money
ow	now	**ay**	day	**ou**	you
oi	coin	**ea**	eat	**ou**	famous
oy	boy	**ee**	meet		
oo	look	**ei**	either		
oo	soon	**ie**	pie		
ei	eight	**oa**	boat		
ey	they	**ou**	soul		
ew	new	**ow**	low		
		ue	blue		
		ui	suit		

Teachers should bear in mind that certain regional influences in English may determine the pronunciation of the vowels as well as decide the extent to which vowel digraphs may be pronounced as diphthongs.

Caveat
When students have learned the phonics of Spanish, they often intuitively apply these decoding skills to English. This ability to recognize English words or word patterns in the reading lesson may give the teachers a false sense of security concerning the students' progress in reading. Unless these activities are followed by opportunities to question and to interpret what has been decoded, the students may continue to transfer their phonic skills to English without making any real sense of what they have been doing. Many of the English reading programs have a heavy emphasis on phonics. Practice in phonics skills may be offered as introductory or preparatory lessons that are intended to lead students to comprehension of the written material. Other reading approaches are arranged to provide the phonics practice after comprehension has been assured. Regardless of the timing or order of sound-symbol relationships as a skill to be learned and practiced, teachers of second language reading in English must be cautious and must know what the possible pitfalls are. A review of the contrastive sound systems will help teachers appreciate the vast difference between a twenty-five phoneme language and a forty-four or forty-five phoneme one. The differences, similarities, and omissions have already been reviewed and presented in the charts of this chapter. Particularly, teachers will want to watch for these potential sources of error:

- The new English phoneme-grapheme has no counterpart in Spanish, and the student may have a tendency to substitute one most nearly like it from the native language, for example, **thin**, becomes **tin** or **jello** becomes **yello**.
- The English and Spanish phoneme-grapheme relationship may be identical but not in all cases. For example, **beam** becomes **bean, check** becomes **cheque.**
- The multiple sound-symbol relationships of English may be confusing for Spanish readers who have learned to rely on the consistency of the speech-print connections in their own language, for example, **cho**colate, ma**chi**ne, **che**mistry.

Teachers may find it useful to stress the ability to **comprehend** the content of the lesson, rather than to make much of an effort correcting students' pronunciation. Silent reading and non-verbal responses may prove most productive in terms of developing the needed skills of understanding what has been read.

One further caution is necessary for teachers who are providing reading instruction for older students. Though the skills to be acquired are the same, the interest level and the suitability of the materials must be considered and adjusted for their age and experience.

References
1. **Lectura en Dos Idiomas.** Northvale, New Jersey: Santillana Publishing Company, Inc., 1977.

2.. Smith, Nila Banton. **Reading Instruction for Today's Children.** New Jersey: Prentice-Hall, Inc., 1963.

3. Thonis, Eleanor, W. **Aprendamos a leer.** Arlington, Virginia: Media Marketing, Inc., 1975.

4. Verdier, Rafael. **La enseñanza de la ortografía en la escuela primaria.** Madrid: Diana Artes Gráficas, 1963.

CHAPTER III

WORD RECOGNITION SKILLS

Word recognition skills are commonly defined as skills that make it possible for readers to make an association between the written word and the spoken one. For beginning readers, the spoken word is a known stimulus, but the written word is unknown. When students can recognize in the visual (written) form those words for which they have meanings in the auditory (oral) form, they can then attach these same meanings from speech to the new forms in print. In this manner, new associations are created and for a **single** set of meanings, students have **two** responses, one auditory and the other visual. Through an associative process, comprehensibility, which formerly was associated with speech, now has been extended to print. Word recognition skills may depend upon memory, visual perception, auditory discrimination, and mental age. There is a variety of strategies that students may use to acquire and to perfect their abilities in word recognition. One major approach is **phonics,** which has been described in Chapter II. Students are taught to listen for differences in sounds in words during the readiness period, and then they are taught the visual appearance, the letters and letter combinations that represent the sounds. Visual training is now matched with auditory training, and the result is the acquisition of hundreds of words through the association of sight and sound. Students who are successful in using this manner of word recognition are able to identify previously learned sound-symbol connections in new or unfamiliar words. For students who can benefit from this type of strategy, phonics can serve as **one** excellent word recognition technique. There are many other means that may be applied to discover what a new word may be. Among these are the development of a sight vocabulary, the use of pictorial clues, the application of structural analysis, the discovery of configuration, the practice of searching context, and the understanding of diacritical marks. With the great popularity of phonics as an introductory approach in Spanish because of the consistency of speech-print connections, these other techniques for promoting word recognition skills are frequently overlooked.

Sight Vocabulary
Sight words are words that are usually presented as **whole** words rather than by their letters or syllables. They are generally learned as the result of the practice in associating a meaningful referent with its form in speech and in print. For example, in a classroom where the teacher has labeled carefully the room environment, the students will have a rich opportunity to acquire a sight vocabulary of objects in the room. They may learn such words as **el reloj, la pared, la luz, el escritorio, los**

libros, las plantas, la puerta, la ventana, and other features of the classroom. Arguments have been advanced that Spanish readers do not have need for the development of a sight vocabulary because the speech-print associations can be made on the basis of sensible, regular associations. There are a few double letters, for example **cc** in le**cc**ión, **ee** in l**ee**r, **aa** in Is**aa**c, and **oo** in c**oo**peración. Such words as these may be learned by sight along with the many words that have the silent **h, hombre, hacer, hogar.** Many students have strong visual memory skills and will learn a large number of words that have been presented visually as complete words. Sight words can be recognized immediately by the reader without any need for slowing down to examine the letters, syllables, or other elements of the words. This instantaneous recognition promotes more rapid, smoother reading and allows for an efficient grasp of meaning. Among the many lists of words suggested as useful for the purpose of developing a sight vocabulary is the one that follows. Many of the words are those that appear over and over again in connected discourse:

sí	a	del	eso	les	ni	sin
un	al	dos	este	lo	no	su
una	así	el	hacia	los	nos	sus
uno	bien	él	hoy	más	para	te
y	casi	en	la	me	por	ti
yo	con	esa	las	mi	se	tu
	de	ese	le	mi	si	muy

These words should be used in a context that will make sense to the students. Also useful as sight words are the many interrogatives that are needed in class:

¿cuál?	¿qué?	¿dónde?
¿cuándo?	¿quién?	¿cómo?
¿por qué?	¿cuánto?	¿cuántos?

As the students learn these words, they are also acquiring an important punctuation mark, the inverted question mark that alerts the reader to the nature of the written message that follows.

¿CUAL ES?

boxeador	Félix
saxofón	taxi
extinguidor	xilófono

1. ¿Cuál es el nombre de un niño?
2. ¿Cuáles son instrumentos musicales?
3. ¿Cuál es un carro?
4. ¿Cuál es el que apaga el fuego?
5. ¿Cuál es el nombre del que boxea?

Umbral, Page 58

¿Qué hacen los patos?

Los patos corren en el mar.
Los patos nadan en el mar.

Trampolin, Page 40

¿QUIEN SOY?

yema	yate	yegua
Yolanda	yuca	yerba

1. Soy un barco de recreo.
2. Soy la hembra del caballo.
3. Soy el nombre de una niña.
4. Soy lo verde del jardín.
5. Soy lo amarillo del huevo.
6. Soy un vegetal que se come.

Umbral, Page 52

Reading teachers usually consider sight vocabulary as a temporary measure that serves a momentary useful purpose. No real reading power can be developed solely on the basis of a sight vocabulary. The words learned by sight are those that should have meaning for the students. The habits that they may develop to fix the sight words in their minds will become extremely useful later in the reading of English when hundreds of words may not be learned through regular speech-print associations. A few techniques for presenting sight words are these:

- Write the word on the board; use it in a sentence; have the student say the word.
- Invite students to come to the board and underline or frame the word.
- Ask students to copy the word (and the short sentence).
- Have students write the words on small cards and place them in a file alphabetically.
- Make a class or personal dictionary of sight words that may be illustrated.
- Prepare charts for use in the classroom of words that are important to the lessons.
- Remove labels from objects in the room and ask the students to replace the labels correctly and quickly.
- Encourage students to refer to their file boxes or personal dictionaries when needed in spelling and writing activities.

In **Lectura en dos idiomas,** occasionally new words essential to the stories may be introduced as sight words. For example:

Alma se pone el **disfraz**.

Estamos **lejos** de la casa.

For beginning readers who are just coming to grips with the decoding process, a presentation of words such as **disfraz** and **lejos** as sight words will give the students opportunities to talk about the meanings of these words and will put them in context. Additionally, the students will have practice in noting that the written endings **s** and **z** have the same pronunciation. Thus, they are dealing with one of the irregular sound-symbol connections, not in isolation, but rather in material that makes sense to them.

Entró en **acción** cuando pidieron auxilio.

Si tienes **voluntad,** tendrás éxito.

When the words **acción** and **voluntad** are taught as sight words, students can see the double consonant **cc** and hear the **k** sound of the first **c** and the **s** sound of the **c** before **i. Voluntad** is also a good sight word because the final **d** is swallowed up in speech and not likely to be heard by the student. These kinds of words are useful for illustrating the few discrepancies between speech and print in Spanish. By identifying them as part of a **sight** vocabulary, the students learn them painlessly and benefit from the speech-print analysis after the words have been acquired.

Picture Clues
In the modern world there are few books and materials for young children that do not contain pictures. One of the first understandings that very young children acquire is the awareness that the writing on the page has something to say about the illustrations. Often, children will pretend to read by inventing stories about the pictures. Children enjoy **seeing** what they have **said** when the teacher writes something and places it under the picture. From these pre-reading and pre-writing experiences, students learn to expect that there is an important relationship between pictures and print. When they are actually engaged in learning to read, the students use this skill to help them recognize words. Sometimes a discussion of what may be found in the illustrations may be productive for the students before they read the selection. Then, picture clues serve as reminders of unfamiliar words that must be identified if the passage is to make sense.

Some of the classroom activities that may serve to promote word recognition through the use of pictures are these:

- Prepare cards with pictures on one side and words on the other. Use these in a variety of card games.
- Have students draw pictures of people, places, or events in the story, and provide the labels for students to copy.
- Provide picture vocabulary cards available commercially for pupil team learning in pairs.
- Send home vocabulary picture cards for students who are out of school because of illness or other reasons.
- Create picture cards for each unit of work and maintain envelopes of them available for the review of a lesson or for the making up of a lesson that has been missed.
- Offer time to use picture dictionaries (commercially published or student developed) to establish the dictionary habit.
- Introduce new reading selections through an examination and discussion of the illustrations.

The selection that follows illustrates how pictures, words, and meanings are brought together.

Los meses del año

Treinta días tiene noviembre,
con abril, junio y septiembre.
De veintiocho o veintinueve sólo hay uno,
y los demás treinta y uno.

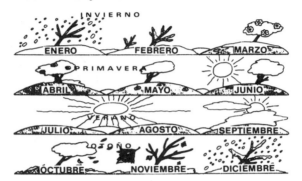

Las estaciones del año son cuatro: la primavera, el verano, el otoño y el invierno.
Cada una de las estaciones es diferente.
Durante la primavera abundan las lluvias y florecen las plantas.
En el verano hace mucho calor y los árboles se llenan de hojas.
En el otoño hay fuertes vientos y las hojas se secan y se caen.
También comienza a refrescar.
El invierno es la estación más fría. En algunos países nieva y en otros no, y los árboles están sin hojas.

Adelante, Page 41

Configuration Clues

Beginning readers may have modest success indentifying words by their general appearance. Such features as the length of the word, the ascending or descending letters, and location of letters in initial, medial, or final position may provide sight clues to word recognition. When the number of words in the student's reading vocabulary is small, the application of the visual perceptual clues offered by configuration may be useful. It is easy to see at a glance that **teléfono** ⌐⌐⌐⌐ has a different shape from **carro** ⌐⌐ . By visualizing the contrasts between these words, the reader has a valuable clue. However, this distinction is insufficient for recognizing each of the words, and the reader must apply additional strategies. Further, as the reading vocabulary expands, many words will have identical configurations — pelo `pelo`, pila `pila`, pato `pato`. A student who depended on word configuration clues alone would soon find too many words with the same shape and would need to search for other clues. Probably the principal advantage of calling attention to the different word configurations comes in the initial stage of reading. The habit of looking at a word in its entirety and of obtaining a sense of the whole word prepares the reader for taking in larger units of print later when skills have been acquired. The use of letter forms and word lengths are illustrated in the activity taken from page 17 in **Estrella, libro de apresto 2, Lectura en dos idiomas.**

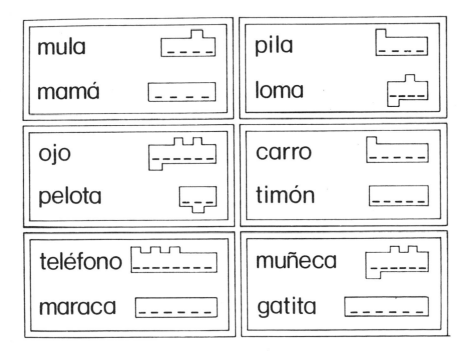

There are a few reading theorists who state that the clues offered by word configuration are minimal and scarcely worth the effort of teaching them. This viewpoint is certainly justified as there are admitted limitations to the word recognition help the mere shape of a word may give the reader. However, there is one advantage in training students to look at all of the word and to focus on the word's total appearance. This practice does serve to establish careful visual response to print. Wise teachers do not ordinarily spend too much time or energy on configuration activities before going on to other productive strategies for unlocking words and their meanings in context.

Structural Clues

The structural elements of language provide valuable clues for recognizing words. Students have learned language patterns and forms as they have been living and growing in oral language. When they come to reading, they have the knowledge of how certain sounds go together to make words; of the order in which words are arranged; and of the basic rules by which their language works. This functional awareness of word formation (the morphology), of word order (the syntax), and the basic rules (the grammar) can be applied to discover words and word patterns in written material. Among the structural features in Spanish that may serve this very useful purpose are these:

- The syllable may consist of one or several letters and may help the student recognize likenesses and/or differences in words.

coro	**co**mo	**co**pa	**co**sa
pa**ta**	la**ta**	na**ta**	ra**ta**

- The root words represent basic words or parts of words that may be varied by adding something to them.

bueno	**buen**os	**mal**o	**mal**a
buena	**buen**as	**mal**os	**mal**as

- The inflectional forms are words that can change in number, gender, tense, person, or other characteristics through changes in or additions to the word. The inflectional endings of the verb system are very significant in Spanish.

habl**o**	habl**amos**
habl**as**	habl**an**

- Derivational processes in words often change the word from one form to another and create a new vocabulary item.

trabajar (verb)	**pint**ar (verb)
trabaj**ador** (noun)	pintor**esco** (adjective)

- The affixes (whatever is attached) to the root or stem may come before (the prefix) or come after (the suffix) the root.

deponer	magistr**ado**
disponer	magist**ral**
superponer	magist**erio**

- The combining of two words into one single word creates a compound word.

rascacielos	**paraguas**	**pasatiempo**
quitasol	**abrelatas**	**salvavidas**

- The augmentative suffixes and the diminutive endings carry not only a connotation of size, but also may suggest endearment, ugliness, or even contempt.

pajar**ito**	Carl**ito**	perr**azo**
cigar**illo**	cuchi**llón**	dormi**lón**

- The Spanish process of **enclisis** in which two word classes are combined into one form is extensive.

dé**melo**	mostrár**selo**
dándo**telo**	mirándo**las**

- The diacritical marks may change the word class and function of certain words.

dé (give)	**de** (of)	**si** (yes)	**si** (if)
más (more)	**mas** (but)	**te** (you)	**té** (tea)
aún (yet)	**aun** (even)		

- The presence of smaller words in longer ones may provide needed clues for recognizing new words.

en**fr**iar (fría)	**persona**jes (persona)
marcha (mar)	con**forma**rse (forma)

Activities that will promote knowledge and skill in using language structure to recognize words are suggested in the pages that follow. They are not intended to be inclusive of every technique that creative and resourceful teachers use in their ongoing efforts to guide students toward an effective understanding of the structural clues that may make reading easier and more enjoyable.

Root Words

The awareness of the constancy of the **basic** word (which remains **unchanged** regardless of the number of affixes that the word may carry) is essential for students before they can be very successful in dealing with the hundreds of inflections that do **change** the meanings of words. The concept of a **root** word should be thoughtfully developed. One of the very first inflectional endings that students encounter is the plural **s.** The root word in its unchanging form may be practiced orally with pictures to illustrate singular and plural. Then the words written on the blackboard or worksheets may be provided for visual practice. Lists of singular and plural words such as these are useful. Words also may be selected from the students' interests or from the material in the reading lessons.

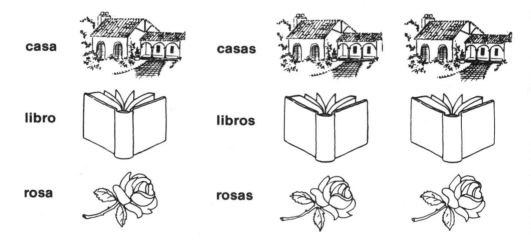

casa   casas

libro   libros

rosa   rosas

To illustrate the concept and the unchanging nature of the **root** word, the lists may be provided with boxes around the root word or the endings.

casa   libro   rosa

casa ⃞s   libro ⃞s   rosa ⃞s

Other plural endings **es** may be demonstrated in the same manner.

papel   papel ⃞es

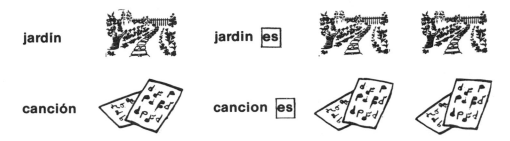

Plurals with orthographic changes may be demonstrated as follows:

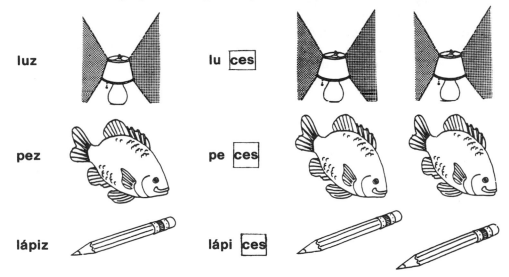

Compound Words

Spanish has a limited number of compound words that are created by the putting together of two words to create a completely new one. A common combination joins a verb form and a noun — **abrelatas; rompecabezas; tocadiscos.** Another less common combination is the linking of a noun and an adjective — **pelirrojo; patizambo; ojinegro.** A few compound words may be formed by two nouns — **arcoiris; bocacalle; plumafuente.** Occasionally other parts of speech may be connected — **compadre; quehaceres; sinvergüenza.** The development of skill in seeing the two smaller words may be of some help to students in decoding longer, more difficult words. The teacher may write the two words separately on the blackboard and then write them as one word using the new word in a sentence. Or, the one word may be given as the stimulus and the two words discovered by the students. Students may be given the words orally and asked to listen for the words within the word given. They may have two words written on cards that can be put together. Teachers should stress the meaning of the newly created word after its component words or parts have been identified. Students should have opportunities to hear and see the word in connected discourse. The students may be asked to draw a line separating the two parts of a compound word or to draw a frame around each part. Practice in identifying whole word units within compound words allows students to perceive and to analyze the formation of words. As spoken and written vocabularies are expanded, the ability to identify parts of compound words becomes a useful technique in word recognition. Recognition alone, however, will not create a meaningful response unless the readers' experiences are related to the word. Students who are reading **Velerín (Pg. 129 Adelante),** for example, and come across the relatively long word **guardacostas** will be helped in their word recognition skills not only from seeing and hearing **guarda** and **costas** as separate words, but also from the context of the story and the understanding of the meaning of **los guardacostas** as a single entity.

Although the formation of new words by the simple expedient of joining the words has somewhat limited application in Spanish, it is an extremely valuable process for students to understand and to have for use later in English where compounding of words is extensive.

Other examples of compound words found in Spanish are these:

Verb-Noun Combinations	Noun-Noun Combinations	Other Combinations
saltamontes	**aguamiel**	**sinpensar**
correcaminas	**madrepatria**	**sinsabor**
cortauñas	**mesabanco**	**anteojos**
lavamanos	**cascanueces**	**paraguas**
trabalenguas	**aeropuerto**	**nochebuena**
matamoscas	**cuentagotas**	**bienestar**

One feature of compound words that may require special attention is the formation of plurals of such words. Some words form the plural according to the regular rules **(bocacalles),** and others add the plural endings to both words **(lenguas madres).** The gender is usually determined by the noun, and in noun-noun combinations by the first noun. Students need to take the time to learn these details.

Context Clues

One powerful strategy for recognizing new words is the effort to find meaning that may be supplied in the sentence or paragraph itself. The student may attempt to identify the unknown word by drawing on personal experiences or by using the words that are known in the surrounding context to predict the unknown. Essentially, the search is for something that makes sense. If students have opportunities and practice in making predictions in oral language activities or in lessons using pictures, they will be better equipped to use context clues as a word recognition technique in reading. Students may be encouraged to complete a sentence — **El pájaro vive en su _____ (nido). El zapatero hace botas y _____ (zapatos). El cielo es _____ (azul). La miel es _____ (dulce) y nos la da la _____ (abeja).** The content of these incomplete sentences may be adjusted for length, complexity, and concept loading according to the maturity of the students. Pictures may be used to elicit responses that require the interpretation of details and actions. The teacher may describe the persons or events as depicted and have the students supply the correct word. Such practice trains students to seek new words from the context of the material that is known to them. The development of skill in using context to discover new words is improved through careful questioning and by supplying additional information. Teachers can ask students about the functions of the unknown word. **¿Qué usamos para _____? ¿Para qué sirve _____? (pintar, barrer, comer, peinar).** They may suggest synonyms. **¿Conoces otro nombre para _____? (cárcel, avión, coche).** They may give definitions of the word. **La palabra quiere decir _____ (listo, fuerte, feliz).** They may suggest that the word is the opposite of a word that is known to the students. **Es el contrario de _____ (frío, suave, agradable). Tiene el sentido contrario de _____.** Sometimes, students may be helped by reminding them of a familiar expression from repeated use of the word in speech — **blanca** como la **paloma; obscura** como **la noche; dura** como **la piedra.** These clichés of language are so well known that students can pick up on the words in written form with very little assistance.

When students are learning to discover unknown words through seeking meaning from context, they should be encouraged to skip the word and read on to see if they can make a sensible prediction on the basis of the additional material. Good readers do not allow themselves to get stuck in one place simply because they cannot understand a word or two. They may obtain useful information from the time of day, the place of the action, the season of the year, the character, or the mood of the character. Words such as **madrugada** or **desayuno** can be predicted in a story taking place early in the day while **nocturno** or **estrellas** may be recognized within the context of evening. Often, the students' logic will serve them in recognizing the temporal relationships so that current, former, or future activities may reveal word differences of **ahora, ayer, anteayer, luego, más tarde, et cetera.** At times, students may obtain meaning from typographical features — question marks, exclamation points, quotation marks. Teachers need to remind students of the usefulness of these context clues. In using context to determine new words, students should be encouraged to bring to reading their personal experiences, their knowledge of speech, their background of familiar expressions, their logic, and their awareness of people, places, and events. Students do need to realize that although they are drawing upon all of these factors to recognize words in print, the act is not a wild guessing game. When students begin to rely excessively on context to help them comprehend, they may not be motivated to acquire other word recognition techniques that could serve them well when the use of context clues alone will not work.

Teachers must also be careful that the material from which context clues may be sought is not too difficult for the readers or too far out of their range of experiences. If the passage contains several unknown words, then the context is unlikely to be of much help to students. The hints as to meaning are efficient to the extent that the new word can be determined from the familiar ones or can be associated with a known experience. The most effective way to develop in students the very useful skill of gaining meaning from context is by preparing them for the passage or story, by reminding them of what they already know, and by applying the various strategies for obtaining clues through **guided** practice and **direct** teaching. Only a few students are somehow able to make good use of context on their own. Most of the students will need guidance and direction if they are to be successful. The ability to use context as a clue to meaning and to the recognition of unknown words improves as reading power increases, as students have more varied experiences, and as they mature developmentally.

Context may provide clues to word meanings through descriptions. Several examples taken from page 46 in **Umbral** follow:

1. Si me pierdes,
   no puedes abrir la puerta.   llave
   Soy una _____.   llanta

2. Si conoces los colores
   y miras el sol,
   ya sabes quién soy.   amarillo
   Soy el _____.   azul

3. Vivo en la finca.
   Pongo huevos
   en el gallinero.   gallo
   Soy una _____.   gallina

4. Si me usas,
   vas peinada
   y arreglada,   caballo
   Soy un _____.   cepillo

Syllabication

The identification of syllables in words may serve as a clue to recognizing an unfamiliar word in Spanish reading. The rules for dividing words into syllables are so steady and consistent that they may be helpful when the students come upon a a long, difficult word. In Spanish, there are eighteen consonants, five vowels, and two (or four) semi-consonants that may combine to form countless syllables. Yet, not all of these potential combinations are permitted. As has been stated, a syllable is formed when there is a vowel or a vowel(s) in combination with a consonant (or semi-consonant). The consonant may precede or follow the vowel. The rules for syllabication derived from an abbreviated examination of the syllable structure* are these:

- Whenever available, a syllable begins with a consonant (**co-ro-nel, pa-so**);
- Two consonants are separated unless the second one is **l** or **r** (**a-bri-go, ta-bla**);
- Three consonants are separated to allow one consonant to remain with the preceding vowel and the two to begin the next syllable (**im-pren-ta, i-gle-sia, ex-tran-je-ros**). Vowels may be separate syllables (**i-de-a, o-a-sis**).

The teacher may not wish to burden the beginning students with these rules of syllabication. It may be more productive for the students to make these discoveries for themselves through practice in forming words and in recognizing syllable elements in words. At an introductory level, students will find delight and wonder in their ability to recognize words formed by the mere repetition of syllables and will readily acquire the habit of searching for familiar syllable combinations when they need to use the syllable as a tool in unlocking new words — **papá, mamá, bebe, Lulú, Pepe, coco.** There are eighty-nine possible combinations of syllables formed by the simple consonant-vowel pattern and identified in over 30,000 words — **pera, loco, tira, toro, casa, mudo, nido, niño.** Consonant-vowel-consonant syllables are also numerous. Thomann lists 392 of them in the **cvc** pattern and

*Donaldo Jose Thomann. **Dictionary of Spanish Syllables.** Stanford University. Unpublished Dissertation, 1968.

pattern and identifies over 15,000 words in which they may be found — **pan; mar; ver; balcón; burlas; pintor; dormir; doctor.** There are thirty-nine vowel-consonant syllables to be found in over 2,800 words — **es; al; un; isla; es**puma, **in**dio; **on**ce; **es**tá. The various types of syllables are frequently found together in words — **bar-rer; na-ran-ja; es-co-ba; chi-rin-ga.**

The work of Thomann and others who have investigated the structure and frequency of the Spanish syllable has enhanced appreciation of the syllable as a useful instrument for word recognition. The decoding of words based on the awareness of the syllabic system, however, will be productive in reading only to the extent that the meanings of these words are obtained from context or are developed in vocabulary instruction. The syllable as a unit of word structure does serve to identify speech-print connections.

Syllables as Units

To assist students in hearing the number of syllables in words, ask them to clap out the rhythm of words in varying lengths. In this manner, students develop the auditory sensitivity needed. They need to know that a syllable is a single pronounceable entity in a word and that it consists of a vowel sound by itself or in combination with one or more consonant sounds. Oral practice should precede written practice. Students may be asked to give the number of claps they made and indicate that this number represents the number of syllables. Words such as **te; pata; México; ladrones; asustados; zapatería** and other words of varying lengths may be used for oral practice. Words may also be selected from the day's lesson. After deciding the number of syllables, the words may be written on the blackboard, and the students may check the number of vowels. Later, when the generalization has been made that one vowel sound creates one syllable, the diphthongs containing **two written vowels** but only **one vowel sound** may be added to the practice in recognizing syllables. Then the words containing diphthongs such as **fiesta, patio, viuda, agua,** and others from the students' listening and speaking vocabularies may be included. In written work, students may supply missing syllables or may take words from dictation and indicate the number of syllables. In order to use the syllable as a clue in analyzing the structure of words, the students need to develop these skills.

- to hear the syllable
- to identify the syllable
- to count the number of syllables
- to generalize the rule that the number of vowel sounds equals the number of syllables.

First, students will find it easy to identify in written form the syllables they have heard in **initial** positions as in the exercise on page 15 from **Estrella**. The students are to circle the syllable that is the same as the one in the box.

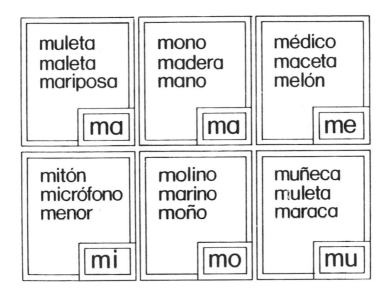

muleta maleta mariposa ma	mono madera mano ma	médico maceta melón me
mitón micrófono menor mi	molino marino moño mo	muñeca muleta maraca mu

Later, they may practice hearing and identifying syllables in **medial** and **final** positions.

bi ci cleta   **de** do   **llu** via   a **ba** nico

ga **lli** na   ar **di** lla   fal **da**   ca **lle**   lo **bo**

Diacritical Marks

The diacritical marks that are part of the Spanish writing system have the important function of guiding the reader to respond accurately to the words, and to pronounce them correctly as needed. Diacritical marks serve another purpose by distinguishing words spelled the same but conveying different meanings. Like most of the principles in Spanish reading, the simple rules may be applied with great constancy and confidence. When the pronunciation of words deviates from the basic guidelines in **oral** Spanish, the orthographic accent signals the reader.

- words ending in vowels **n,** or **s** are stressed on the **next** to the last syllable — **clas**es, **or**den, **bue**no;
- all other words are stressed on the **last** syllable — profe**sor,** volunt**ad,** albañ**il;**
- when the stress falls on some other syllable a written accent mark indicates where the stress falls — **violín, jamás, algodón, Perú, maní, árbol, café.**

Students can learn these three basic rules and practice their application in writing and spelling from the very first lessons. Other very important marks are the tilde over **ñ** as in niño and the dieresis over **ü** as in **pingüino.** Teachers would be wise to consider the omission of the diacritical mark an error and encourage students to master these straightforward requirements early so that good habits can be growing. Gentle reminders of the rules governing the use of diacritical marks can be placed in the writing and spelling areas of the classroom for students to consult as needed.

Rules for accentuation in **speech** may be presented if appropriate for the learners.

Palabras **agudas** llevan el acento con la última sílaba — **nariz, comer.**

Palabras **llanas** llevan el acento en la penúltima sílaba — **lindo, juego.**

Palabras **esdrújulas** llevan el acento en la antepenúltima sílaba — **vámonos, México, lástima.**

Rules for accentuation in **print** may also be provided in charts placed near the writing activities corner of the classroom. The teacher needs to be careful about overdoing the presentation of rules, but the charts do serve as silent reminders when students are writing. Practice lessons such as the sentences that follow are useful in helping students understand the **acento prosódico** and the **acento ortográfico.**

1. Lila usa el termómetro.
2. Lila usa el teléfono.
3. Manolo usa el teléfono.

1. La niña está en la fila.
2. El niño está al final.
3. El niño está en la fila.

Cascabel, Libro de Actividades, página 27.

Deben llevar el acento ortográfico

café **maní** **corazón** **jamás**	1. las palabras terminadas en vocales, **n** y **s,** si el acento cae sobre la última sílaba.
sílaba **cántaro** **albóndigas** **luciérnaga**	2. las palabras terminadas en vocales y en otras consonantes si el acento cae sobre la antepenúltima sílaba.

These are the major rules for using the written accent. When students have become comfortable with these requirements, they may be given the additional information such as:

- singular words sometimes lose their diacritial marks when they become plural — **lección - lecciones**
- plural words sometimes lose their diacritical marks when they become singular — **jóvenes - joven**

97

- when **mente** is added to a word to create an adverb, the diacritical mark is retained — **fácil - fácilmente**
- when pronouns are added to verb forms, the verb carries the stress — **pagando - pagándosela.**

A few common words that have diacritical marks to distinguish them from other words of the same spelling are these:

dé	give	**de**	(preposition) of
él	(subject)	**el**	(article) the
sí	yes	**si**	if
sé	know	**se**	(reflexive pronoun) you
té	tea	**te**	(personal pronoun)
tú	you	**tu**	your
sólo	only	**solo**	sole
mí	me	**mi**	my
aún	yet	**aun**	even
más	more	**mas**	but
aquél	(pronoun) that	**aquel**	(adjective) that

Transferability of Word Recognition Skills to English

Students who are literate in Spanish at a level commensurate with their grade placement have strong word recognition skills to bring to the reading of English. They have learned to apply a variety of strategies in discovering words, phrases, and sentences. They are now ready to use many of the same techniques to recognize the print of English. They may have acquired a sight vocabulary; used sound-symbol associations; sought clues from pictures, maps, or other graphic materials; considered structural changes in words; recognized configural differences; gained meaning through context; determined word identity through syllabication; and noted the system of diacritical marks. This ability to employ such word recognition tactics is the very same ability needed in recognizing English words in second-language reading. Every skill that has been carefully nurtured while learning to read in Spanish can be applied to the new task. Some skills may have greater or lesser application in English reading, but **all** of them will be useful and productive.

Sight Vocabulary in English Transfer

The development of a sight vocabulary in English may be of greater usefulness than a sight vocabulary in Spanish, because there are in English so many words that cannot be recognized through other methods of word analysis. The visual memory, visual perception and visual discrimination activities offered in learning to read Spanish can be provided again. The content of word packs, word games, blackboard practice, and seat work is drawn from the English reading materials. The students know how to make the responses, how to play the word games, and how to follow through on the tasks as assigned. If the English listening and speaking vocabularies of the students have been promoted through sound oral language opportunities, then they will acquire the written forms as they **see** what they have been **hearing** and saying.

Especially useful as a sight vocabulary for second-language learners are the words suggested by the late Walter McHugh. He states that these words represent fifty percent of all written material.

on	the	them	then	make	of
but	any	out	today	to	we
so	very	leave	only	or	see
must	under	on	had	upon	what
into	in	they	great	shall	can
that	are	if	take	these	it
this	our	such	my	was	who
him	how	most	which	were	more
ever	us	as	been	is	me
now	be	will	when	go	part
by	for	one	where	say	know
not	all	other	than	often	he
at	some	though	there	have	would
said	do	after	their	use	whose
like	come	with	may	you	give
many	his	should	does	has	made

The interrogative words are especially important to learn in order that the students may understand questioning in the classroom activities and can respond appropriately.

From: Walter J. McHugh. **Words Most Useful in Reading.** California State University, Hayward, CA., 1972.

The words — **Who? When? Where? Why? How?** — need to be learned as English expressions for the same purpose of asking questions that have already been learned using Spanish interrogative words. Students will have enjoyed extensive practice in framing questions and in responding to questions in the Spanish reading program. Now, they will have to realize that in English the inverted question mark before the interrogative statement is dropped, but the question mark at the end of the sentence is kept. They will **not** have to learn the function of interrogative words because they already have acquired the most common interrogative words, their meanings, and their function. They will have interpreted the context in which the various interrogatives may be indicated and will have these essential understandings available to use as they acquire the English terminology for this identical function of questioning. Oral practice of these words **in English** will have built a background of language information needed to apply interrogative forms in speech.

Essentially, Spanish speakers and readers will have followed this sequence of language acquisition and learning:

- listening to and understanding the function and form of interrogatives in **oral Spanish**;
- reading, writing, and understanding the visual, **written** forms in Spanish;
- learning the conventions of the written system relative to interrogative words — the spelling, the beginning inverted question mark, the accent required on **all** interrogatives, the conventional mark of the punctuation at the end of an interrogative expression;
- listening to and understanding the function and form of interrogatives in **oral English**;
- reading, writing, and understanding the visual **written** forms in English;
- learning the conventions of the written system of English relative to interrogative words — the spelling and punctuation changes presented by dropping the inverted question mark and the orthographic accent that are **not** part of English writing.

Other sight vocabulary activities in English may involve the traditional word lists that native speakers of English are given early in their reading experiences. Despite the fact that the development of a sight vocabulary may not have been a major concern in the Spanish reading program, the students will have developed some basic strategies for recognizing words by sight. They will transfer to English **at least** the following:

- awareness of the visual appearance of the word;
- attention to the details of individual letters and their sequence;
- sensitivity to the importance of meaning in words;
- interest in words as a clue to obtaining meaning from larger units of written material;
- facility in using a variety of skills that promote retention of words.

Phonics as a Word Recognition Tool in English

Phonic analysis of words in English may be only relatively useful for students who have benefited from the development of this skill in Spanish. As has been mentioned, the pitfalls of non-transferable sound-symbol associations and of non-existing sound-symbol connections for the second language reader can create reading difficulties. A teacher who is using a phonic method in the word recognition activities in English will have to be very sensitive to the obvious discrepancies between Spanish and English phonics. However, the most serious concern of the teacher is that phonic analysis does **not** always lead students to meaning. It may help to some extent in the pronunciation of words but is no guarantee of word meaning for any reader, especially for a non-native speaker of English. In the early introductory phase of reading English, the teacher may make a reasonable assumption that the approximate (as opposed to absolute) accuracy of pronunciation leads the student to the recognition of the word. From word recognition to word meaning can be assured only **if** the student has that word available in his or her receptive vocabulary. Phonic analysis can be assisted by pictorial material as illustrated in the exercise designed to provide practice in hearing, seeing, and recognizing words with short sounds on page 15 and 31 from **Able To Read:**

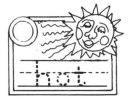  

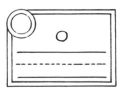  

Phonic elements taught in isolation and devoid of **real** meaning in **real** words from understandable sentences are not especially useful. Only when students are able to apply such phonic skills to discover words that can then make sense is the practice of value. In using English phonics as a word recognition strategy, the Hispanic student must check the context to verify that his or her discovery, derived through phonic analysis, is suitable. If the word does not fit the context, if it does not make sense to the reader, then the analysis is futile and other strategies must be used.

Centuries of language usage and change have altered spelling and pronunciation patterns of English words. Meanings of words have also been modified drastically. English presently has the dubious distinction of being considered a language that has a very irregular and inconsistent system of connections between sound and symbol. Despite the well-recognized number of speech-print exceptions to phonic rules, there is considerable merit in encouraging Spanish readers to try out their phonic skills as **one** word recognition approach. Students may be told that if the word they have recognized by phonic analysis fits into meaningful context, fine! If not, they should go on to try some other means of discovery. The context serves as a check or proof of the readers' decision. For example, students may have difficulty recognizing the word **jockey.** The application of phonic analysis alone will be a challenge to remember that the **j** of English is a new sound for their own familiar **jota.** The **ck** in medial position may represent another unknown, and **ey** may represent a diphthong for them. If they are somehow able to come up with an approximation of the word **jockey,** they still are not going to have anything useful until the word is understood in the sentence: **Jockeys are people who ride horses in a horse race.** * If the word is mistakenly thought to be **jackets, journey,** or **juicy,** the use of the word in the sentence will reveal the error and force the students to think of alternatives.

Phonic analysis should be silent. Students should be encouraged to look not at the individual letters or clusters of letters first, but at the **whole** word. Then, after a look at the word in its entirety, students can begin with their knowledge of sound-symbol associations for the consonants and vowels. The application of phonic skills as a word recognition method in English involves at least the following ways of thinking about words:

- a search for the word from those known to the student — the listening and/or speaking vocabulary in English;
- a search for the parts of the words — letters, digraphs, syllables;
- an attempt to pronounce the word after or during the analysis process;

*Lickety-Split, Page 178.

- an effort to put the word in context to see how it works;
- a new attempt if the context does not make sense;
- an alternate word recognition strategy.

Structural Analysis as a Strategy in English Word Recognition
The commonalities in structure between Spanish and English offer many transfer opportunities for the students. There are many prefixes and suffixes that are shared. The concept of a **root** word is the same in both languages. Inflectional forms are fewer in English than in Spanish. In particular, the verb forms do not change in English to the extent that they do in Spanish. English does a great deal of word compounding whereas Spanish does only a little. The augmentative and diminutive forms that create such colorful and creative imagery in Spanish are relatively few in English. English does not have an enclitic form nor does English make use of orthographic accentuation. The contrasts and comparisons should be brought to the attention of students as the English reading program is being presented. Some of the structural elements that are **identical** in both languages can be pointed out as follows:

- plurals are formed by adding **s** to the singular form

libro	—	libro**s**
book	—	book**s**

- some words add **es** to form the plural

flor	—	flor**es**
church	—	church**es**

- some words are the same in their plural or singular forms

lunes	—	**lunes***
sheep	—	**sheep**

- some irregular plurals exist in both languages and must be learned as they are met in reading.

The addition of a prefix to a root word for the purpose of forming a new word with a different meaning is a practice common to both languages. Many of the prefixes

*The article **los** indicates the plural

are spelled the same or nearly the same and carry the same connotation. For example:

ab	**ab**stener	**ab**stain
ante	**ante**cedente	**ante**cedent
anti	**anti**congelante	**anti**freeze
contra	**contra**decir	**contra**dict
inter	**inter**ceder	**inter**cede
post	**post**umo	**post**humous
pro	**pro**nombre	**pro**noun
re	**re**conocer	**re**cognize
sub	**sub**marino	**sub**marine
super	**super**abundancia	**super**abundance

Some of the prefixes have slight variations in spelling but carry the same meanings. For example:

circun	**circun**scribir	**circum**	**circum**scribe
entre	**entre**mezclar	**inter**	**inter**mingle
hiper	**hiper**crítico	**hyper**	**hyper**critical

Suffixes in **both** Spanish and English are numerous. At times they are identical in spelling, and at times the suffixes differ only slightly. A few examples follow:

al	can**al**	**al**	can**al**
or	act**or**	**or**	act**or**
ar	lun**ar**	**ar**	lun**ar**
able	formid**able**	**able**	formid**able**
ión	relig**ión**	**ion**	relig**ion**

Many of the suffixes are recognizable from one language to the other because of the very little change in spelling.

ador	sen**ador**	**ator**	sen**ator**
gio	presti**gio**	**ge**	presti**ge**
ción	na**ción**	**tion**	na**tion**
ica	mús**ica**	**ic**	mus**ic**
ismo	comun**ismo**	**ism**	commun**ism**
ito	infin**ito**	**ite**	infin**ite**

Although it is true that the prefixes and suffixes of Spanish and English have a great deal in common, it is wise to move cautiously when teaching the comparisons. The use of the affix system is great for word recognition purposes because students who may have the words available in their Spanish and written vocabularies can apply this knowledge to discover words and their meanings in English reading. However, when students are using the same information to write English, they must be more careful because not all the prefixes **or** suffixes can be applied wholesale in both languages. For example, in Spanish the ending **ista** can be considered without the **a** and the words flaut**ist** (flaut**ista**); dent**ist** (dent**ista**); art**ist** (art**ista**); novel**ist** (novel**ista**) can be formed, but there is no such word as **fondist** in English to be created from **fondista,** which means innkeeper in Spanish.

Compound Words in English

If the students have learned the principles of word compounding and have had practice in recognizing them in their Spanish reading activities, the skill should be an extremely useful one for managing the hundreds of words that exist in English as a result of the fondness English has for putting **two** words together to create a new one. Instead of new words coming into existence by a combination of root word and prefix or suffix, compound words are formed by the combination of **two** root words. Very simple compound words for students who are new to the reading of English are these:

sunset	lookout	gunman	godson
sunrise	dishpan	popcorn	tomcat
classroom	campfire	hilltop	workbook

The important characteristic of these words is that they are usually written as **one** word but actually contain **two.** The teacher should ascertain that the students know **each** word singly and have a good understanding of each before putting them into their new form and giving them new or additional meanings. A classroom is a **room** where the **class** works. A campfire is a **fire** that is built in the **camp.** A **sunrise** is when the **sun** comes up or **rises.** Some compound words have completely new meanings. A **godson** cannot be explained by the two given words alone, and a **gunman** is not merely a man who carries a **gun!** In English some compound words are hyphenated. Words that are made up of **self** and another word, such as self-confidence, self-control, self-satisfied, use the hyphen. Words combined with **well** — well-intentioned or well-known — may also be hyphenated compounds. As students become more familiar with this feature of the writing system, they should have practice with these variations of compounding in English:

- some compound words are one word with meanings taken directly from the words put together — classroom;
- some compound words are one word with meanings different from the words put together — godson;
- some compound words are written as two words connected by a hyphen — well-known, self-esteem;
- some words are kept as separate words **but** have a compound meaning — ice cream;
- number words from twenty-one to ninety-nine are hyphenated compounds.

For the Hispanic student, it may be important to point out that the tendency to compound is not always the same in both languages. **Abrelatas** and **canopener** are parallel combinations, but **comedor** is **one** word for the English **dining room;** and **el correo** has two words, **post office,** and **arco iris,** two words in Spanish for the single word **rainbow.** Activities that help students draw upon their Spanish language and literacy will enhance reading word recognition skills in English.

Context Clues to Words in English

The students will have had a variety of opportunities to use context to discover unknown words in their Spanish reading lessons. They will have had practice in their search for the words that make sense in the sentence or passage. The process of completing sentences, responding to questioning, finding synonyms and antonyms, and using their own knowledge of the setting, people, or other events is one that has developed logic and reasoning abilities. This skill is applied in the same manner to identify unfamiliar words in the English reading classes. Students will be engaging in the very same process. They will be asked by the teacher these same kinds of questions: What word fits? What word makes sense? What is the word we use to describe **winter** or the **snowy mountains?** The word is another word for **cold;** or it is the opposite of **hot.** Students will be searching for the typographical clues, the punctuation and capitalization. The teacher will be stressing constantly the comprehensibility of the words selected as they relate to the context provided. Good habits from Spanish reading will have diverted the time-wasting practice of wild, random guessing, and students will not have developed the practice of depending solely on context for meaning. The teacher, too, will wish to be especially patient in building the background information for the passage and will have introduced concepts and vocabulary as needed. In searching context for clues to unfamiliar words in English, students may need considerable guidance because:

- words in English often have multiple meanings;
- words used frequently appear to have many, varied meanings;

- words tend to have more meanings for persons who have more encounters with many people, places, events, and ideas;
- words may be discovered by several means other than through context, but the discovery must always be checked in meaningful context.

Syllabication in English

The fairly steady and economical syllable units of Spanish that have proved eminently manageable for the readers of Spanish will serve as a most valuable understanding when the students meet English syllables. They will know that the number of syllables in a word can be determined by the number of vowel sounds **heard** in the word. Thus, the first rule acquired in Spanish can be applied to English as well. Students will have to learn additionally that some vowels are **seen** but not **heard** — c**oa**t, cr**ea**m, h**ai**l, f**oe**. They will also have to deal with the silent vowel **e** — fad**e**, shin**e**, hop**e**. The English vowel sounds may be influenced by the type of syllable, open or closed, and Spanish speakers are unfamiliar with this description of open syllables ending in vowels and closed syllables ending in consonants. There are several basic procedures that may guide the students in the division of words into syllables, and to these basic principles there are some exceptions. For the non-native speaker of English, the concept of the **speech consonant** is important. Hispanic students already know that consonant blends are not divided, but they will have to learn to be careful about the consonant digraphs that cannot be divided either, e.g. mot**her**, fat**her**. The **two** basic rules for dividing words into syllables in English will be comfortable for Spanish readers because they are used to beginning a syllable with a consonant whenever possible. The first rule states that when two consonants come together, the word is usually divided between the two consonants. The second rule states that when there is only one consonant it usually goes with the next syllable. There are the seven* exceptions that need to be taught as the words are met in reading and become important to the students' reading vocabulary. Awareness of the syllables as the component parts of words is a valuable skill in spelling and reading, and will transfer to English to the extent that it has been well taught and well practiced during the acquisition of reading and spelling skills in Spanish.

There are some skills that may have limited usefulness for transfer. For example, the syllable system of English is far more complex and operates under several guiding principles that may not immediately make much sense to Spanish speakers and readers. They may certainly transfer totally the concept that for each vowel sound there is a syllable and may hear the number of syllables as they count. However, the silent vowels as well as the silent consonants will need to be dealt with directly. As has been mentioned, words such as **beam, huge, appeal,**

*Emerald Dechant. **Improving the Teaching of Reading.** New Jersey: Prentice-Hall, Inc., 1964.

saddle, may at first pose problems. The many past tense forms of commonly used words may evoke an extra syllable as a response. The English variant **ed** may be pronounced as **ed** in paint**ed,** count**ed,** repeat**ed,** but there are many **ed** verb forms in which **ed** is pronounced as **d** or **t** — mark**ed,** hook**ed,** jump**ed,** play**ed,** explain**ed.** These are more likely to be spelling and pronunciation problems than reading difficulties. Still, it may be helpful to mention these potential stumbling blocks during lessons on syllabication. The division of syllables between double consonants a **p-p** eal, inte **l-l** igence, ac-co **m-m** o-date may also be pointed out since Spanish has only **one** double consonant le **c-c ción.** Occasionally, an **en** prefix may create a word such as **ennoblecer,** but ordinarily, students are not accustomed to seeing double consonants in Spanish and will need specific instruction in English. The **rr** and **ll** are single letters of the alphabet and would **never** be separated. Another pronunciation difference is found in the many English words ending in **le** where the **e** is silent.

Caveat
The principal concern that teachers may have in developing the word recognition skills in English is the students' tendency to be **too** good at transferring their word-unlocking strategies from Spanish to English. Because the techniques have served them well in Spanish, the students may become very successful at **calling words.** This apparent prosperity must be monitored thoughtfully to ensure that students are obtaining meaning from the English words they have recognized. Teachers will want to continue to develop the broad foundation of oral English that will support the written program. They will be checking from time to time the levels of English comprehension in both speech and print to prevent confusion or misunderstandings.

Another decision that teachers will have to make with great caution is one concerning the rules of language. Both oral and written forms are governed by specific arbitrary conventions that ultimately have to be acquired. Teachers will need to consider the age and developmental status of students before adding the burden of rules governing syllables, structural variants or other aspects of language. Usually, the third grade students are able to manage rules and their exceptions. At the early stages of learning to read and to write, the students appear to benefit more from active practice with examples of material from which rules may be generalized.

Unless the teacher is using oral reading for diagnostic purposes, it is prudent to avoid overemphasis on the pronunciation of English words as recognized. Usually, non-native speakers improve their control of the sound system as they enjoy additional opportunities in English language settings. Silent reading followed by questions, discussions, and seatwork will give the teacher enough information to determine whether or not the word recognition skills have been learned. Sensitive teachers will want to avoid putting students in the embarrassing position of struggling with the capricious pronunciation of English. The major goal of instruction is to help students develop efficient and effective ways of identifying words in written form so that ultimately they may explore their meanings.

In summary, the skills of recognizing words in print may be acquired through a variety of strategies. Students who have good auditory integrities may apply phonics and learn to unlock unfamiliar words first in Spanish, and later, use this same technique successfully in English. Students who have strong visual skills may acquire sight vocabularies in **both** Spanish and English. Picture clues, context clues, and structural clues are very effective means of word identification in both languages. They draw upon the same intellectual process and require the same kind of language practice. The mere recognition of the words, however successful, will not ensure competence in comprehending what has been read. Word recognition is, nonetheless, the **first critical step** on the way to word meaning and beyond to the comprehension of words in connected written discourse. Skills, practiced and brought to a level of automatic response, first in Spanish and then transferred to English, permit readers to get on with the heart of reading instruction, which is comprehension.

References

1. Dechant, Emerald. **Improving the Teaching of Reading.** New Jersey: Prentice-Hall, Inc., 1964.

2. **Lectura en dos idiomas.** Northvale, New Jersey: Santillana Publishing Company, Inc., 1977.

3. McHugh, Walter. **Words Most Useful in Reading.** Hayward: California State University, Mimeographed, 1972.

4. Stockwell, Robert P., Bowen, J. Donald, and Martin, John W. **The Grammatical Structures of English and Spanish.** Chicago: The University of Chicago Press, 1965.

5. Thomann, Donaldo José. **Dictionary of Spanish Syllables.** Unpublished Dissertation, Stanford University, 1964.

CHAPTER IV

BASIC COMPREHENSION SKILLS IN SPANISH

Reading theorists are highly indebted to Edward Thorndike, who cut through many complex definitions of reading when he stated plainly that **reading is thinking.*** Thorndike's judgment in the early years of this century can be expanded today in the statement that reading **is** thinking in **any** language. Teachers who are guiding students toward excellence in English through the development of their native Spanish language and literacy skills will want to consider thoughtfully the wisdom of Thorndike and its implication for teaching. As students have been acquiring the readiness skills, the knowledge of the writing system, and the ability to recognize words in Spanish, they have been thinking. They have learned to remember and to reason, using their proficiencies in oral and written Spanish. They have been in the process of acquiring the tools to comprehend larger amounts of written material of increasing complexity. Comprehension of written material takes place on at least three levels — the literal, the interpretive, and the creative. Literal comprehension occurs when the reader obtains the basic meanings of what the author has written. The words, phrases, and sentences are understood because the reader recognizes them and is able to associate them with his or her own experiences. The language used to express the author's thoughts is known to the reader, who can then retrieve them from a background of information encoded in the same language. In comprehending at a literal level, the reader will discover the direct and the obvious. Literal comprehension makes few demands that the reader go beyond what is explicitly stated in the written material. Students are expected to understand what the selection is about (the main idea); what facts are given (the details); and in what order the narrative progresses (the sequence). Students may also be asked to identify specific words or expressions. Each of these acts of comprehending the literal meaning of written discourse demands thought. When students are understanding written material at an interpretative level, they are responding to ideas **not** explicitly stated by the author. They are expected to read between the lines, to make inferences, to see cause and effect relationships, to make generalizations, or to engage in a number of other practices that demand thinking. Responses are highly personal and vary according to the reader's motives, experience, and ability. The discovery of richer, deeper meanings is a search for the indirect and the subtle. Comprehension becomes multi-dimensional as the student goes beyond and between the written words in mental activity known only to the reader. The concepts and word knowledge drawn from encounters with a specific environment and made sensible through a specific language are brought

*Edward L. Thorndike. **"Reading As Reasoning."** Journal of Education Research, Volume 8, June, 1917.

together with the author's words and determine the extent of the reader's comprehension. Meaning is not **on** the page but, rather, is to be found **in** the mind and heart of the reader.

Students are reading creatively when they can take the author's ideas, add them to notions of their own, and develop something fresh and new. They may fill in happenings between events or may anticipate what may occur next. They may compare or contrast a person or an event with one that they have previously known. They may extend the author's point of view to outer boundaries or frontiers of thought. As students develop the skills of making sense of written discourse at the literal, interpretative, and creative levels, they are growing in an awareness of the many facets of comprehension. The appreciation of content develops as the reader matures in skill and in age. Intellectual power increases as students grow older and are capable of moving away from the concrete and the simple to the abstract and the complex. This developmental nature of the task of comprehending suggests that the early emphasis in reading instruction be placed on providing the background of concepts and language necessary for success. The teachers of Hispanic children who are learning to read in Spanish should feel very comfortable about taking the time to offer strong and systematic practice in comprehending Spanish print. Each organizational and analytical skill is completely transferable as an intellectual activity to the reading program in English when needed. As Thorndike has reminded teachers everywhere, **reading is thinking.** For students in either Spanish or English reading programs, the lessons to promote skill development are the same. They are presented in a similar manner; they require comparable materials and teaching strategies; and they involve identical cognitive processes. The only difference is the language, both oral and written, of instruction. The intellectual activity is not changed. Students are involved in memory, perception, concept formation, problem solving and other thinking skills as demanded by the lesson.

When written material is introduced, the teacher checks on the students' comprehension by means of questions, discussions, and explanations. Students may respond orally, in writing, by following directions, or through drawing. The fundamental responsibility of the teacher is that of an active, involved partner who guides and directs students toward the comprehension of written discourse. For **literal** comprehension, the students may be encouraged to examine the illustrations. They are asked to talk about the picture and to think about what may be observed in the picture. Time is provided for a discussion of concepts, ideas, or words that may emerge from the discussion. Then the story or part of the story is assigned for silent reading. The questioning and conversing continue as illustrations and parts of the story are presented at a pace comfortable for the students.

The students receive guidance and direction from the teacher whose purpose is clearly understood. The activities designed to engage students in obtaining **literal** meanings explicit in the pictures and print should include opportunities as follows:

- observe the details in the illustrations
- respond to factual data available in pictures
- recognize the words in the story
- answer direct questions about material explicitly stated
- identify specific details and the words or expressions that denote them
- use their knowledge of oral language to make the appropriate connection in print
- provide any information given in the text including
  (a) the main idea
  (b) the characters (Who?)
  (c) the time (When?)
  (d) the place (Where?)
  (e) the events (What?)
  (f) the order or sequence of events.

The interpretative level of comprehension requires the students to respond further to the author's ideas and statements as given and to discover meanings that are implicit in the context and are **not** explicitly stated.

The teacher's questions serve several purposes. Questions stimulate interest and focus the students' attention on the people or events they may expect to meet in the story. Questions give the students some direction in guiding their thoughts about the story. Questions also serve as a way of checking the extent to which the students are understanding what is going on in the reading lesson. Questions intended to elicit literal comprehension responses require minimal intellectual involvement. They ask students to provide factual information that stands out in bold relief if the students can recognize the words. Variations of the question-answer format are requests to decide whether a statement is true or false; to complete a missing part of a statement; to choose the correct response from several alternatives; or to reply in **yes — no** form to descriptions of story content.

Types of Questions
Comprehension checks are generally carried out through questions and discussions. The type of questioning and the nature of deliberating determine the kinds of comprehension that the students develop. If the questions are simple recall tasks designed to encourage the students to identify, locate, discover, or

match facts, then only explicitly stated material will be examined. This essential skill of **finding out** is used most of the time that students are in class. Questions that may require the students to **make use of** information that they have found will promote the skills of applying the material. Students may respond through projects of construction, preparation of reports, simulation, creation of experiments, or through a variety of other activities that apply the knowledge and make use of the known. Analysis questions are those that ask students to consider the material as a whole and then **take it apart** and identify its component parts. Analysis questions suggest the separation into classes, categories, or groups. These inquiries may also require comparisons or contrasts. The comprehension skill to be practiced by students is the facility of recognizing and dissecting in a logical manner the various elements as given. Synthesis questions are those that expect the students to go beyond recalling, applying, and analyzing. In synthesis, the students respond by putting the material together into **something new.** They may invent, create, produce, imagine, or predict **new** information on the basis of that which has been provided. Comprehension skills nurtured through synthesis questioning are those that may extend the learnings and that may result in greatly expanded use of the original knowledge. Evaluation questions are those that are intended to make the students more critical readers. They are to consider how things may turn out and **to judge the outcomes** carefully. The students may be asked to decide the relevance, to discuss the relative values, to choose from among alternatives, and to recommend solutions. The evaluation activities are designed to encourage students in the skills of practical judgment.

The strategy of questioning appears to be the most common technique for developing reading comprehension. Teachers ask their students to read the selection and then question them to verify that the students understand what has been read. If teachers are wise in the **variety** of questions posed, then students will have opportunities to grow in their skills of recall, application, analysis, synthesis, and evaluation. Unfortunately, many of the comprehension activities in reading classrooms focus almost exclusively on the **recall** type of questions. These lessons in **finding out** are valuable skills but are insufficient for many of the reading demands in the content areas of the curriculum. When students are acquiring these essential comprehension skills in the Spanish reading program, they are also practicing and growing in their ability to think. Different kinds of questions will require different kinds of thinking. The chart that follows has been organized to describe the purpose, the process, the products, and the thinking skills that may result from each type of question.

Las Preguntas de la Comprensión

El tipo	El propósito	El proceso	El producto	El conocimiento
Revocación	saber/ reconocer	colocar/ identificar/ observar	libros/ pruebas	traer a la memoria
Aplicación	usar/ practicar	construir/ notar/ informar	modelos/ mapas/ dibujos	aplicar los principios
Análisis	separar/ desunir	clasificar/ comparar/ comprobar	materias gráficas/noticias	dividir el compuesto en sus varias partes
Síntesis	juntar/ componer	inventar/ combinar/ imaginar	poemas/ cuentos/ juegos	reunir de substancias separadas
Evaluación	decidir/ escoger	juzgar/ discutir/ contender	cartas/ redacciones/ discusiones a cargo de un panel	considerar el valor de resultados visibles

Framing questions that will serve to focus attention and to guide thinking is not a simple task. Questions that have the answers already embodied in the content of questioning will not be especially effective in stimulating even slight mental activity. Furthermore, if most of the questions require only that the students recall facts, then opportunities for application, analysis, synthesis, or evaluation of information will not be provided. Discussions and explanations that accompany or follow the reading may draw out from students many clues relative to their levels of thinking. Since teachers cannot directly observe the nature of their students' thoughts, they must infer what those thoughts are from discussions and responses in the classroom. Purposeful questions will tap as many levels of thinking as reasonable for the developmental maturity of the students and will encourage students to do more with what they have read than merely repeat it from the text.

In the following exercise, page 24 from **Libro de Actividades — Cascabel,** the only response required is **sí** or **no.**

Escribe **Sí** o **No.**

1. El niño baña el burro.
2. El señor está sentado.
3. El niño baña el lobo.
4. Los niños juegan a la pelota.
5. El perro tiene botas.
6. La mamá pasea a la niña.

One alternative to teacher questions is the practice of having students formulate their own questions. These questions may be written on the blackboard for class discussion and response. Another option is to divide the class and have one group frame the questions and the other group provide the answers. Discussion may follow, and students may have the opportunity to decide on the nature of the questions and appropriateness of the responses. Students may be reminded that questions requiring a mere yes-no answer or a reply in a very few words close down further mental activity. Questions that expect longer, more detailed answers are likely to keep the thinking going on and may generate additional ideas. During such exchange, the teacher can check the clarity of the students' concepts and provide additional information as needed. As soon as the students are mature enough to recognize the different kinds of questions as illustrated on the chart, a simplified version with the same questions may be placed in the classroom for students to refer to when they are thinking of questions.

Preguntas de memoria

¿Qué _____?   ¿Qué animales pueden vivir en una finca?

¿Quién _____?   ¿Quiénes van a la escuela?

¿Dónde _____?   ¿Dónde está la niña?

¿Adónde _____?   ¿Adónde va el niño?

Preguntas de aplicación

¿Para qué usamos _____?   ¿Para qué usamos el cepillo?
                              ¿Para qué necesitamos el azúcar?

Preguntas de análisis

¿Cuántos aspectos de _____?   ¿Cuántos grupos de personas se pueden notar?

¿Cuáles son las partes _____?   ¿Cuáles son las partes de la poesía?

Preguntas de síntesis

¿Cuáles _____?   ¿Cuáles se relacionan con el otoño?

¿Qué _____?   ¿Qué harías tú para ayudar a tus amigos?

Preguntas de evaluación

¿Qué _____?   ¿Qué flor le gusta más el geranio o el girasol?

¿Cuál _____?   ¿Cuál es el más rápido?
                                                        ¿Cuál es más grande?

One method of encouraging students to improve their reading comprehension skills is to ask them to retell a short story or a part of a longer one in their own words. In order to accomplish the retelling, students may have to engage in some of these cognitive activities:

- to recall the story line (memory)
- to order the events (sequence)
- to put together the separate details (synthesis)
- to arrange and classify material (analysis)
- to judge the relevance of the story (evaluation)
- to invent and create (divergent thought)

When students have had little experience in retelling a story, they find it difficult to summarize and to state briefly the essence of what they have read. Young students, especially, are capable of making the retold story longer than the original. They tend to recite a litany of whatever they have remembered without taking the care to order, arrange, or group the facts. The teacher's guidance and prompting may help the students to stay on track and to learn how information may be distilled and combined. Such skills become increasingly important as the students advance through the grades and have the responsibility of processing larger amounts of written material.

The purpose of instruction is to lead the students beyond the written material itself and to make inferences relative to the persons or events described in the story.

Students are persuaded to consider the how and the why of the events. They are asked to read for discoveries of how the characters feel, or why the child was sad, or whether the story was real.

The activities designed to promote comprehension at an interpretative level and to discover implicit meanings in pictures and in print should include opportunities as follows:

- to consider details not present in the illustration
- to suggest descriptions not stated in the story
- to propose other ways of saying or doing what the characters said or did
- to answer questions about feelings or values
- to compare the story setting with other familiar places
- to give reasons for changes that occur in the story

Creative comprehension must be nurtured especially in the beginning stages of early reading. The stories are usually short, they have a highly restricted vocabulary, and the syntax is very simple. Some teachers consider the simplicity of content and language a barrier to creative thinking about material at this level. As Constance McCullough* points out, although such limitations do exist in the stories, the ideas as reflections of the children's experiences are many. When the students are urged to draw upon their personal experiences to extend notions of how people feel and what they value, they are reading creatively. Activities designed to increase creative comprehension skills should include opportunities as follows:

- to consider themselves in the illustrations
- to see relationships in a series of events
- to foresee what might happen next
- to suggest what might have turned out differently
- to decide what kind of person a character is
- to give reasons for an event taking place

Comprehension Activities in Spanish
Careful observation of reading instruction in almost any classroom will lead to the conclusion that practice in the skills of reading comprehension is not very consistent. Although a great deal of direction is usually provided in word recognition lessons or in vocabulary building, students are quite often on their own when working on lessons aimed at the improvement of comprehension. The teacher frequently guides and encourages the students using direct and monitored

*Constance McCullough. **Handbook for Teaching the Language Arts.** San Francisco: Chandler Publishing Company, 1969.

118

instruction in phonics, structural analysis, and syllabication but may offer little direct instruction in the strategies to increase understanding at several levels of thought. The persistent use of worksheets, seatwork, and other individual tasks as assigned prevents the students from receiving the guided practice that will enhance thinking skills. For these reasons, it is suggested that the teacher remain actively involved in the search for meanings as discussions, questions, and responses are taking place. The activities that follow are only representative of the kinds of lessons that could be productive for each of the purposes stated.

The Main Idea

When Hispanic students are reading to determine **la idea principal,** they must have an accurate picture of what the words, phrases, and sentences mean in total context. During the lessons in oral Spanish, they will have had opportunities to listen to oral discourse and to recognize the main idea. In reading, the main idea may not immediately reach out and capture the readers' attention. They may have to search for it in several sentences or paragraphs. After reading a selection, students may do one or more of the following:

- descubrir la idea principal en una oración
- escoger de cuatro títulos el título mejor
- sugerir un título en sus palabras propias
- subrayar las palabras claves
- identificar la oración importante

**Adelante
Segundo libro
de lectura
Página 140**

Lee este cuento:

Ayer caminaba por la calle y vi humo. Oí la sirena y corrí a ver qué pasaba.
De pronto, llegó el carro de bomberos y todos se bajaron.
Un bombero apoyó la escalera en la pared, mientras otro subía por ella.
Al mismo tiempo, otro desenrollaba una manguera, por donde salía un chorro de agua.
La gente gritaba:
—¡Qué rapidez!
—¡Qué valientes!
Y en pocos minutos el fuego estaba apagado.

Ahora contesta estas preguntas:
¿Qué aprendiste de este cuento?
¿Qué título le darías a este cuento?

Lee las palabras claves en el cuento.
Lee la oración más importante.

The Details

The recognition of specific details to be found in writing requires careful attention to the material. The skill of reading for details becomes more important as the students mature and need to locate specific information. The students also have to give a thoughtful reading to instructions that may involve several steps. If one step is overlooked, then the project may not be carried out successfully. Noting details begins with training the students to observe the people, places, and happenings around them. Then they may be encouraged to examine pictures and objects with care. Finally, they need to look for specific details in print. After the reading and discussion of a selection, the students may decide on the main idea and then look for facts that support the choice. They may apply some of the strategies that follow:

- responder a unas palabras específicas
- reconocer unas oraciones que no son aplicables o a propósito
- preparar un recorte
- hacer una lista de los datos
- colocar unas palabras específicas

The following excerpt illustrates the manner in which the teacher asks questions concerning the details:

Era una noche de mucho calor.
Andrés se entretenía mirando por la ventana.
Veía una luna grande y muchas estrellas.
"Quizás algún día pueda llegar hasta allí", pensó.
—¡Andrés, vete a la cama! —le dijo su mamá desde el otro cuarto.
Andrés obedeció. Siguió pensando en la luna y las estrellas y al ratito, volvió a abrir los ojos.
¡Qué sorpresa! ¡Unos brazos largos y finitos como mangueras de regar, le hacían señas!
Salió al jardín y vio algo como un carro redondo y muy reluciente.
Aquel extraño personaje se metió dentro del carro y Andrés lo siguió.
Al rato, el carro redondo se perdía en el cielo . . .
Los señores tan raros le dijeron que venían del planeta Ji-Ji, donde todo el mundo se reía.
Le dio tanta risa que volvió a quedarse dormido.

¿Dónde es la aventura?
¿Obedeció Andrés a su mamá?
¿Qué vio en el jardín?

To extend the students' skills using the specific reading content, the teacher asks for antonyms of certain words:

Busca un antónimo de **cerrar,** otro de **cortos** y otro de **frio.**

The syllable **ji** found in the title of the story is used for perceptual practice in the direction:

Busca palabras con la sílaba **ji.**

Conventions of the writing system are pointed out in the questions:

¿Qué signos ven antes y después de "**¡Qué sorpresa!**"?
¿Qué nos dicen esos signos?

The Sequence

An awareness of the sequence or order of events in a passage helps the readers to organize their thoughts as they read. This sense of reasonable time allows for the readers to relate to the material in a logical manner. Students may benefit from practice in putting a series of happenings in order of their occurrence. They may be asked to respond to questions concerning what happened at critical times in the narrative. A few examples of sequencing practice are these:

- arreglar los eventos en una secuencia adecuada
- hacer un mapa o una carta de los eventos
- preparar una lista de orden en el desarrollo del cuento
- dar instrucciones para hacer un traje o cocinar unos dulces

Ejemplo:

**Libro de
Actividades
Adelante,**

Página 47

---

1. VAMOS A PONER EN ORDEN

Δ   Juan nos contó lo que hizo antes de ir a la escuela. Pero es tan distraído, que nos lo contó de una forma desordenada. Al lado de cada una de las frases que dijo hay un recuadro. Escribe los números del 1 al 6, de acuerdo con el orden apropiado.

[ ] Desayuné jugo, cereal y leche.

[ ] Me puse el pantalón y la camisa.

[ ] Hice la cama.

[ ] Me lavé la cara y los dientes.

[ ] Me desperté a las siete.

[ ] Salí de la casa.

---

2. OTRA HISTORIA DESORDENADA

△   Un amigo nuestro leyó el libro de Robinson Crusoe. Pero no supo contárnoslo bien. Nos dijo todas las cosas en desorden. Ordénalas. Escribe los números del 1 al 5, de acuerdo con el orden apropiado.

☐ El barco se hundió.

☐ Allí vivió solo durante muchos años.

☐ Robinson llegó nadando a una isla desierta.

☐ Por fin, un barco que iba por allí lo recogió.

☐ Robinson Crusoe era un hombre que iba en un barco.

Other methods of helping the students perceive logic and organization may include teaching students the essential temporal expressions — **ahora, después, próximo, durante, más tarde, cuando** — and others.

Inference

Inferential reading is an important part of interpreting in the light of one's own experience what the author has said. When the students are encouraged to explore the information and ideas that are not explicitly stated, they are adding what they already know to what the author has written. Readers may infer something about the characters in the story, the events as described, the setting in which the action takes place, or the person who wrote the story. Students may improve their inferencing skills through practice in the following:

- considerar los sentimientos de una persona
- pensar en **el cómo** de un evento
- descubrir los cambios en el héroe
- formar una opinión sobre alguien
- escribir una pregunta de inferencia

¿Creen que le gustó la idea
al ji-jigiano?

¿Por qué se despertó Andrés
con miedo?

¿Dónde ocurrió la aventura
de Andrés?

¿Cómo había sido el sueño
de Andrés?

Andrés salió corriendo hacia donde se veían
los carros redondos. ¡Corría pero nunca llegaba!
Como se había quitado las gomitas, no entendía
lo que los otros niños trataban de decirle.
—¡Qué te pasa, Andrés!… ¡Despierta!
¡Andrés abrió los ojos con mucho miedo! Pero
al ver a su mamá se puso muy contento y siguió
durmiendo muy tranquilo.

168

Cause and Effect

One of the important skills to be developed in reading comprehension is the ability to perceive the relationships that may exist between one set of facts and another. If certain circumstances or conditions produce certain results that can be traced directly back to the earlier information, then a cause and effect relationship may be understood. Comprehension of the connection between both sets of data helps the students look back to the specific events that may have precipitated specific consequences. The reader must group and order one set of data and then consider the actions that may follow. If the students read that despite the enthusiastic plans of the children they were unable to go on their picnic, then they have to find reasons for their **not** going. Did it rain? Did the river overflow? Was someone sick? Did something happen to their lunch? Did Father's car fail to start? Was there any other possible factor that caused the picnic to be cancelled? Practice with direct and obvious cause and effect relationships offers many opportunities to deal with simple content before applying their reasoning to more complex relationships.

Questions to guide the students in their skill development are these: Why did it happen that _____? What made Tom say that _____? Can you think of the reason that _____? When exploring story content for the purpose of helping the students organize the facts and of seeing relationships among them, the teacher needs to guide the discussion. Framing the questions correctly is important, but of even greater significance is the teaching of the vocabulary and sentence structure required in the response. To express relationships, students need certain words and specific syntactical patterns. The if-and-result construction: If it rains, we cannot go on a picnic. If you are sick, you cannot go on a picnic. Words such as consequently, as a result of, because, thus, and therefore are **glue** words in expressing relationships. At early levels the why-because patterns apply. Why did he _____? Because he _____. As the students grow in their abilities to manage more abstract material, the advanced vocabulary, appropriate structure, and adequate practice will offer stimulating mental activities that nurture intelligence. The students may be asked to decide the relevance, to discuss the relative values, to choose from among alternatives, and to recommend solutions. The evaluation activities are designed to encourage the students in the skills of practical judgment. An exercise for seeing cause and effect relationships from **Adelante, Page 54,** follows.

A LIMPIAR EL LAGO

△ Mira el dibujo. Tacha con una X todas las cosas que han ayudado a contaminar el lago.

Contesta las preguntas:

a) ¿Qué cosas han contaminado el agua de este laguito?
1. El aire puro.
2. El jabón, los detergentes y la basura.
3. El humo.

b) ¿Qué les ha pasado a algunos de los animales que allí viven?
_____

c) ¿Qué cosas han contaminado el aire? _____

d) ¿Dónde se debe arrojar la basura?
1. En la calle.
2. En el jardín.
3. En los basureros.

e) ¿Es saludable vivir en una ciudad como la de arriba? ____
¿Por qué?
_____

f) ¿Qué harías tú para aliviar la contaminación de un lago y de un parque?
_____
_____

Trata de dibujar el lago. pero que se vea sin contaminación.

Other Interpretative Skills

Once the students have become skillful in reading for the literal meanings to be found in print and have begun to search for the relationships expressed in written discourse, they are capable of dealing with higher level thinking skills. They may be encouraged to consider the logic, the consistency, and the relevance of what they have read. In order to comprehend at this level of abstraction, they must exercise judgment based on their own experiences and values. Decisions and choices must be made and measured according to personal standards. The readers are judging the author's message and accepting or rejecting it in the light of their own criteria. The teachers need to help the students sort through their values, attitudes, and feelings in order to make judgments that are logical and consistent with such standards. The students will need to have practice in abstracting from data and drawing generalizations.

An example of the variety of thinking skills that may be nurtured is found in Ronald Singerton's **1848: ¡ORO! EN CALIFORNIA.** The narrative weaves historical characters and fictional ones together against an authentic background of the gold rush era. The discourse is narrative and dialog. One section deals with the relationships of the American and the Chinese miners:

Narrador: Poco después, un grupo de mineros chinos vinieron al campamento. No fueron bienvenidos por los americanos. Terminaron por ir a una zona del río que nadie tenía interés en explotar. Bayard Taylor se hizo amigo de Wang Lee y de su hijo Sam.

Wang Lee: Los chinos trabajamos muy duro, señor Taylor. Encontraremos oro.

Taylor: Pero nadie ha encontrado nada en esta parte del río.

Wang Lee: Nosotros encontraremos oro. Muchos americanos no tienen paciencia.

Taylor: Supongo que siempre estamos apurados. Nos gusta el éxito rápido.

Sam Lee: Sí, pero a veces las cosas necesitan tiempo. Como las semillas que plantamos y que crecerán y se convertirán en un hermoso árbol. Se llama el Arbol del Cielo.

Taylor: Ese es un buen regalo para América.

Sam Lee: Entonces, ¿por qué no le gustamos a su pueblo?

Taylor: Quizá porque hablan un idioma diferente y porque usan ropa distinta. También porque están dispuestos a trabajar por menos dinero. Quizá ellos se sienten superiores. Este es un país joven en pleno crecimiento. Tenemos que madurar.

Wang Lee: Los chinos llamamos a nuestro país el Reino Medio porque pensamos que es el centro del mundo. Los chinos nos sentimos importantes por tener un país tan antiguo. Quizá podamos aprender unos de otros.

The answer to the factual question — **¿Qué árbol trajeron los chinos a California?** may be found in the words of Sam Lee.

Responses to the very sensitive question of relationships between the American and Chinese miners may be elicited by discussion and questions as follows:

> **Las culturas americana y china son muy diferentes. ¿Qué podrían los americanos aprender de los chinos? ¿Qué podrían aprender los chinos de los americanos?**

Yet another kind of fortune was made during this period by Levi Strauss, creator of the blue jeans so popular with contemporary youth.

> **Narrador:** Hacia 1853, Joseph Luntz tenía una buena sastrería. Un día un joven comerciante visitó su tienda.
>
> **Strauss:** Mi nombre es Levi Strauss. ¿Me puede hacer un par de overoles que pueda vender a los mineros?
>
> **Luntz:** Claro. ¿Cómo los quiere?
>
> **Strauss:** Bueno, deben ser hasta la cintura y deben ser muy fuertes y durables.
>
> **Luntz:** Les haré doble costura en los bolsillos, señor Strauss. Los mineros siempre los llenan con muestras de rocas y los bolsillos se rompen.
>
> **Strauss:** Usaremos esta tela que he comprado. Es muy fuerte. Quiero vender pantalones que duren.
>
> **Luntz:** ¿Cómo los llamará?
>
> **Strauss:** Levis. Overoles Levis hasta la cintura.
>
> **Luntz:** Está bien. Probablemente resulte.

When the students are asked to answer the question — **¿Quién comenzó el negocio de hacer pantalones para los mineros?** — they are merely recalling the name of the person. Further discussion of his fortune made in blue jeans as compared to fortunes made and lost in searching for rich deposits of gold demands more mental activity. The students will have to see relationships between the two endeavors, mining and manufacturing. They will need to compare risks involved, differences in activity, commonalities in both, and the other contrasts or comparisons that may be made. They may be encouraged to speculate which persons they would like to have been in 1848 — a miner or Levi Strauss.

The figurative language used in the expression — **Voy en busca del elefante!** — has to be interpreted in the light of the gold fever of the times.

La época y sus acontecimientos:

"Oiga forastero, ¿a dónde va tan apurado?"

"¿Por qué? ¿No lo nota? **¡Voy en busca del elefante!**"

"Buscar el elefante" significaba buscar fortuna en las minas.

Estamos en 1848 al comienzo de la fiebre del oro.

The question — **¿Qué significaba "ir a buscar el elefante"?** — may lend itself to a discussion of one of the major themes in literature — man's search for his dream. Questions of this nature should evoke varied and multiple responses from students.

Even a short paragraph has the potential for drawing out several kinds of comprehension skills. **Un Cuento** from **Adelante** asks students to consider the main idea, (a) the details (b) and (d); inference (c); and personal interpretation (e).

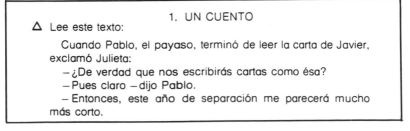

1. UN CUENTO

△ Lee este texto:

Cuando Pablo, el payaso, terminó de leer la carta de Javier, exclamó Julieta:
— ¿De verdad que nos escribirás cartas como ésa?
— Pues claro —dijo Pablo.
— Entonces, este año de separación me parecerá mucho más corto.

Pronto se interrumpió aquella conversación, porque Juan, el dueño del circo, quería empezar el viaje.

—¡Vamos, muchachos! ¡Que se nos hace tarde! —exclamó Juan.

Julieta y su hermano se despidieron de sus amigos. Y los carros del circo siguieron su camino.

— Ahora comprendo que despedirse de los amigos no es tan triste. Especialmente, porque por medio de las cartas podemos saber de ellos — dijo Julieta.

2. ¿QUE DICE EL CUENTO?

△ Contesta las preguntas. Escribe las respuestas de acuerdo con el texto que has leído.

a) ¿Qué título le darías a este texto?

_____

b) ¿Quiénes son los personajes?

_____

c) ¿Cómo se sintieron los niños al ver alejarse los carros del circo? _____

d) ¿Qué medio usarán los niños para comunicarse con sus amigos? _____

e) ¿Qué otros medios de comunicación conoces?

_____

Another example follows.

LENGUA NACIONAL 2

1. Lee esto que cuenta Antón Retaco:

Era Carantoña, nuestra mona, que se estaba divirtiendo asustando a las ovejas. Les hacía muecas y saltaba detrás de ellas, y las ovejas corrían y balaban espantadas. Mi padre llamó a la mona y la ató con una cadena.
—Se está volviendo muy enredadora —dijo mi madre— y nos va a complicar la vida en el pueblo. Lo mejor será que se la lleve el tío Badajo! ¡Tío Badajo! ¡Tío Badajo, espere! ¡Llévese la mona!

MARIA LUISA GEFAELL

2. La madre de Antón Retaco dijo que la mona se estaba volviendo muy enredadora.

Quería decir

☐ Que la mona se enredaba en una cuerda.

☐ Que la mona les hacía muchas travesuras.

☐ Que la mona se subía por las enredaderas.

Marca la respuesta que creas correcta.

3. El padre de Antón Retaco ató a la mona

☐ con una cuerda

☐ con un hilo

☐ con una cadena

Marca con una cruz la respuesta correcta.

Fecha _____

4. Busca en el diccionario las palabras siguientes:
Escribe su significado.
Muecas _____
Balar _____
Escribe dos oraciones. En cada una, que entre una de estas palabras.
a) _____
b) _____

5. Mira estos dibujos.
¿Cuál te parece que es la mona Carantoña?

Tacha las que no son Carantoña.

① ② ③

6. Di todo lo que se te ocurra de Carantoña. ¿Cómo es? ¿Cómo son sus ojos? ¿Y sus patas?, etc.

_____
_____
_____

7. Carantoña se va con el tío Badajo.
Escribe lo que tú creas que les pasa después.

_____
_____
_____
_____
_____
_____

Transferability of Comprehension Skills to Reading in English

When the students have had sound opportunities to develop their comprehension of written Spanish, their thinking skills are one hundred percent transferable for comprehending English. The concepts of determining the main idea, of noting supportive details, of locating specific information, and of discovering the proper sequence need only the terminology of English. The knowledge and skill required to understand what they have been reading at the several levels of comprehension are part of the students' intelligence. There is, of course, the requirement of recognizing the words through the application of a variety of word attack techniques, and the need to make sense of the English words, themselves, in terms of the referent system in English. However, there is no reason for the students to employ new thinking strategies. A main idea or the surrounding details; an appropriate sequence or a cause and effect relationship; a judgment of relevance or an analysis of essential factors are the same in any language and will, once the written code is cracked, be ascertained by the use of those very same cognitive processes. The students should be reminded that they already know how to read. They will become more confident in their approach to the second language reading activities if the teachers will reassure them that reading is thinking, and that they are competent readers and effective thinkers now. A prominent classroom sign might state: **You read only once!**

The chart of reading comprehension skills used in the introductory Spanish reading program for formulating questions may be displayed to good advantage with the descriptive terminology provided in English.

COMPREHENSION QUESTIONS

Type of Question	Purpose	Process	Product	Mental Activity
1. RECALL	knowing recognizing	identify locate	books tests	memory
2. APPLICATION	using practicing	construct inform	models drawings	reasoning
3. ANALYSIS	dividing separating	classify compare/ contrast	charts tables	organization
4. SYNTHESIS	joining putting together	combine invent	games poems	part-whole relationships
5. EVALUATION	deciding choosing	judge recommend	panels editorials	judgment

*Adapted from Bloom's Taxonomy

Sample Questions

1. Recall questions simply ask for the students to supply information — Where did the boy live? Who was the hero? What did they do about the river?

2. Application questions ask the students to use data — What would you need to follow the explorer's route? What would you do to get ready for such a journey?

3. Analysis questions ask the students to consider all the essential elements and put them in perspective — What are the essential needs of people living in the cities? How are their needs different from people living in the country?

4. Synthesis questions ask the students to take separate facts or ideas and put them together — How do all the events that occurred lead to the final outcome? Could the result have been different if the events had happened at another time?

5. Evaluation questions ask the students to make judgments — Is this a reliable report? Should one man have the right to choose another man's future? Could this event happen here?

Although comprehension skills have the potential for complete transfer, there is need for the teacher to recognize that transfer cannot be taken for granted. The transferability of skills will not occur automatically without careful organization and purposeful planning on the part of the teacher. Among the several concerns that must be addressed are these:

- the importance of experiences — rich and varied encounters made sensible in Spanish;
- the need for direction, guidance and monitoring while the transfer of skills is going on;
- the deliberate intent to draw upon Spanish comprehension skills and bring them forward for use in English;
- the awareness of significant clues to meaning in **both** Spanish and English;
- the identification of specific elements common to **both** Spanish and English;
- the application of appropriate strategies and comfortable pacing as skills do transfer to the second reading system.

Main Idea Transfer

As the students have learned to identify **la idea principal** in Spanish, they have discovered the basic thought in a sentence. They have had opportunities to summarize the central message in longer passages of several sentences. They have considered titles as relevant and appropriate for the material they have read. They have selected from among alternative statements the one that best contained the essential idea. They have acquired and have understood the definition of **a main idea.** They have practiced finding **main ideas** in different forms of written discourse of varying length and complexity. **Such comprehending is thinking.** When the students are ready to engage in this same mental process using English, they should be reassured that they are already good thinkers, competent in identifying the main idea. The sequence of skill development in English is the same. Teachers first must make certain that the key words in a sentence are comprehensible. Then, they provide practice in lengthy, more complex discourse. Activities to nurture the skills needed to identify the main idea are the same: select a title from several given, choose a descriptive statement, make a brief summary, suggest a topic sentence, or provide a title for untitled materials.

For effective main idea transfer the teacher will wish to consider the following factors:

- the extent to which the students can identify main ideas in their stronger language;
- the level of difficulty of written Spanish that they have successfully comprehended;
- the breadth of their English listening comprehension vocabulary;
- the index of reading difficulty of the written English that considers at least the number of multisyllabic words and complexity of sentences;
- the concept burden of the content from which the **main idea** is to be extracted;
- the existence of idiomatic or figurative language with which the non-native person may not be familiar.

By giving thoughtful attention and by preparing the way for the students, teachers will promote excellent main idea transfer. The students need to experience the excitement of successful transfer of skills. They should hear often the sincere reassurance that these are exactly the same thinking skills that they applied so well in Spanish. The students should be helped to appreciate how well they think, how effectively they responded to the comprehension demands of Spanish, and how rapidly they will become readers of English. **¡Sí, se pueden!**

A simple exercise in finding the main idea is given on **Page 84, Activity Book, Navigating.**

What?

A great cat sat on top
of a mat.
The mat was on top of
my hat.
I got my hat from under
the mat,
And then ran away from the
hat bell cat

My bunny hops and hops.
He hops on top of my mop.
I yell at my pet.
I say "Don't hop!"
But my bunny will not
hop stop stay

The hens stay in their
house all day.
They eat their food.
They do not play.
So they are not good
players.
But they are good egg
layers sayers sellers

Finding Details Transfer

When second language readers are engaging in activities that require a search for details, they once again need to be reassured that the task is precisely the same one as previously learned. New vocabulary will now cue them in their search: The **who** is the person(s) or animal(s); the **where** is the place; the **when** is the time; the **what** is the event or action. The teacher can encourage the accuracy and speed of finding significant details by asking **very specific** questions at reasonable **intervals** and by suggesting that the students write down important details as they are encountered in their reading. Teachers may also give the students a statement of the author's main idea and ask the students to prepare a list of facts that support the idea. When English reading material is introduced, the assignment should be short, direct, and obvious in order to build confidence, but as skills mature, the pupils may advance to finding evidence that may not be so clearly stated and to composing their own questions concerning details.

Emma looked for her yellow ball. She looked in her mitt. She looked under her hat. Jim helped her look too. But they did not see the yellow ball.

Then Emma looked under her book. "I got it!" she said.

Where was the yellow ball?
Who saw the yellow ball?
Who helped Emma look for the ball?

Sequence Transfer

Once the concept of the ordering of events has been understood in the reading of Spanish, no new comprehension skill is involved **except** the vocabulary of sequence in English. Again, the students need to be told that putting actions in an appropriate sequence is a skill that they have already mastered. Sequence words of importance to the reading of English include first, second, third, next, last. Other useful signals are then, after, before, yesterday, tomorrow, and other temporal expressions. A little practice in sequence will go a long way because the skill has already been well internalized. The major stumbling block to transfer of sequence skill in English is the new words to indicate time and order. Wise teachers will make certain that their students know these words by introducing any vocabulary items needed ahead of time.

Imagining, Page 57

a. _____ I ran out of the house.
   _____ I get my hat.

b. _____ So I sit.
   _____ Ma says I have to rest.

c. _____ Tommy hops in the mud.
   _____ Tommy runs into the house.
   _____ Tommy gets muddy.

d. _____ Teddy gets the food.
   _____ Teddy cooks the food.
   _____ Teddy is not hungry now.

e. _____ Penny got the rabbit.
   _____ The rabbit runs from Penny.
   _____ Penny runs after the rabbit.

f. _____ They make a hat for me.
   _____ Patty and Winny have hats.
   _____ I have a hat.

A simple sequence exercise from page 76, **Activity Book, Navigating,** follows:

Yes or No?

1. Yes   No   ☐ Ralph was playing ball.
                    ☐ He was at bat.
                    ☐ He ran.
                    ☐ Then he hit the ball!

2. Yes   No   ☐ Lily gets an apple.
                    ☐ She eats the apple.
                    ☐ Now she doesn't have an apple.

3. Yes   No   ☐ The boys play ball at the picnic.
                    ☐ The boys go to the picnic.
                    ☐ The boys go away.

4. Yes   No   ☐ Mat got the yellow hat.
                    ☐ Mat saw the yellow hat.
                    ☐ He ran for it.

5. Yes   No   ☐ The ball hits the wall.
                    ☐ Then it falls.

Rewriting a short story is another activity that affords practice in sequence, from **An Ant About Town:**

Name _____

BOOK 7
WORKSHEET 6

THE LIFE
OF A CAN . . .

This is the story of a can of soda. The story got mixed up. It's in the wrong order. Read it carefully and write it in the correct order.

Lisa drank the soda.
Mom got money for the can at the recycling center.
Dad got a six pack of soda at the market.
Tony crushed the can.
Lisa put a bag full of empty cans in the car.
The can was melted so the aluminum could be recycled.

1. _____
2. _____
3. _____
4. _____
5. _____
6. _____

THE LIFE OF A NEWSPAPER . . .

The story you see above tells about a can of soda. Write a story about a newspaper. You can think about these things before you write your story.

    –Who has the newspaper?
    –Where did this person get the newspaper?
    –What will happen to the newspaper?

Copyright 1982 Santillana Publishing Company, Inc

The students should be encouraged to test the reality of information they have read. Could this really happen? Is it true or untrue? Is it fantasy? Is it imaginary? Is it logical or illogical? Checking on the content serves to develop a questioning attitude about what may be found in print. The search for the discrepant, the ridiculous, the incongruent, and the obscure offers valuable opportunities for reading critically. When second language readers bring good, strong intellectual processing skills to Spanish reading, they need English speech and their written connections. The thinking skills are already in place.

A few exercises for illustrating the practice of comprehension skills are taken from the English component of **Lectura en dos idiomas.**

136

A cause and effect practice from page 60, **Activity Book, Imagining,** follows:

1. Tilly and Milly are not well today.
   So they are resting.
   Tomorrow they will be well.
   Then they will go out of the house.

2. The bunny hopped onto a lamp.
   It fell.
   When the lamp fell, it hit a can.
   All the tin men in the can are spilling.

3. It is not hot out.
   So I get a hat.
   Then it gets hot.
   So I make a fan.

An exercise in making inferences from page 89, **Activity Book, Navigating,** follows:

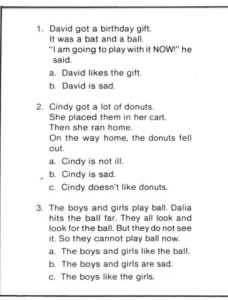

1. David got a birthday gift.
   It was a bat and a ball.
   "I am going to play with it NOW!" he
   said.
   a. David likes the gift.
   b. David is sad.

2. Cindy got a lot of donuts.
   She placed them in her cart.
   Then she ran home.
   On the way home, the donuts fell
   out.
   a. Cindy is not ill.
   b. Cindy is sad.
   c. Cindy doesn't like donuts.

3. The boys and girls play ball. Dalia
   hits the ball far. They all look and
   look for the ball. But they do not see
   it. So they cannot play ball now.
   a. The boys and girls like the ball.
   b. The boys and girls are sad.
   c. The boys like the girls.

An exercise in making predictions from page 77, **Activity Book, Navigating,** follows:

What To Do!

Mat was playing ball. He hit the ball on top of the Gonzalez house. Now he can see the ball. But he can't get to it.

What is Mat going to do?
a. Call the Gonzalez family.
b. Run away.
c. Hop on top of the house.
d. Help Ben get on top of the house.

Tommy got a new hat. But it didn't fit well.
"This hat is for a tall boy!" said Tommy.
"I am tall, Tommy!" said Bill.

What is Tommy going to do?
a. Sit on the hat.
b. Let Bill have the hat.
c. Get a NEW, new hat.
d. Make the hat not so tall.

Other Comprehension Skill Transfer
Students who have learned to determine the significance of context in Spanish may transfer their abilities to English in the following activities:

- restate sentences in their own words
- suggest titles or headlines for articles
- describe a character in the story
- illustrate a story
- prepare a short oral summary of a story
- predict how a story will turn out
- build a vocabulary of English words for concepts encoded in Spanish
- express an opinion relative to the material
- consider the author's views in contrast to their own
- understand differences between fantasy and reality.

Whether the students are learning to read in Spanish or in English, they are engaging in one of the major neurological tasks of the school. Speaking, reading, and comprehending demand an intact central nervous system and a brain. The students must remember, perceive, form concepts, reason, and transfer learning. This ongoing mental activity will result in intellectual growth and an improved capacity to manage ideas. To comprehend anything, the students first have to **pay attention** to the manner in which the words are formed, the way they are arranged, and how they are regulated. To think, students must **listen** to **instruction** and **follow directions.** They must **recall** what they have heard and seen. They need **to locate** and **to retrieve** information. They must **sift** and **select** among data. They need **to sort** and **to organize** knowledge. They must **order** learnings in a logical sequence. Students in **any** language and in **any** content area at **any** level are involved in these intelligent actions when they are comprehending written material. The following activities illustrate the use of a variety of comprehension questions.

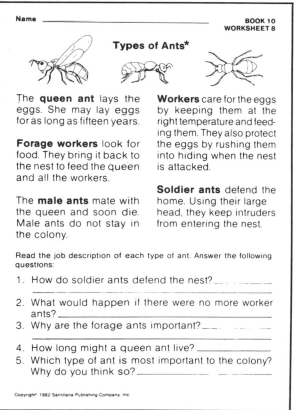

Name _____
BOOK 10
WORKSHEET 8

Types of Ants*

The **queen ant** lays the eggs. She may lay eggs for as long as fifteen years.

Forage workers look for food. They bring it back to the nest to feed the queen and all the workers.

The **male ants** mate with the queen and soon die. Male ants do not stay in the colony.

Workers care for the eggs by keeping them at the right temperature and feeding them. They also protect the eggs by rushing them into hiding when the nest is attacked.

Soldier ants defend the home. Using their large head, they keep intruders from entering the nest.

Read the job description of each type of ant. Answer the following questions:

1. How do soldier ants defend the nest? ___ _ _____
   _____
2. What would happen if there were no more worker ants? _____
3. Why are the forage ants important? ___ _ ___ ___
   _____
4. How long might a queen ant live? _____
5. Which type of ant is most important to the colony? Why do you think so? _____ _ __ _

Copyright 1982 Santillana Publishing Company, Inc

*An Ant About Town, Book 10 — Worksheet 8.

He Painted What He Felt*

Have you ever drawn a Halloween witch in art class? Perhaps the teacher put some of the students' drawings on the board. Although everyone drew the same subject, some of the drawings probably looked different than others. Many of the artists put into their pictures some of their feelings about witches.

When the famous Spanish painter Pablo Picasso (pa'blō pē ka'sō) went to art school, he and his classmates painted the same subjects. They drew trees, flowers, and people. They made sketches of the sea and of buildings. Many of their paintings looked alike.

Picasso discovered many things about painting in school. He studied the works of famous artists and learned from them. But he was be-

ginning to express himself in his own way. In time, his paintings were so different that they could be picked out from the drawings of the other artists. He had developed a style of his own.

It has been said that Picasso never set out to paint carrying his easel and paintbrushes. When he felt like painting, he painted, even if it was the middle of the night. Sometimes he made a quick drawing with his fingers or with a rusty nail he had picked up.

He never painted an object just the way his eyes saw it, as if he were taking a photograph. But his paintings still had meaning to many who saw them. His art became so special that Picasso no longer belonged to the group of artists who thought and painted alike.

FIND THE ANSWERS

1. Pablo Picasso is a famous painter from
   - a. Italy
   - b. Spain
   - c. France
   - d. America

2. The word in paragraph 4 that means *a three-legged stand that holds a painting* is _____.

3. The words "never set out to paint carrying his easel and paintbrushes" in paragraph 4 describe _____.

4. The story does not say so, but it makes you think that
   - a. all artists do not paint the same way
   - b. new artists do not learn from famous artists
   - c. Halloween witches look the same to everyone

5. Picasso painted
   - a. every morning at 9:00
   - b. with a feather
   - c. when he felt like it.

6. Picasso painted an object just the way his eyes saw it.
   Yes   No   Does not say

7. On the whole, this story is about
   - a. drawing Halloween pictures.
   - b. how Pablo Picasso painted.
   - c. painting in the middle of the night

8. Why were Picasso's drawings different than those of other artists?
   - a. He had developed a style of his own.
   - b. He always used the same colors.
   - c. He always painted the same objects.

9. Which statement does the story lead you to believe?
   - a. Picasso's paintings have meaning for everyone.
   - b. Different people see the same object in different ways.
   - c. Picasso started out by painting people's photographs.

*Reading for Concepts

140

For excellent comprehension skills to be developed in English, the students must have had excellent guidance and instruction in comprehending Spanish. The teacher's **active** presence and **direct** instruction are the keys to the nurturance of strategies that will assist the students get the most out of what they are reading. Teachers must provide explicit directions and explanations when giving a lesson in reading comprehension. They must tie the practice specifically to the skill expected. They need to stress the vocabulary that signals the particular kind of understanding anticipated in practice. They must be certain that the opportunities for practice are not fragmented, insufficient, or irrelevant to the comprehension objective. They need to keep uppermost in their planning the tight relationship between instruction and practice.

Caveat
The major hazard in the transfer of comprehension skills in Spanish to English lies in the unwarranted assumption that transfer will occur without deliberate teaching for transfer. For each skill at every level, teachers need to emphasize the underlying thinking process common to both languages while they work diligently to teach new word meanings, different structural patterns, unfamiliar idioms, and other potential barriers to comprehension.

References
1. **An Ant About Town.** Northvale, New Jersey: Santillana Publishing Company, Inc., 1982.

2. **Lectura en dos idiomas.** Northvale, New Jersey: Santillana Publishing Company, Inc., 1977.

3. **Lengua Nacional Fichas de trabajo 2.** Northvale, New Jersey: Santillana Publishing Company, Inc., 1972.

4. Liddle, William, Ed. **Reading for Concepts, Book F.** New York: Webster McGraw-Hill, 1970.

5. McCullough, Constance. **Handbook for Teaching the Language Arts.** San Francisco: Chandler Publishing Company, 1969.

6. Smith, Frank. **Comprehension and Learning: A Conceptual Framework for Teachers.** New York: Holt, Rinehart and Winston, 1975.

7. Thorndike, Edward L. "Reading As Reasoning." **Journal of Educational Research, Volume 8.** June, 1917.

CHAPTER V

RELATING ORAL AND WRITTEN FORMS OF SPANISH

There is no debate over the close relationships that speech bears to print. Connections between oral and written language form the basis for a considerable amount of instruction in reading classrooms anywhere. In Spanish, as in any language, oral language tends to be informal and subject to many variations from several sources. Written language, on the other hand, generally remains the same over long periods of time. Once words have been immortalized in print and have met the arbitrary conventions of a writing system, they persist as **proper** written forms until they are discarded by the language experts. Everyone is familiar with the regional influences that change pronunciation, vocabulary items, and semantics. English is spoken in many ways by millions of individuals who consider themselves members of the English language community. Though there may be serious difficulties in understanding one another in speech, the written forms present far fewer problems despite spelling variations and lexical differences. Reading, writing, and spelling uncertainties are more likely to occur when the speech patterns of a particular group are loosely related to the so-called standard written forms.

Hispanic students in English-speaking countries have been described by John Staczek as having language skills influenced by Spanish, influenced by English, or randomly influenced. In relating what they hear and say to what they read and write, students apparently draw upon the dual language systems available to them at home and in school. The result of such freedom of choice may promote a degree of creativity of expression, but may be a stumbling block for many students in an educational setting. With what appears to be an incomplete development of two language systems, the students often find that they have inadequate skills in both. Many school practices in the past have considered this condition the fault of the student. The "blame-the-victim" point of view has resulted in a proliferation of compensatory and remedial programs that seem to aggravate the condition. Thus, many Hispanic students feel less rather than more capable and continue to fill the deficit labels unfairly assigned to them. The language diversity found among Hispanic students has received scholarly treatment from linguists and socio-linguists.* Detailed discussion of the Puerto Rican Inner City Spanish or Chicano Speech Patterns are beyond the scope of this book. What does appear relevant for the classroom teacher who is providing reading instruction for Hispanic students is a solid appreciation of Spanish oral forms as they relate to their written representation. Armed with sensible reminders of these relationships, the teacher

*See **Bilingual Education for Hispanic Students in the United States.** Editors: Joshua Fishman and Gary Keller. New York: Teachers College Press, 1982.

may then pursue a reasonable course based upon the particular kind of oral language usage that the students demonstrate. Among the several oral-written associations that may be valuable for students to work through are these: (l) plural forms; (2) concept of agreement; (3) verb inflections; (4) possessives; (5) apocópe; (6) enclisis; (7) derived forms; (8) pronouns; (9) punctuation; and (10) capitalization.

When the students acquire these skills in Spanish and have a good understanding of the speech-print relationships in their own language, they are in a much stronger position to manage the speech-print connections of English. The better their Spanish, the greater is their potential for fluency and literacy in English. **As has often been stated: The best predictor of success in a second language is competence in the first.**

Plural Forms
Awareness of number emerges early in speech development, and students use plural forms with relative ease long before they enter school and begin formal instruction. Hispanic students have a good grasp of the singular and plural forms used in everyday speech. When they come to the graphic representation of these forms, they may need additional reminders and/or direct teaching to improve their reading and spelling of forms that they have previously used automatically. Among the rules governing plurals that students should know and practice are these:

1. Nouns that end in vowels usually add **s** to the singular form.
   The article also adds **s**

la boca	las bocas
la calle	las calles
el hombre	los hombres
la foto	las fotos

2. Nouns ending in accented vowels usually add **es** to the singular form and the **s** to the article*

el rubí	los rubíes
el tabú	los tabúes

   *exceptions:

la mamá	las mamás
el sofá	los sofás

144

3. Nouns ending in consonants usually add **es**. The article adds **s** as usual.

la ciudad	las ciudades
el ratón	los ratones
la flor	las flores
el frijol	los frijoles

4. Nouns ending in **z** change the **z** to **c** and then add **es**. The article adds **s**.

la vez	las veces
el lápiz	los lápices
el pez	los peces
la luz	las luces

5. Nouns ending in **s** have the same written form for singular or plural. The article adds the **s** in the plural.

la tesis	las tesis
el martes	los martes
el lunes	los lunes

6. Compound nouns usually form their plurals in the regular manner as given.

el ferrocarril	los ferrocarriles
el sobretodo	los sobretodos

Some have the same form in singular and plural and indicate number by the plural article.

el rompecabezas	los rompecabezas
el rascacielos	los rascacielos

A few compound nouns carry the plural **s** or **es** in **both** component words according to the rules for each word.

el gentilhombre	los gentileshombres
el ricohombre	los ricoshombres

7. For proper names, the **s** is **never** added to the **last** name, and the plural is indicated by the plural article.

la señora Montenegro   los Montenegro

First names take the regular plurals.

Pedro	los Pedros
Luis	los Luises

8. There are a few exceptions to these basic rules for plurals, but they are usually words borrowed from other languages and can be taught as they are met in reading.

There is such consistency in the principles of writing the plural form and recognizing plurals in print that the teacher can provide practice whenever an opportunity exists in the reading instruction. **Mi Libro de lenguage 5° curso, Begoña Bilbao** gives an excellent summary of the rules for the formation of plurals.

> ***Número es el accidente gramatical que indica si la palabra expresa una o más personas, animales o cosas.**
>
> El nombre sustantivo tiene dos números: **singular** o **plural,** según indique una o más de una persona, animal o cosa.
>
> **FORMACION DEL PLURAL**
> —Añadiendo una **s** al singular:
> a) los nombres terminados en vocal no acentuada:
> **libro — libros;**
> b) los nombres terminados en **é** acentuada:
> **café — cafés.**
>
> —Añadiendo **es** al singular:
> a) los nombres que terminan en consonante:
> **compás — compases;**
> b) los nombres que terminan en vocal acentuada que no sea **é: jabalí — jabalíes.**
>
> —Sin modificar el singular:
> a) las palabras graves terminadas en **s:**
> **dosis — crisis;**

b) las palabras esdrújulas terminadas en **s**:
análisis — éxtasis;

c) los días de la semana terminados en **s**:
jueves — lunes.

HAY NOMBRES QUE SOLO SE USAN EN SINGULAR

—Los que expresan **cualidades morales: la fe, la pureza.**

—Los que expresan **materia: el mármol, el cobre.**

—Los que indican **especie en general: el manzano, el olivo.**

HAY NOMBRES QUE SOLO SE USAN EN PLURAL

—Algunos nombres que tienen **valor colectivo: los víveres, las tienieblas.**

—Los que se refieren a **objetos compuestos** por varias partes: **las tijeras.**

An exercise to practice in forming plurals follows:

Pon en plural los siguientes nombres

ferrocarril — cutis — perdiz — tribu — huésped — diócesis — porta-
monedas — limpiabotas — máscara — ciempiés — compás — gafas — madera
bóveda — mar — abad — análisis — libro — casa — palacio — martes —
máquina — actriz — héroe.

*Page 47

Some specific activities are suggested as follows:

- select one or two words that have been read and understood in context from the lesson and ask the students to write the plural forms if the singular is given or the singular forms if the plural is given;
- point out any exceptions to regular practice and have the students put the singular and plural forms in their personal dictionaries.
- dictate plural forms of words the students have in their listening and speaking vocabularies and ask the students to write the singular;
- write the words in sentences on the board in the singular and ask the

students to change them to plurals;

- play singular-plural games in which a member of one group gives a singular word form and a member of another group gives the plural or vice versa. The group with the most correct forms wins;
- prepare worksheets for individual practice in correctly forming and using plurals;
- select appropriate worksheets from publishers' materials as available to practice formation of plurals;
- whenever words are used to illustrate singular or plural forms, provide their meanings through pictures, objects, diagrams, illustrations, and use in meaningful context. Students will then be acquiring not only the correct form of the word or words, but also the meaning(s).

Concept of Agreement

The **concordancia** of Spanish is an important feature of correct usage in oral and written discourse. As teachers know, words that explain or describe nouns must agree in gender and in number with the word so qualified. In the course of language acquisition, the students have developed an intuitive grasp of the changing forms of the articles and adjectives. They have learned to accommodate certain expressions — **los gatos, las ventanas, el libro, la pluma.** They ordinarily demonstrate an expected range of differences in proficiency as a result of their own Spanish language opportunities. Like **all** students of **any** language, they have **not** studied or analyzed the rules of agreement. They have not usually had extensive experience in seeing or expressing in written form the words and phrases that have become second nature to them. Teachers in reading classrooms have many occasions to weave into the reading, writing, and spelling activities the concept of agreement and the basic guidelines for improving these speech-print connections. Among the lessons in noun-modifier agreement, the following few appear useful to incorporate as appropriate for students:

- The articles have several forms

el	**los**	**un**	**uno**	**unos**
la	**las**		**una**	**unas**

Ordinarily these forms must agree with the word they are designating.

el soldado	**la clase**
los soldados	**las clases**
un soldado	**una clase**
unos soldados	**unas clases**

- Words used to describe nouns have several forms

  bonito   bonitos
  bonita   bonitas

  Ordinarily the forms are used to agree with the nouns they are describing.

  un día bonito   **unos días bonitos**
  una blusa bonita   **unas blusas bonitas**

- The plurals of adjectives are formed in the same manner as the plurals of nouns.

  el niño feliz   **los niños felices**
  los vinos buenos   **las comidas deliciosas**
  los profesores inteligentes

- There are some special forms for words that end in **án, ín, ón,** or **dor.** These may be best managed as they turn up in the material used in the reading lesson.

  una señora muy habladora
  una niña dormilona

The concept of agreement in Spanish extends beyond noun-modifier. Eventually, students will need to learn that

- subjects agree with predicates;
- pronouns agree in number and gender with the noun they represent;
- certain classes of words have requirements for grammatical agreement in number, gender, tense, and person.

As students are encouraged to improve oral production of Spanish, they will be better able to recognize and use language in written form.

Verb Forms

The most complex system of word formation and use is found in Spanish verbs. Not only are they changed for person, number, tense, mood and voice, but they are also subject to spelling variations and irregular forms. The potential for more than forty-five distinct forms of a single verb exists. Students need to have opportunities for learning the basic rules for predicting verb forms at some point during their acquisition and use of oral Spanish which provides the foundation for their reading and writing skills. For Hispanic students who are growing in fluency and literacy in a country where Spanish is the dominant language, their daily lives and their instructional program are totally Spanish and may be expected to contain abundant practice in verb forms. Hispanic students in English-speaking milieux, however, are rarely given the direct teaching necessary to acquire skills in using the verb forms correctly. Ordinarily, the study of verbs is relegated to the later language classes in secondary schools or colleges. It seems reasonable to suggest that gentle direction and judicious practice in verb forms offered as part of the reading classes would be in the best interests of students. Lessons begun during their primary school years and carried out systematically as literacy and fluency improve would result in improved competence. For example, students may practice selecting the correct form from several given.

Students may be asked to match finite forms with the correct infinitive. **Adelante, Página 44**.

___

1. UNA PARA CADA UNA

△ Lee las palabras de la columna **A**. A cada una le corresponde una palabra de la columna **B**. Escribe esa palabra de la columna **B** en la línea dada.

COLUMNA A		COLUMNA B
cobrar	cobramos	encontré
sembrar	_____	abrió
abrir	_____	cuadrará
comprar	_____	celebramos
celebrar	_____	entró
encontrar	_____	sufrió
ladrar	_____	compré
entrar	_____	cobramos
cuadrar	_____	ladra
sufrir	_____	sembré

Students may fill in correct form of verb to complete the sentences. **Adelante, Página 44**

2. ¿QUE PALABRA FALTA?

△ Completa estas oraciones. Escoge la palabra apropiada en la columna **A**.

a) Si el perro oye un ruido, va a _____ .

b) Vamos al mercado a _____ la carne.

c) Si la puerta está cerrada no puedes _____ .

Students may be directed to underline the action and indicate the time of the action — **ayer — ahora — mañana.**
Lengua Nacional, Página 209

Completa estas oraciones:
Usa estas palabras:

cavaron	cavarán	cavan

Los piratas _____ Los piratas _____ Los piratas _____

Students may be given experiences with simple future forms. **Lengua Nacional, Level 2, Página 180**

Completa:

arán	ará	ará	arán	ará	ará	arán	arán

— Toño cant ☐   — él cant ☐

— Lupe cant ☐   — ella cant ☐

— Toño y Pancho cant ☐   — ellos cant ☐

— Lupe y Anita cant ☐   — ellas cant ☐

Students may practice using the more common idiomatic verbs.
Lengua Nacional, Level 2, Página 208

Dice el texto que el capitán mandó esconder el **ron** para
que todos **tuvieran la cabeza clara.**

¿Qué es el ron?

☐ Un sombrero especial de pirata.
☐ Una bebida alcohólica, parecida al vino.
☐ Un jabón para lavar la cabeza.

Marca la respuesta acertada.

¿Qué quiere decir **tener la cabeza clara?**

☐ No estar borracho.
☐ Tener el pelo limpio.
☐ No llevar sombrero.

Marca la respuesta acertada.

The many variations in verb forms that may be found in written discourse include not only the changes resulting from the familiar verb attributes of person, number, tense, and mood, but also from the spelling variations, the irregular forms and the stem changing verbs. When these differences are added to the infinitive, the present participle, and the past participle, the multiple learnings that are possible from a **single** verb are overwhelming. Memorization of verb paradigms or of cumbersome rules, particularly at the early levels of instruction, does not appear very productive or interesting for students. As they encounter the various verb forms in their reading, however, there is value in pointing out to them any essential characteristic that may serve to signal meaning in some other context. If the students have some knowledge, for example, that **cono** ⟨zco⟩ represents a first person form of **conocer,** when they encounter **produ** ⟨zco⟩, **pere** ⟨zco⟩ or **mere** ⟨zco⟩, they will recognize the same person, number, and tense cued by the verb ending.

Teachers will have to exercise prudence and judgment in their **formal** teaching of verb forms. Students in the third grade and beyond are generally able to understand language generalizations and rules. Furthermore, by this age they usually have had enough experience with language in oral and written forms to benefit from additional descriptions of familiar forms. Information about verbs that may be offered as relevant and supplementary to the reading lessons from the third grade through high school **when such learning is appropriate** may include the following:

- the family to which the verbs belong — first, second, or third conjugation
- the concept of the root and ending of the verb
- the attributes of the verb — person, tense, number, voice, mood
- the groups or classes of verbs — transitive, intransitive, reflexive, copulative, etc.

Such skills enhance not only the students' reading vocabularies but also extend their listening and speaking proficiency as well.

An excellent summary of salient features of the verbs in Spanish is given in the book **Mi Libro de Lenguaje.** Teachers of reading in Spanish may wish to keep these thumbnail sketches on hand and use them when verb variations occur in the reading and writing activities.

REPASEMOS LOS VERBOS: **Las tres grandes familias.**

Rosita **tenía** la frente recta
El autor **retrata** a Rosita
Rosita **reía** a menudo

Busca el infinitivo de los tres verbos y separa la raíz de la terminación. Cada uno de ellos pertenece a cada uno de los tres grandes grupos de verbos: los que terminan en **ar,** los que terminan en **er** y los que terminan en **ir.**
- **No copies más que los verbos de la 2ª conjugación:**
leer, escribir, reflexionar, oír, dibujar, comprender, disfrutar, tener, llegar, aplaudir, abrir, obtener, suponer, redondear.

- **No copies más que los verbos de la 3ª conjugación:**
conducir, creer, curar, oír, madurar, dormir, escribir, montar, madurar, poder, gemir, sentir, sufrir, contener.

- **Forma cinco oraciones que contengan verbos de la 1ª conjugación. Subráyalos junto con sus sujetos.**

REPASEMOS EL VERBO: **Las personas en la conjugación.**

Ya hemos dicho que la terminación de los verbos indica el tiempo, el modo, el número y la persona en que están empleados.
Hay tres personas en singular o en plural que pueden realizar la acción del verbo:

	yo (el que habla)		**nosotros** (los que
Una . . .	**tú** (a quién se habla)	Varias..	hablamos)
	él (de quien se habla)		**vosotros** (con quienes
			hablamos)
			ellos (de los que
			hablamos)

● **Observa las terminaciones de los verbos siguientes y escribe la persona que le conviene:**

. . . tiene buen caracter. . . . admiro su virtud. . . . fueron muy amables. . . . tenía una voz dulce. sonreirás con agrado. . . . volvieron a ayudarle. . . . seremos siempre generosos. . . . estudiaréis este asunto. . . . llegarás muy lejos.

● **Pon la terminación que conviene a estos verbos:**
Yo lleg. . . tarde. Mis hermanos tien. . . mucha gracia. Ellos s. . . muy optimistas. Nosotros comprend. . . su buen humor. María lleg. . . tarde a las lecciones. Tú volver. . . mañana a vernos. Vosotros demostr. . . vuestro buen corazón. Ellos pens. . . las cosas bien.

No olvides que el verbo varía según la persona, o lo que es lo mismo, el verbo concuerda **con su sujeto.**

REPASEMOS EL VERBO: **Los tiempos.**

—Recuerda que los tiempos del verbo son fundamentalmente tres, porque las acciones pueden producirse: **en el momento** en que se habla (presente); **antes** del momento en que se habla (pasado), y **después** del momento en que se habla (futuro).

Los tiempos fundamentalmente son, pues: **presente, pasado** y **futuro.**

● **Emplea en presente los verbos que en las oraciones siguientes, están empleados en futuro (separa raíz y terminación):**

Yo encontraré placer en el campo. Allí hallaremos goces muy grandes. María apreciará la belleza de las flores. Tú distinguirás las variadas clases de árboles. Todos contemplaremos el bello paisaje.

● **Busca en la lectura los verbos que haya. Emplea en pasado los verbos que estén en presente o en futuro y ponles un sujeto.**

● **Clasifica los siguientes verbos en los tres tiempos fundamentales:**
juego, llegaremos, volará, cantó, contemplaron, pintaré, miras, fotografió, saldrán, advirtieron, distinguiremos, percibió, sufrimos.

REPASEMOS EL VERBO: **Los modos.**

Recuerda que el **modo** es un accidente que indica **cómo** el verbo expresa la acción.

En efecto: La voz de los sapos **suena** monótona en la espesura (expresa la acción enunciándola como un hecho real.) Es el modo **indicativo.**
Cuidad bien vuestra vista (presenta la acción como ordenada). Es el **imperativo.**
Si estuviera la noche clara **veríamos** las estrella (no indica el hecho como real, depende de una condición). Es el **Potencial.**

Yo **quisiera** pintar bien (expresa la acción como deseable). Es el **Subjuntivo.**

Estos cuatro modos se llaman **personales.** Se conjugan en las diferentes personas.

Ver, oír, llegar, cantar. Son nombres de verbos. Enuncian la acción de abstracto, sin hacer más que nombrarla. Están en modo **Infinitivo.**

● **Con el infinitivo expresa las acciones de un escolar, de un maestro, de un buen amigo.**

● **Indica entre paréntesis después de cada verbo, el modo en que está empleado:**
El sol brilla mucho. Si hiciese bueno saldríamos al campo. No trasnochéis. Es mejor dormir mucho. Ponte las gafas. El Sol se ocultó pronto. Es necesario mirar con atención. Si saliera el Sol . . . Acostémonos pronto. Se cayó al colocar el toldo. El calor molestaba mucho. Callad, se oyen los pájaros.

These charts listing important features of the verb system may be placed in the writing or library corner. These gentle reminders serve to assist students throughout the year.

Possessive Forms

Possessive forms in Spanish may be adjectives. Furthermore, they may take a short or long form. They inflect for person, gender, and number to indicate to the hearer or reader the possessor and the possessed. Their position in relationship to the noun they modify may be before the noun, — **mi libro; tu amiga; sus tíos** —, or they may follow the noun — **Estos libros son tuyos; La culpa ha sido mía; Padre Nuestro.** The longer stressed forms generally are used to emphasize a point or in direct address, — **Hijita mía, ¿qué te pasa?** Possessive forms may also be pronouns, formed by the addition of the appropriate definite article to the **long** form of the possessive adjective and agree in number and gender with the **possessed** not the possessor, — **Sus niños están en la escuela; Los nuestros se han quedado en casa. Necesito una pluma; Elena tiene la mía.** Knowledge of this system of possessive adjectives and pronouns will help students recognize in written form the signals that cue them to the discovery of possessor and object or person possessed. Another indicator of possession is the construction **de** followed by the noun, — **Es el libro de María.** This same use of **de** with pronouns may be used frequently to clarify the referent particularly in third person, — **El coche de usted; La casa de ella; El abrigo de él.**

Activities for the development of the **concept** of possession and for the **practice** in reading these forms will offer students both knowledge and skills for English transfer. The English **forms** will differ, but the **function** of possessives in **both** languages is the same. Here are a few examples of lessons to promote the understanding of form and function in Spanish.

¿Qué quiere decir la palabra **mi** en **mi** tina? **mi** tomate; **mi** tulipán?
¿Qué quiere decir la palabra **tu** en **tu** teléfono? **tu** taza?
¿Qué quiere decir la palabra **de** en la taza **de** Manolo?

Cascabel, Página 7

Rodea con un circulo la palabra.

1. mi tomate
2. tu taza

1. mi teléfono
2. tu tamal

1. mi mapa
2. tu moto

1. tu teléfono
2. mi tulipán

1. mi tapa
2. tu pato

1. mi tina
2. tu tomate

The multiple meanings that are possible in the third person possessives **su, sus, los suyos,** and **el suyo** frequently require the addition or replacement of these words since it may not be clear who the third person is. Students should be given some practice in the replacement **de él, de ella, de usted,** and so on to, eliminate confusion or to clear up any uncertainty.

Cascabel, Página 8 y 33

Escribe los números.

☐ la taza de Ema

☐ el tulipán de mamá

☐ el tomate de Pancho

☐ el teléfono de papá

☐ la moto de Manolo

1

2

3

4

5

El _____ es de Ana.
La _____ es de Manolo.

Shortened Forms

El apócope refers to change in descriptive words used to describe people, places, or events when such words precede instead of follow the nouns they are modifying. Words such as **uno, bueno, malo, grande, alguno, ninguno,** may be shortened — **El buen hombre; Su mal humor; Algun dia.** The **o** is dropped before a masculine singular noun. The **de** of **grande** may be dropped before either a masculine or feminine singular noun beginning with a consonant — **la gran profesora, el gran desengaño.** Sometimes the **de** may be dropped before nouns beginning with vowels — **la gran actriz, el gran orador.** These forms carry the meaning of **great** not **large.** In the plural forms the **de** is not dropped — **los grandes presidentes.** The words **uno, primero, tercero, postrero** also drop the **o** when they precede a masculine noun even if there are other intervening words — **el primer buen dia, el tercer verso, un postrermal dia.** The words **cualquiera** and **cualesquiera** may also be shortened and may drop the final **a** before **either** singular or plural forms of the noun of either gender — **cualquier casa, cualesquier datas.** Two other words that students may encounter in their reading should be mentioned — **ciento** and **santo. Ciento** always drops its **to** before **mil** — **cien mil almas** and before plural nouns of either gender — **cien patos, cien máquinas de coser,** but keeps its full form in **dos cientos pájaros,** or **tres cientos estudiantes. Santo** may mean sacred, holy, or saint. The form is shortened before a saint's name unless the name begins with **Do** or **To** as in **Santo Domingo** and **Santo Tomás,** but **San Pablo, San Isidro** and **San Martin. Santa** is never shortened, thus, **Santa Clara, Santa Teresa** and **Santa Ana** are correct.

These forms, like the shortened forms of the possessive adjectives, are restricted by their placement. The governing rule permits them to be shortened **only** if they **precede, not follow** the noun. It is highly unlikely that students will know this rule or discover it for themselves even if they have used the forms with a fair degree of accuracy. Practice and opportunities to generalize from varied activities can improve speech patterns and increase reading rate. Knowledge of the rule will also assist students in written expression when they are creating their own connected discourse and have to make decisions about correct word order and spelling. Two other important shortened forms that the students are well accustomed to hearing and using in speech are the **del** of **de** plus **el** and the **al** of **a** plus **el.** They need to recognize these in writing **al** — **María va al salon,** and **del** — **Me gusta el color del coche.** Because the article and the vowel are often elided in oral form, students may not use this written distinction when required. They may be helped in spelling and written expression if they are told that despite the many oral combinations, only **de** and **a** are combined with **el** in writing.

Enclisis

Enclitic forms practically do not exist in English but are extensive in Spanish. The process is one in which words are formed by combining two classes of words. A pronoun may be added to the infinitive — **María, quiero ayudarte.** A pronoun may be added to the participle — **Están pintandolo.** Pronouns may also be added to the command forms — **Dámelo, ayudame, por favor,** but if the command is negative, enclisis does not occur. **Pedro, no me ayudes por favor — No me lo des.** When students have been provided with activities that illustrate the various enclitic forms in writing, they may be expected to make more rapid associations with the spoken forms and grasp their meanings more readily.

Derived Forms

Many words are formed through the process of adding prefixes or suffixes to the stems or root words. New words may be created through the additional endings.

sol	solana	nube	nuboso
	solazo		nublado
	solearse		nubecillo
criar	criado	vestir	vestidura
	crianza		vestimenta
	criatura		vestido

New words may also be formed by using prefixes to change meanings. The verb **poner** is a classic example of the many words formed in this manner — **deponer, disponer, entreponer, exponer, imponer, posponer, proponer, reponer, sobreponer, superponer.**

These derived forms have great potential for vocabulary enhancement and are discussed as one means of extending both the oral and written vocabulary skills of students in Chapter VI. The derivational forms are also mentioned in this brief summary of oral and written language connections because students may overlook the word recognition and/or the comprehension possibilities that exist in these associations. If the readers, for example, know the infinitive **poner** and have meanings stored for this word, by recognizing **super** from some other context, they may be able to extract meaning.

Pronouns

Pronouns are usually defined as words that refer to a noun — a person, place, object, or event known to the hearer or reader. There are several classes of pronouns that serve a variety of language functions. Pronouns in Spanish make distinctions of person, number, gender, and case. There are also specific forms for the conventional and the intimate use of the second person pronoun. When students are learning to recognize and to understand pronouns in print, they do not necessarily need elaborate declensions of the personal, reflexive, demonstrative, possessive, and relative pronouns. As they find pronouns in written discourse, the important learning is an unambiguous connection to the referent represented by the pronoun. If there is lack of clarity in the reader's response, then the meaning carried by the pronoun may be lost. If in the teacher's judgment, the students may benefit from a few exercises in identifying, supplying, or using pronouns in sentences as an extension of a reading lesson, excerpts from elementary Spanish materials may be provided. For example, from **Mil Libro de Lenguaje, Página 103.**

—Los pronombres personales sustituyen a los nombres de personas: **yo, tú, él, ella, nosotros, vosotros, ellos, ellas.**
—Los pronombres sujetos utilizados en la conjugación de los verbos, son pronombres personales.
—Los pronombres personales cambian de forma **en el plural.**
—Algunos pronombres personales de la 3.ª persona cambian de forma en el femenino.
—Los pronombres personales pueden ser sujeto del verbo y complemento del verbo.
—Las formas de pronombre personal **me, te, se, nos, os, se,** cuando reciben la acción de los verbos reflexivos, es decir, cuando el sujeto es la misma persona que ejecuta y recibe la acción, se llaman pronombres personales reflexivos:

Yo me lavo

—No confundamos **él, la, lo, los, las,** artículos y formas del pronombre personal.
Delante del verbo son siempre pronombres; delante de un nombre son artículos.

Subraya los pronombres personales sujetos y los pronombres personales complementos indicando, entre paréntesis, la persona a quien se refieren (repasa el cuadro y recuerda la clase de complementos que has estudiado, con preposición y sin preposición):

Yo estoy contento de vosotros. Yo os invitaré mañana. Ellos llegaron tarde. Ellos le encontraron pronto. Juan iba con él. Mañana saldrán conmigo. Vosotros os laváis con frecuencia. Llamad pronto a ellos. Vendrán a jugar con vosotros.

Completa las oraciones siguientes, sustituyendo los puntos por el pronombre personal que conviene:

Cuando . . . hayas acabado el carrete de fotografía . . . llevarás a revelar.
Si las fotos han salido bien . . . mandarás que . . . amplíen. Si . . . sois estudiosos.
Si las fotos han salido bien . . . mandarás que . . . amplíen. Si . . . sois estudiosos
. . . premiaremos con una excursión. Pablito es pequeño, pero quizá . . .
llevemos también con . . . Margarita es ordenada: . . . arregla su habitación
. . . barre y limpia el polvo.

The form and placement of pronouns comprise a relatively elaborate system and may be more comprehensible to older students. A brief, simple explanation that goes beyond the usage in the reading lesson will keep the knowledge of the language growing. Over a period of time, the several grammatical categories may be acquired. For Hispanic students to read and to write correctly in their native language, they need to have some instruction in these **ideas claras:**

—Los pronombres sustituyen al nombre para evitar su repetición y en muchos casos para determinarlo.
—Los pronombres pueden ser: **personales, demostrativos, posesivos, indefinidos, relativos** que estudiaremos más tarde, **interrogativos** y **numerales.**
—Los pronombres tienen el mismo **género** y **número** que el nombre a quien sustituyen.
—No se debe confundir un adjetivo con un pronombre. Los primeros **acompañan** al nombre. Los segundos lo **sustituyen.**

ATENCION: No debes confundir los pronombres estudiados con los adjetivos de igual denominación. Es muy fácil distinguirlos: **los pronombres van siempre solos; los adjetivos van siempre acompañando a un nombre.** Obsérvalo:

Este (adj.) monte es muy alto.   **Este** (pron.) es bajo.
Su (adj.) bicicleta es buena.   **La suya** (pron.) es mejor.
Aquí hay **muchas** (adj.) flores.   También allí hay **muchas** (pron.).

—El pronombre relativo sustituye a un nombre que es su atecedente. Une una oración subordinada con una principal:
           María tiene una herida **que** inquieta a su madre
—El pronombre relativo es, pues, el comienzo de una oración subordinada.
—Los pronombres relativos son: **que, cual, quien, cuyo,** y sus plurales.
—No debemos confundir el pronombre relativo **que,** con la conjunción **que.**
—Los pronombres interrogativos tienen las mismas formas que los pronombres relativos.
—El pronombre relativo toma el género y número de su antecedente. **Que** es invariable en género y número. **Quien** y **cual** son invariable en género.

Punctuation

An important element in Spanish writing is the punctuation system. The written signs are taken as indicators of pauses, intonation, and other features of oral language. Punctuation marks, however, represent more than aides to speech. They suggest a purposeful logic regarding the marking of the end of a thought. The thought may be a statement, a question, or an exclamation, but there has to be some written notice to the reader suggesting where one thought ends and another is about to begin. Linguists have noted that although alphabets may differ enormously among languages, there are many commonalities in punctuation systems. Logical thought appears as a universal property that enhances all languages. In Spanish, the **signos de puntuación** are listed and explained well in **Mi Libro de Lenguaje** as follows:

La Ortografía no consiste sólo en escribir correctamente las palabras por el acertado empleo de las letras, sino también en emplear debidamente los signos auxiliares de la escritura, llamados, en general, **signos de puntuación.**

Los signos de puntuación tienen gran importancia porque sirven para aclarar el sentido del texto que leemos.

Unos signos sirven para señalar en la escritura las **pausas** que debemos hacer al leer. Son: **coma (,), punto y coma (;), dos puntos (:), y punto final (.).**

Otros signos indican la **entonación** que hemos de dar a algunas oraciones. Son: el **paréntesis (( ))**, la **interrogación (¿?)**, la **admiración (¡!)** y los **puntos suspensivos (. . .)**

Se usará la coma:
—**En las enumeraciones:** En el cajón había plumas, lápices y cuadernos. (La coma se suprimirá cuando alguna de estas palabras vayan enlazadas por **y, e, o, u**).
—**Después de los vocativos:** Juan, ven aquí. Acércate, Pedro, hasta la casa.
—**Cuando en una oración se intercala un inciso** que aclare o amplíe lo que se está diciendo: Los hielos, en el mes de abril, destrozaron las cosechas.
—**Cuando se invierte el orden lógico de los elementos de la oración:** Cuando empezó a llover, saqué el paraguas. A la mañana siguiente, María volvió.
—**Delante de las conjunciones mas, pero, aunque,** cuando **el párrafo es breve.**

Se usará el punto y coma:
—Cuando el párrafo sea extenso, para separar las distintas oraciones que lo componen y que, a veces, llevan ya ellas alguna coma: En la Biblia están escritos los anales del cielo, de la tierra y del género humano; en ella se contiene lo que fue, lo que es y lo que será. (Donoso Cortés).
—Delante de las conjunciones **mas, pero, aunque,** siempre que el párrafo tenga alguna extensión, pues de lo contrario llevará coma: Estaba dispuesto a enrolarse en la excursión; pero una pulmonía le impidió tomar parte en esta aventura que tanto deseaba.

Se usan los dos puntos:
—Cuando se citan palabras textuales de un autor o personaje:
  El profesor dijo así: "La excursión está prevista para el jueves".
—Después de saludar en las cartas: Querido hijo: Estimado amigo:
—Después de las expresiones: **Por ejemplo, son las siguientes, verbigracia, a saber...:** Los ríos principales de España son cinco, a saber: Duero, Tajo, Guadiana, Guadalquivir y Ebro.
—Ante una enumeración de hechos o de objetos — Las flores que más me gustan son: las rosas, los claveles, y los gladiolos.

El punto indica una pausa mayor que la del punto y coma. Podemos considerar dos clases de puntos: **punto final** y **punto y seguido.**

Se empleo el **punto final** cuando una oración o un párrafo ha terminado y el que sigue no tiene relación con ella.
  "En el centro está el quiosco de los músicos y los domingos por la tarde tocan cuatro piezas. Enfrente tenemos la botica y a la derecha la pastelería, así que estamos muy bien."
  Borita Casas. "Antoñita la Fantástica"

Se emplea punto y seguido, cuando una oración ha terminado y la siguiente habla del mismo tema, es decir, tiene relación con ella. (Puede servirte de ejemplo, el párrafo del ejemplo anterior).

También se emplea el punto en la escritura abreviada de algunas palabras: Sr. D. ptas. Excmo. Ilmo.

Los signos de interrogación (**¿?**) y de admiración (**¡!**) se colocan antes y después de las oraciones admirativas:
  ¿Cuándo vienes? ¡Qué bien estás!

Hay cocasiones en que la pregunta o el sentido admirativo no comienza al principio de la oración. En estos casos los signos interrogativos o admirativos han de colocarse justamente donde comienza y no al principio de la oración:
  Si tardas en desayunar, ¿no llegarás tarde a clase?
  Si sacas malas notas ¡qué pena me darás!

En una oración se **interrumpe** a veces el sentido de ella intercalando otra oración aclaratoria. Esta oración se suele poner entre paréntesis.
  Cuando llegamos a Madrid (y llegamos con mucho retraso) nos esperaba mi familia.
  Mañana —dijo mi padre— saldremos para Barcelona.
  El descubrimiento de América (octubre 1492) es una fecha importantísima en la Historia de España.
Modernamente se tiende a suprimir el paréntesis y a emplear más las rayas.

Los **puntos suspensivos** son signos de valor expresivo y pueden indicar:
a) Que el sentido de la oración queda incompleto porque no **queremos** continuar, no **sabemos** continuar o consideramos que no **es necesario,** puesto que el que nos escucha lo entenderá.

Me gustaría decirte... Las partes de la Gramática son: morfología, sintaxis, fonética...

b) Que lo que vamos a decir causará sorpresa: Nos llamaron, fuimos asustados y... no ocurría nada.

It will be necessary for the teacher to decide which marks of punctuation to teach and when to teach them. Usually, young students begin with the period **(.)** and question marks **(¿?).** They then acquire the meaning for and the skill in using the exclamation points **(¡!).** As students mature, they learn to manage the logic that accompanies other forms of punctuation. They will need to know which marks indicate the speaker and changes of speakers in a dialogue, and they ultimately should have skill in recognizing the intent of the other marks. When they are writing their own thoughts, they will need to use the many written indicators with reason and with skill. Isolated lessons in punctuation drills do not appear too exciting or beneficial. If, however, students may be led to the realization that **puntos, comas, comillas,** and other marks serve a vital purpose in assisting the readers in organizing, arranging, and otherwise ordering their thoughts then, regular but brief excercises may be of great instructional benefit. Practice, such as that provided in the short exercise from **Adelante, Page 78,** is a good introduction for young students.

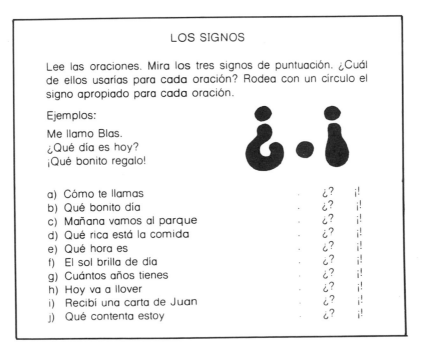

LOS SIGNOS

Lee las oraciones. Mira los tres signos de puntuación. ¿Cuál de ellos usarías para cada oración? Rodea con un círculo el signo apropiado para cada oración.

Ejemplos:

Me llamo Blas.
¿Qué día es hoy?
¡Qué bonito regalo!

a) Cómo te llamas . ¿? ¡!
b) Qué bonito día . ¿? ¡!
c) Mañana vamos al parque . ¿? ¡!
d) Qué rica está la comida . ¿? ¡!
e) Qué hora es . ¿? ¡!
f) El sol brilla de día . ¿? ¡!
g) Cuántos años tienes . ¿? ¡!
h) Hoy va a llover . ¿? ¡!
i) Recibí una carta de Juan . ¿? ¡!
j) Qué contenta estoy . ¿? ¡!

After the students have circled the correct response, they may select one sentence representing each type and copy the **three** sentences complete with their correct **signos de puntuación.** Gradually, students need to move beyond to more difficult exercises using the **coma,** the **punto y coma,** and the **dos puntos.** Teachers will need to watch for opportunities as they occur in the students' reading and writing.

Capitalization

Spanish is very frugal in its use of capital letters. The few words that require the use of the capital letter are these:

- the names of countries — **el Perú, los Estados Unidos**
- the proper names — **Garza, Tomás**
- the abbreviations for titles — **Sr., Sra., Srta.**
- the words in titles of literary or artistic works — **Don Quijote, El Pensador.**

These requirements for the use of **las letras mayúsculas** are not difficult to learn in the usual course of reading instruction. The teacher may point out the difference in the size of the letters when encountered in the daily lessons. They may also help students edit their own writing by reminding them of these easy capitalization rules.

Lengua Nacional, Level 2, Fichas de trabajo.
   Copia estas oraciones:

Toño, Pancho y Lupe viven en México.
_____

Pancho tiene un tío que vive en el Perú.
_____

Toño pasó unas vacaciones en Cuba.
_____

A Lupe le han traído un regalo de Brasil.
_____

Escribe los nombres de países que has visto en esas oraciones.
_____

> **Todos los nombres de países se escriben con mayúscula.**

Escribe el nombre del país que corresponda:

español	_____
alemán	_____
francés	_____
guatemalteco	_____
argentino	_____
peruano	_____

In classrooms beyond the third grade, students may copy this information in their language notebooks. If the teacher considers the writing of rules too abstract or too difficult for the levels of the students, then the rules may be written on a chart and placed in a convenient corner. The chart may be moved to a more prominent place in the room when the students are working on a particular oral-written connection and may benefit from a gentle reminder of the applicable rule.

EJERCICIO ACERCA DE LAS MAYÚSCULAS

Coloca la letra mayúscula en los espacios señalados:

1. "___n esto de gigantes, respondió ___on ___uijote; hay diferentes opiniones si los ha habido o no en el mundo; pero la ___anta ___scritura, que no puede faltar un átomo a la verdad, nos muestra que los hubo, contándonos la historia de aquel filisteazo de ___olías, que tenía siete codos y medio de altura."

2. "___eñor, replicó ___ancho, yo imagino que es bueno mandar, aunque sea a un hato de ganado." "___on vos me entierren, ___ancho, que sabéis todo, respondió el ___uque; y yo espero que seréis tal gobernador como vuestro juicio promete."
El Ingeniero Hidalgo Don Quijote de la Mancha, por Miguel de Cervantes Saavedra.

3. ___varisto había hecho conocimiento con toda la mala gente del rumbo, sin que esa mala gente, de quien desconfiaba, conociese ni frecuentase ___l ___ancho de los ___oyotes.
Los Bandidos del Río Frío, por Manuel Payno

4. ___e pie, frente a ___u ___ajestad, ___ristóbal ___olón, hablaba, dejándose llevar por su sueño de ___ndias.

5. ___e trata de la gloriosa época que los hombres han convenido en considerar como la más bella invención italiana, ___l ___enacimiento, y que comprende los treinta o cuarenta primeros años del siglo XVI. ___n este breve periodo florecen los artistas ___onardo de ___inci, ___afael, ___iguel ___ngel, etc.
Historia del Arte, por Hipólito Tane

Nombres propios y títulos usados en los párrafos anteriores:

Don Quijote	Cristóbal Colón
Santa Escritura	Indias
Golías	El Renacimiento
Sancho	Leonardo de Vinci
Evaristo	(pronúnciese Vinchi)
El Rancho de los Coyotes	Rafael
Su Majestad	Miguel Angel

Debe usarse letra mayúscula:
1. Al comienzo de un escrito.
2. Después del punto.
3. Cuando se escriben nombres propios, sean de personas, animales, países, ciudades, ríos, etc. Ejemplos: Pedro, Rosalinda, Pérez, Alvarado, Sultán, Laika, Minino, Inglaterra, París, Rhin, Volga.
4. En los dos o más nombres reunidos para designar países, estados, instituciones, empresas, etc. Ejemplos: San Luis Potosí, Compañía Fraccionadora del Sureste, Estados Unidos de Norteamérica, Instituto Politécnico Nacional, Instituto Tecnológico de Monterrey, etc.
5. En la misma forma debe emplearse cuando se trata de títulos de obras literarias o artísticas: **El Ruiseñor y la Rosa** (cuento de Oscar Wilde), **El Patito Feo** (de Christian Anderson), **El Ingenioso Hidalgo Don Quijote de la Mancha** (de Miguel de Cervantes Saavedra), **La Trinchera** (mural del pintor mexicano José Clemente Orozco), **La Gioconda** (lienzo de Leonardo da Vinci), **El Pensador** (escultura de Rodin).
6. En los epítetos con que suelen sustituirse los nombres de ciudades, montañas, ríos, personajes célebres y que, en ocasiones, sustituyen a los originales. Ejemplos: La Ciudad Eterna (Roma), La Ciudad de los Palacios (Mexico), La Montaña que Humea (el Popocatépetl), Los Hijos del Sol Naciente (los japoneses), El Caudillo de Sur (Zapata).

Transfer of Oral-Written Connections to English

Students who have had strong opportunities for seeing how spoken discourse is represented in written form have a background of wonderful skills to bring to the reading and writing of English. Fluent and literate Hispanic students are well on their way to fluency and literacy in English. The teachers can be very optimistic as they remind students that many of the oral-written connections that they have been practicing and learning are identical to or very similar to the oral-written connections needed in the second language. The principles for forming plurals have great generalizability. The concept of agreement may be applied, though in a more limited sense. Possessive indicators are different in English, but the apostrophe cue and placement signal the same information that students have understood in Spanish. There are far fewer verb forms to manage in English so students who have learned the many inflected verbs of Spanish should have no difficulties leaning the English verb forms. The enclitic and apocopated (shortened) forms will not have much application to English. Understanding the derivational process, however, should have great potential for building an extensive reading vocabulary in English. The capitalization and punctuation skills practiced in Spanish will have some transfer and some non-transfer possibilities. There will be a general awareness of the common function of these features of both writing systems. This knowledge will provide a solid basis for presenting the specific requirements of written English.

*Information that serves as a reminder in the use of capital letters is from **Enseñanza lógica del español.**

English Plurals

Hispanic students should be told that there are **only** a few new skills to be introduced in order to have English plurals under complete control. Teachers will find it very gratifying to reassure the students that they already understand the concept of number and know the two most important signals of the plural — the **s** and the **es**. Happily, these are the same two signals for forming plurals most of the time in English — mats, benches, dishes.

Some words that end in **o** add **es** to form their plurals — hero, heroes — cargo cargoes — potato, potatoes.

Some words that end in **o** preceded by a vowel add only **s** — cameo, cameos — folio, folios.

Some nouns ending in **o** preceded by a consonant form their plurals by adding **s** — piano, pianos, — burro, burros — banjo, banjos.

When nouns end in **s, z, x, ch** or **sh,** they add **es** to form their plurals — box, boxes — church, churches — loss, losses.

A few nouns add **en** or **ren** to form their plurals — ox, oxen — child, children.

A few nouns are very irregular and change their vowels completely. These practically defy regular rules and must be learned — man, men — foot, feet — mouse, mice — goose, geese — tooth, teeth.

Some nouns change their spellings before forming their plurals —

    fly — change y to i add **es** flies
    berry — change y to i add **es** berries
    wife — change f to v add **es** wives
    wharf — change f to v add **es** wharves

A few nouns have the same singular and plural forms —

    the deer (singular) the deer (plural)
    the sheep (singular) the sheep (plural)

Compound nouns usually take the plural according to the rule governing the last part of the word — spoonful, spoonfuls — bathhouse, bathhouses. Some few of them give the plural signal to the first word — editors-in chief, sons-in-law.

A particularly troublesome plural cue is the apostrophe s (**'s)** which is used to indicate the plural of letters and numbers — p's and q's, d's and b's, 3's or 8's.

There are several other plural rules that may be mentioned if students meet these forms in their reading: foreign language plurals — alumnus, alumni — erratum, errata — thesis, theses. The plural of proper names is formed by the specific requirements of title and name.

A few nouns are never used in the **singular** — trousers, athletics, annals, stocks.

There are some English words that are plural in form, but they carry a singular meaning — measles, mumps, politics.

Occasionally, a noun will have two plural forms, but the different words carry a difference in meaning.

die	dies	— used in manufacturing
die	dice	— used in games
fish	fish	— collectively
fish	fishes	— individually
head	heads	— usual plural
head	head	— of cattle

From this cursory review of the indicators of number in English, it may be easily recognized that the students will have to learn several additional forms to recognize or to express the plural in their second language. They should not attempt to learn the variations of form in isolation but, rather, may be given the information and skill practice with these differences as they are met or needed in their reading lessons. The principal learning is one that they already have — There are **two** numbers in English, the singular and the plural. The singular number denotes **one** person, place, thing, or event. The plural number denotes **more than one** person, place, thing, or event. The big message for second language readers is that they know the rule and function of number. All they need is skill practice with capricious English forms.

Practice may be offered in English plural forms.

---

1. The pet food is in the cart.
   The chocolate is in the cart.

2. The man is running after our rabbits.
   The man is running after the rabbit.
   The rabbits are running.

3. All the bananas are in the bowl.
   A banana is not in the bowl.
   All the bananas are in the bowls.

4. The rabbits are getting wet.
   A rabbit is getting wet.
   Not all the rabbits are getting wet.

5. All the pots and pans are hot.
   A pan is not hot.
   The pans are hot.
   The pots are hot.

The Concept of Agreement in English

The matter of gender agreement between nouns and their modifiers is not a requirement in English except in the system of pronouns and demonstrative adjectives. The major rule of concord in English is that of number agreement between subject and predicate. For Hispanic students this concept has been well learned and generally practiced during the instruction and use of their own language. A few agreement problems do exist for them and will need attention as they make the transfer to English.

- A number of apparently plural subject nouns are used in the singular sense. Measles is a childhood disease. Civics is part of the social sciences.
- The s marker for a plural noun is the same marker used to indicate the third person singular form of the verb. She dances well. He plays ball every day.
- The word order of Spanish sentences is far more variable and flexible than in English. A simple sentence may have as many as four optimal forms in

Spanish. These are a few of the agreement difficulties that may be expected. Hispanic students may not recognize plural and/or singular elements when word order changes have been made or when the sense of number has not been understood.

Teaching second language students to deal with the differences in number may be improved by calling the students' attention to the specific meanings carried by the word or by the group of words used in oral and written discourse in English. Other commonalities as well as differences may be highlighted. For example, both English and Spanish have parallel forms for the demonstratives — **this, these, those;** pronouns agree with the noun in apposition — we, Americans believe; the relative pronouns agree with their antecedents in both languages but there are some tricky points of usage that have to be learned. There may also be stumbling blocks for students who are learning the distinctions among words such as **some**body, **most, any**body, **a few, no**body, **each, none.** Native speakers of English often have the same problems in deciding whether to use a singular or plural verb. The English pronoun **you** always takes the plural form of the verb in contrast to the singular or plural requirements when using the pronoun **you** in Spanish. Teachers may observe carefully any problems in comprehending written material and any errors in the students' production of written English. Lessons may then be arranged to offer practice that is specifically related to the identified grammatical difficulty of the students.

Verbs
The English verbs do not inflect for person and number except for the third person singular. Hispanic students are familiar with the many variations found in the Spanish verb system. They understand the concept of changing the verb form to indicate person and number. They do not have to learn this principle again. They merely need to know that they are going to use a verb system with five forms as a general rule instead of one with the potential for forty-five or more. Some additional problems may be anticipated in moving from a language in which the verb itself may contain the prepositional form. Spanish often has the economy of using **one** word to express **two: (colgar) hang up; (arrojar) throw out; (buscar) look for; (poner) put away.** These differences occasionally cause errors in oral or written expression when students may transfer such usage statements such as **throw** the trash; **look** the money; or **put** the clothes. These are language production problems, however, and should not seriously interfere with the reception of meaning when students are reading. Teachers, however, need to check for possible misunderstandings.

English has its share of irregular verbs and verbs with spelling variations in a number of forms. The students gradually acquire them in speech, read them, and write them usually with scant attention to the rules and their many exceptions. Teachers need occasionally to point out these verb forms and make certain that second language readers understand them. In time, with sufficient exposure and practice, most of the students will learn to respond to them correctly and to use them with relative ease. Native speakers of English have the same challenge as they develop and refine their language skills in using verb structures. A totally new requirement may be found in the present progressive (**is** working **is** singing), and in the use of the auxiliary verb forms **shall, will, do, does, should, would.** These words must be learned and understood by students whose native language has incorporated such meanings into the inflected endings of the verb system. These are but a few of the contrasts that exist between the two verb systems. If the teacher discovers problems in reading comprehension that may arise, then, specific instruction regarding the commonalities and the differences can be presented briefly. If the moment is not appropriate for interrupting the flow and interest of the narrative, the teacher may wish merely to provide meaning and make a note of the need for later, separate instruction.

Possessives

English nouns are inflected to indicate the possessive case. Since the gender is already in the noun and has been determined logically on the basis of a masculine and feminine (or neuter) gender system, the possessive pronoun must agree — the man broke **his** leg; the lady lost **her** hat. Nouns add **'s** to the singular form — John's book, Mary's hat; the girl's name. Plural nouns ending in **s** take only the **'** — the girls' names; the birds' nests. Plural nouns **not** ending in **s** take the **'s** — the children's play yard; the firemen's hats. There are some special requirements for other plural nouns — the deer's tracks or family names ending in **s, x** — the Thonis' family, the Dix's, and these variations may be treated as they turn up in students' writings or as they are encountered in print. Ordinarily in English, the **of** possessive construction **(el libro de Juan)** varies with the need to avoid ambiguity and the intent to use the expression idiomatically — the governor of California; the outbreak of the epidemic; the cares of the ladies. The tendency of Hispanic students to overuse the **of** construction in English — it is the house **of** John instead of John's house — can be anticipated in written expression and can be easily corrected in time and with additional opportunities to use possessive forms. For accurate comprehension in reading, the students need to recognize and interpret the **'s or s'** as possessive markers and make the appropriate determination of the possessor and the possessed.

Shortened Forms and Enclisis

The apócope of Spanish has no counterpart in English. Furthermore, there is practically no enclisis. Some expressions formed through the combination of two word classes appear in English, for example, layman, but such words probably would not occur frequently in the ordinary course of instruction in the school. The most common shortened forms for Hispanic students to learn are the contractions. English frequently allows the omission of letters in two words to create one word — don't, can't, I'll, wouldn't, he's, where's, that's, and so on. For non-native speakers, these words may simply be taught as sight words. Then, after the students have learned them and have understood them in context, the word may be analyzed for its structural elements, and the two shortened to create the single one may be discovered.

don't	— do not		can't	__ can not
I'll	— I will		aren't	— are not
where's	— where is		couldn't	— could not
how's	— how is		there's	— there is

Students may be taught that contracted forms are very common in informal speech and writing but are generally not found in more formal language. The use of the apostrophe to indicate the omitted letters is an essential learning.

Derived Forms

The derivational process in English is very comparable to that of Spanish. When students have learned that a root word can have several affixes to create other words — **librero, librería, librito, librote, libreto, libresco** — or **marino, marinero, marinería, marítimo, marea** — then they are in a position to transfer the principle of derivation to a great many English words. They improve in their ability to recognize words and to seek their meanings through the awareness of the **word families** created by the process. For example, **joy — enjoy, enjoyable, joyful, enjoyment** can be perceived as carrying some connotation of the word **joy.** The wealth of words that may be available to students who understand the concept of word derivatives is described in Chapter VI. For the singular purpose of improving the students' awareness of the connection between oral and written forms, the teacher may wish to note some of the differences and some of the commonalities of derivation in both languages **if** such analysis is appropriate for the backgrounds of the students.

• Spanish and English share many equivalent forms which both have inherited from Latin.

172

- New words are often created in both languages because the process is a continuing one.
- Derivation may result from use of **both** prefixes and suffixes in **both** languages.
- The derivational process in both languages may change the word to another word class.

Transfer of Pronouns to English
The pronouns of English serve the same function in most instances as the pronouns of Spanish. Students who have acquired the system of personal pronouns, possessive pronouns, demonstrative pronouns, interrogative pronouns, and relative pronouns have an abundance of language understanding to apply in English. They have used pronouns as direct objects of verbs, as indirect objects of verbs, and as objects of prepositions. There are, of course, some important distinctions that must be made in correct usage of both languages. The differences can be taught in manageable form **if** the students have had satisfactory opportunities and good teaching of the Spanish pronouns. Notable among the likenesses and differences are these:

- Pronouns that are the subjects of verbs have separate forms in both languages except **you.**
- English and Spanish have only one form for both direct and indirect objects of verbs except for the pronoun **you.**
- Spanish has a second form for the object of a preposition, but English uses the same pronoun form, which serves as indirect or direct object of the verb.
- Placement of the pronoun in relation to other words in the sentence is very prescriptive in Spanish and is often in a **very** different word order than in English.
- The gender of possessive pronouns (formed by adding the definite article to the long form of the possessive — **la mia, los mios**) does not apply in English except in the third person **his, hers, its.**
- The single relative pronoun **que** may refer to **who, whom, which, that** in English and since it may be either singular or plural and may refer to either persons or things, there may be some confusion in English.
- The elaborate use of reflexive pronouns in Spanish, particularly as part of the system of reflexive verbs, is not generally needed in English.

As students grow in their ability to read, write, spell, and use English, they become increasingly aware of the grammatical rules governing the use of pronouns. Transfer of the knowledge of the classes of pronouns, their function in sentences, their referents, their forms, and their meanings can be pointed out when such words are part of the reading and writing lessons. The teaching of declensions or elaborate rules does not appear productive or exciting, but judicious mention of a grammar principle shared or suitable notice of a contrastive use may be very valuable for students in the middle grades or beyond.

Punctuation Transfer
Except for the need to learn new terms for the punctuation marks, there are few differences to be found in the punctuation of English. The logic to be discovered in the punctuation marks of Spanish is the same logic governing the use of punctuation marks in English writings. The **period** still functions to signal the end of a sentence; the comma to indicate enumeration, inverted order of a sentence, to suggest a parenthetical idea, and to use before certain connective words. Other punctuation marks are shared in form and in function.

There are a few differences that students must learn.

- The inverted marks ¡! in exclamatory sentences do not apply; only the ending ! is needed.
- The inverted question mark ¿? in interrogative sentences is not used; only the ending ? is needed.
- The change of speaker in a dialogue is not signaled by the dash; the new speaker is indicated by a new set of quotation marks. Change in speaker is usually indicated on a separate line, however, in Spanish.

Except for reminding students of these contrasts, the teacher is not likely to need much time in helping students understand the punctuation of English. If it can be assumed that the students have learned the **signos de puntuación,** have understood the reasons for their use, have responded to them intelligently in reading, have practiced them frequently in writing, then good transfer may be expected.

Capitalization Transfer
For the acquisition of skill in using capital letters when necessary in English, there may be positive and negative transfer. Students are accustomed to a more frugal use of capital letters and will need to be provided with direct instruction in the capitalization of English words. Positive transfer will occur in these instances:

- the first word in a sentence begins with a capital letter.
- the name of a country or continent begins with a capital letter.
- the abbreviation of a title begins with a capital letter.
- the names of persons begin with capital letters.

Negative transfer may occur as a result of **not** having to use a capital letter for these words:

- the days of the week.
- the months of the year.
- the nationality of persons.
- the names of languages.
- the names of religions.
- the words following the first word in titles.

The transfer principle that applies is the understanding of the **purpose** of capitalization. English makes a careful distinction between common and proper nouns, and the capital letter signals this distinction. The need to learn the capitalization requirements of English is greater for writing skill than for reading. However, when proper nouns, titles, days of the week, months, nationality, or other words that are capitalized are found in the course of reading instruction, the teacher may highlight them, point out the capital letters, and explain why they are used.

There are many other oral-written connections that might be included in this chapter. Adjectives and their placement differ in their word order patterns in Spanish and English. The nominalization of adjectives occurs in Spanish but not necessarily in English. The fact that Spanish nouns cannot be used as adjectives is another difference. Spanish expresses the comparison of adjectives in a different manner usually. Other parts of speech to consider include the complexities of prepositions and conjunctions in the both languages. However, the purpose for calling teachers' attention to the speech-print requirements of Spanish is to point out that reading improvement in Spanish can be expected only to the extent that oral language improves in correctness and complexity. The few examples given are not inclusive but, rather, are representative of grammar points to be considered as part of the instructional program in reading.

A major supplement to the reading program in English is the instruction in other aspects of language. The regular and systematic lessons in grammar, spelling, literature, composition, and structure make a tremendous contribution to reading improvement. Students are learning the rules of **English** and are adding to their understanding of how **English** works. This knowledge permits them to make generalizations about many complex language phenomena and helps them to predict form or content. For native speakers of English, reading, language study, and experiences beyond the classroom unite within the same linguistic framework to enhance thinking. In the classrooms where Spanish reading is taught, however, language study is usually conspicuously absent. There are few opportunities for students to enjoy planned instruction in **Spanish** grammar, composition, or literature. Some of the phonics, spelling, and writing principles are generally woven into the reading activities as they appear relevant. Some **incidental** or **accidental** grammatical learning may accrue to a few bright and perceptive students. However, if students are to become truly proficient readers in Spanish, they need the understanding of how oral forms relate to written forms and the knowledge of what principles guide these speech-print connections. The study of their own language will serve them well and even accelerate their acquisition of skills in English. Many of the descriptions of the Spanish language will transfer and can be used without change in English. Some technical information will be different in English. Some descriptors will be new, and some of them may not apply.

If the reading program is part of a comprehensive language arts plan for Hispanic students, the teacher may have materials and methods available for further study. Programs such as **La Lengua Nacional; Mi Libro de Lenguaje** have been designed to assist students in learning the grammar and composition of the Spanish they have as an inheritance. It is prudent for the teacher to consider that specific instruction in the grammar of the language represents a different language dimension. Language analysis is **not** language acquisition, **nor** is it language use. The study of grammar logically follows the acquisition and use of language. There is no benefit derived from the formal teaching of grammar rules to students who have poorly developed language and minimal skills in the use of that language.

Perhaps there would be fewer arguments over the place of grammar in language teaching if teachers would make a careful distinction among the separate objectives of language acquisition, language use, and language study. Language is rule-governed behavior, and the rules that apply are incorporated in the grammar of the language. As students acquire skills and use them in comprehending speaking, reading, and writing, they are gradually refining a kind of **functional** grammar. Additional opportunities to pull together the generalizations or principles that apply to specific language forms may result in the understanding of how the language works. The role of grammar has been controversial because of extremes in points of view regarding its usefulness. When grammar rules are drawn inductively from a variety of rich and interesting experiences with language, students are able to generate rules that may then serve them well on other occasions.

Teaching reading in Spanish to Hispanic students enrolled in a traditional English curriculum represents a quantum leap from the past practices of submersing them in second language reading for which they have had few oral referents. Yet, the reading, writing, and spelling opportunities in Spanish with scant attention to systematic, careful instruction in a full language arts program may still short-change many Hispanic children. The youth of any language must **acquire** that language, learn to **use** it as an instrument for carrying content, and for **learning about** the language. Acquisition, use, and analysis of oral and written forms are **three** separate yet interrelated fields of study. To ensure high-quality skills in Spanish, teachers may wish to take time to teach the basic grammar, the syntax, and the morphology of Spanish along with the skills of reading and spelling. When students have a firm grasp of the requirements of their own language, they have a wealth of structures and patterns to bring to English.

Caveat
Although this chapter has made a very strong recommendation regarding the necessity of including some elements of grammar in the reading program, it should not be interpreted as a plea for the traditional grammatical approach to language fluency and literacy. The intent has been to point out to teachers that written forms must be recognized by Hispanic students as representing oral forms, first in Spanish and later in English. When oral forms are excessively informal and/or ungrammatical, they may not be perceived correctly and meaning-fully in written language, which tends to be less subject to variation over time. Furthermore, all language is rule-governed behavior, and if teachers can gently point out the rules along the way, reading proficiency and language competence will develop for most students. Grammar rules in Spanish may be approached inductively when students have encountered enough examples of the rule to arrive at a generalization. The principles derived can be transferred in large measure to many of the rules in English. When and how to encourage transfer becomes a matter of teacher judgment. Among the criteria for making transfer to English of the many grammatical features of the Spanish language are these:

- the student is able to abstract and generalize the rule.
- the student has skill in functional usage required by the rule.
- the student can recognize the similarity of elements present in both languages.
- the student can understand non-transferable features and is able to avoid negative transfer.
- the student has opportunities to practice the application of the transferred skill in English.

References
1. **Enseñanza lógica del español.** Mexico: Trillas, F. (Editorial), S.A., 1970.

2. Fishman, Joshua and Keller, Gary (Editors). **Bilingual Education for Hispanic Students in the United States.** New York: Teachers College Press, 1982.

3. Gleason, H.A. **An Introduction to Descriptive Linguistics.** New York: Rinehart, Winston, 1961.

4. **Lengua Nacional, Fichas de trabajo.** Northvale, New Jersey: Santillana Publishing Company, Inc., 1972.

5. **Lectura en dos idiomas.** Northvale, New Jersey: Santillana Publishing Company, Inc., 1977.

6. **Mi Libro de Lenguaje.** España: Hijos de Santiago Rodriguez (Editorial), 1971.

7. Politzer, Robert. **Foreign Language Learning.** New Jersey: Prentice-Hall, 1965.

8. Stockwell, Robert P., Bowen, Donald J., and Martin, John W. **The Grammatical Structures of English and Spanish.** Chicago: The University of Chicago Press, 1965.

CHAPTER VI

DEVELOPING A SPANISH READING VOCABULARY

From the earliest moment of exposure to human speech, children are developing their vocabularies. During the years from two through eight, the acquisition of words is extraordinary. Estimates of the size of an individual's vocabulary upon entrance to school vary according to the descriptions of what constitutes a word, and whether derivatives of words should be considered separately. Another problem in estimating how many words students know at certain stages of their development resides in the discrepancies that may exist between oral and written vocabularies and between receptive and expressive vocabularies. Students often understand words they do not use in speech, or they may read words they cannot put in writing. The students in the primary grades usually have only **two** vocabularies, listening and speaking. As they learn to read, to spell, and to write, they add two more vocabularies, reading and writing. Their listening and reading vocabularies comprise their **receptive** vocabulary, and their speaking and writing ones make up their **expressive** vocabulary. An effective instructional program in reading has as a major goal the marked increase in the number of words the students know and have the functional use of in all four vocabularies. These vocabularies are intimately related and interdependent. Improvement in a listening vocabulary carries great promise for an increase in a reading vocabulary. Additions to a speaking vocabulary strengthen the foundation for an extended writing vocabulary. Hispanic students need Spanish words to label their reality as it has been encountered. They also need Spanish words to communicate with the significant people in those encounters — parents, grandparents, relatives, friends, neighbors, and, **if they are fortunate,** teachers. The development of vocabularies, then, serves the personal purposes in **thinking** about the world and about one's self, and serves the social purposes of **communicating** with others.

To develop a reading vocabulary, students must seek meaning from their listening and/or speaking vocabularies. They have to have something to bring to the written material in order to add the dimension of new vocabulary in print. Words in reading, once they have been decoded, have to have significance in the listening vocabulary. The meaning has to fit the context of the written discourse. As the linguists often remind us, definitions of words alone will not provide the richness and nuance of meanings to be discovered in context. Word lists, vocabulary exercises, and dictionary drills designed to provide practice in defining words have some limited usefulness. Students also need to be encouraged to listen to words in a variety of contexts, to discuss the many possibilities of meaning, and to explore as many leads to understanding as available. In this manner, they may have opportunities to get beyond definitions of words to improved vocabulary development. Reading teachers need to offer a variety of word-building strategies while keeping in mind the realization that a reading vocabulary bears a close connection to a listening vocabulary.

Homonyms

Words that sound the same, but have different meanings and spellings, are called homonyms, as all teachers know. Such words can be difficult and confusing for beginning readers because the meaning is made clear only in context. In Spanish, homonyms are relatively few, and many meanings may be obtained through knowledge of the orthographic accents that distinguish one word from another. Words pronounced the same, such as, **té** and **te; dé** and **de; más** and **mas** are generally recognized in context. The knowledge of the spellings complete with diacritical marks is an additional clue to the meaning of the word.

Another feature of **oral** Spanish that may need attention in reading lessons is the practice of carrying a final consonant sound over to the next word if it begins with a vowel. The words **el loro** and **el oro** sound exactly the same, and whether the written forms refer to **oro** (gold) or **loro** (parrot) must be determined. **Un ovillo** and **un novillo** are the same in speech but have totally different meanings. Students will need to be reminded to search first in context after recognizing the word and to ask themselves: Does this word make sense? Other words commonly considered as homonyms are these:

gallo	**gayo**
ablando	**hablando**
cesta	**sexta**
azar	**asar**
baca	**vaca**
leyes	**lees**
pillo	**pío**

Learning to deal effectively with the relatively few homonyms in Spanish is important because the concept, definition, and illustrations of them in guided practice provide the knowledge and understanding needed for the sensible reading of the many English homonyms when they occur later in second language reading.

El bote de vela navega.

La vela se apagó.

Trampolin, Página 36.

Synonyms

The dictionary defines the word synonym as a word that means the same or almost the same as the given word. Students' listening and reading vocabularies may be enhanced through encouraging them to find other words that could be used in the passage or sentence. Snynonyms may emerge in a class discussion as students pool their word knowledge. Synonyms may be developed in specific follow-up lessons drawn from the daily reading. Synonyms also may be discovered through judicious use of the dictionary.

Lengua Nacional, Página 132

Haz una cruz junto a la palabra que signifique lo mismo que la palabra destacada.

En la cochera había un coche **antiguo**.

☐ moderno
☐ viejo
☐ usado

Es una cosa **difícil** de creer.

☐ complicada
☐ necesaria
☐ imposible

Antonyms

Antonyms are words that have an opposite meaning to the word given. Once the students have acquired the sense of how many words can be used to express the same or about the same meaning, they can increase their word knowledge considerably by learning their opposites. **Lengua Nacional, Página 84.**

Observa los dibujos. Completa.

LO CONTRARIO

Un niño **contento** ————————→ Un niño <u>triste</u>

Un niño **pobre** ————————→ Un niño_____

Un niño **pequeño** ————————→ Un niño_____

Una niña **triste** ————————→ Una niña_____

Una niña **rica** ————————→ Una niña_____

Una niña **alta** ————————→ Una niña_____

Lee esto:

Pasaban los días. El sol calentaba más que nunca y el pobre jitomatito seguía de color verde amarillento. Los niños de la casa venían al huerto a cortar verduras para la ensalada y al verlo decían:

—No, ese no, que debe de estar muy desabrido . . . Esperemos que madure.

Era muy triste verse despreciado así. Sin embargo, él no perdía las esperanzas de convertirse algún día en un jitomate apetitoso y conservaba el buen humor en medio de su desventura.

CARMEN VAZQUEZ VIGO

Lee estas palabras:

| calentaba | triste | pobre | venían |

Búscalas en el texto anterior. Subráyalas.

Ahora subraya la palabra que significa lo contrario de cada una.

a) **calentaba** | quemaba   enfriaba   hervía

b) **pobre** | bueno   listo   rico

c) **venían** | iban   salían   caminaban

d) **triste** | alegre   bonito   blanco

Phrases

Meanings are not carried by single words but by groups of words in larger units of thought. A phrase is such a unit of meaning as the words alone do not always make sense. Such expressions as — **on the bus, down the road, over the rainbow** — fit in meaningful context **only** as they are perceived together as one message. Furthermore, reading words, rather than groups of words, impedes comprehension and reduces the potential for improving reading vocabulary and reading speed.

Trampolin, Página 36

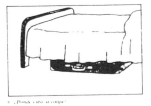

La valija está sobre la cama.

La valija está debajo de la cama.

El pavo está debajo de la mesa.

El pavo está sobre la mesa.

183

Inflected Forms

Words in Spanish can be identified as belonging to specific parts of speech. Certain characteristic forms have rule-governed changes from the system of affixes that exists in the language. Formation of plurals is one example of the inflection in nouns. **Number** represents the **only** category of inflection for Spanish nouns and is usually learned easily by the students. Vocabulary exercises designed to provide practice in the singular and plural forms of new nouns that students are adding to their lexical storehouse should be easily slipped into most reading lessons. Adjectives have inflected endings for both **number** and **gender.** They may also add the diminutive or augmentative endings. These variations have the potential of adding the luxury of many words to the vocabularies of Hispanic students. The pronoun class of words has a distinct set of requirements for changes in forms to denote **person, number, case,** and **gender.** In addition, there is a formal and an informal class in the second person pronoun. The reading teacher needs to consider the importance of various meanings as expressed by the many changes in forms. Pronouns are among the last speech forms acquired in the development of language. They continue to be difficult for students for a long time. Opportunities to use pronouns in speech and in print will improve the understanding of what is expressed by pronouns and will, at the same time, add to the listening and reading vocabularies.

Lengua Nacional, Level 2, Página 112

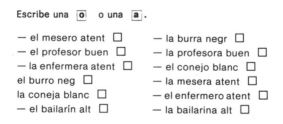

Escribe una ⬜o⬜ o una ⬜a⬜.

- el mesero atent ☐   — la burra negr ☐
- el profesor buen ☐   — la profesora buen ☐
- la enfermera atent ☐   — el conejo blanc ☐
- el burro neg ☐   — la mesera atent ☐
- la coneja blanc ☐   — el enfermero atent ☐
- el bailarín alt ☐   — la bailarina alt ☐

Of all the classes of words in Spanish that have inflected forms, the verb system is the most complex. Verbs change to indicate **tense, person, number, mood, and finity.** According to Stockwell, Bowen, and Martin*, these five categories are capable of producing as many as forty-seven separate and distinct forms. In addition to these variations of inflection, verb forms are also changed according to their description as regular or irregular verbs. The vocabulary development that accrues from an ever-improving control of the constituent elements of verb forms is tremendous. Colorful and creative use of language expands as students acquire the knowledge and skill in managing the inflectional categories. At every level in reading instruction, teachers should endeavor to incorporate frequent practice in

*Robert P. Stockwell, J. Donald Bowen, and John W. Martin. **The Grammatical Structures of English and Spanish.** Chicago: The University of Chicago Press, 1965.

verb forms as appropriate for the language background and maturity of their students.

Lengua Nacional, Level 2, Página 152

Escribe debajo de cada dibujo lo que ves en él.

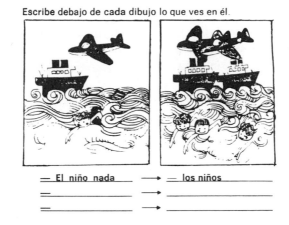

— El niño nada   ⟶   — los niños _____

_____ ⟶ _____

_____ ⟶ _____

Termina de hacer este ejercicio:

a. el coche corre ⟶ **los coches corren**

b. un pájaro pasa ⟶ _____

c. la abuela come ⟶ _____

d. el árbol crece ⟶ _____

e. una mula anda ⟶ _____

Escribe lo que quieras. Utiliza estas palabras.

| sale | cantó | cantaron | salen |

_____

_____

Derived Forms

Derivational affixes may produce new words and follow some rules of Spanish inherited from its earlier Latin roots or borrowed from other languages as needed. The process is an exciting one for vocabulary development as literally hundreds of words can be added to the students' receptive and expressive vocabularies when they are learning to read. New endings for words that may be already known to students will serve to add new words with extended meanings. The suffixes as learned have considerable generalizability, but rules for derivational forms are not always applied according to rigorous criteria. The suffix **ería,** meaning the place where something is made or sold, is useful for recognizing words such as **librería, zapatería, panadería,** and **lavandería;** but the same suffix may also refer to a profession as **ingeniería. Ero** added to words may suggest a container — **granero, florero;** or may be used to indicate a characteristic — **guerrero, parlero. Eda — edo,** when added to something that grows, denotes the place where it is grown — **árboleda, alameda.** Sometimes a suffix added to a verb creates a name out of an action — **salida, entrada, llegada.** Other additions, such as **mente, able, oso, aje,** or **ucho,** make new words that may function as different parts of speech.

Lengua Nacional, Level 2, Página 194.

LAS FAMILIAS DE PALABRAS

La familia de la palabra **libro.**

libro librero librería librazo librito

También se llama **librero** el mueble donde se guardan los

Escribe la familia de cada palabra.

pan _____ _____ _____

Escribe la familia de cada palabra.

coche   sal   silla   barco

Lengua Nacional, Level 2, Página 195

ADIVINA QUE ES

Contesta:

> trastero · papelera · plumero · ropero

¿Qué es

    — una cosa hecha de plumas ? _____

    — una cosa para echar los papeles ? _____

    — un sitio para guardar la ropa ? _____

    — un sitio para guardar los trastos ? _____

Contesta:

¿Quién es

    — el hombre que cuida el jardín? _____

    — la mujer que cuida el Jardín? _____

    — la mujer que vende dulces? _____

    — el hombre que vende dulces? _____

Contesta:

¿Qué hace

    — el campanero? Vende _____

    — la cocinera? Trabaja en la _____

    — el farolero? Trabaja en la _____

    — la lechera? Vende la _____

Prefixes, too, have their contribution in modifying the literal and suggested meanings of words — **dis**culpar, **dis**gregar, **inter**cambiar, **inter**ceder. The derivational forms in Spanish have boundless potential for stretching the students' vocabularies and giving them a colorful, useful reading vocabulary.

Lengua Nacional, Level 2, Página 183

Lee esta frase:

> Hubo un revuelo en el lago.

Revuelo quiere decir alboroto.

Añadiendo **re** a la palabra vuelo se ha formado la palabra revuelo.

Añade re a las siguientes palabras y escribe la palabra que resulte.

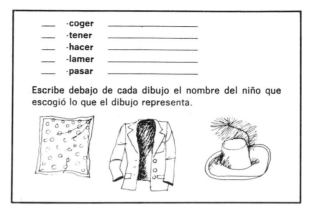

```
___  ·coger      _____
___  ·tener      _____
___  ·hacer      _____
___  ·lamer      _____
___  ·pasar      _____
```

Escribe debajo de cada dibujo el nombre del niño que
escogió lo que el dibujo representa.

Diminutives and Augmentatives

The vocabulary enrichment that is available through the addition of the many
diminutive and augmentative suffixes of Spanish is abundant. These variations
offer liveliness, humor, and interest as descriptors of people, animals, places, and
events. Given a single descriptive term, the student may change the meanings to
suit diverse situations by using the appropriate suffix. Hispanic students have
become familiar with the gentle and tender words — **hijito, abuelita, angelico,**
and they have probably acquired some of the less affectionate vocabulary items —
perrazo, monigote. The connotations of contempt may have escaped some of
the younger ones — **palabrotas, madraza.** Examples of activities to offer practice
in these suffixes are from **La Lengua Nacional, Level 2, Página 187.**

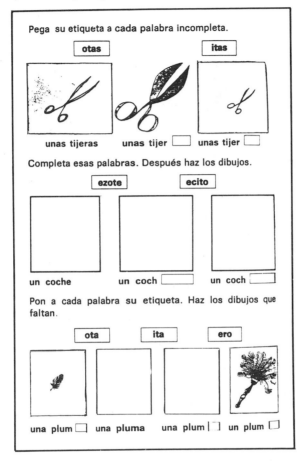

Pega su etiqueta a cada palabra incompleta.

otas		itas

unas tijeras   unas tijer ☐   unas tijer ☐

Completa esas palabras. Después haz los dibujos.

ezote		ecito

un coche   un coch ☐   un coch ☐

Pon a cada palabra su etiqueta. Haz los dibujos que faltan.

ota	ita	ero

una plum ☐   una pluma   una plum ☐   un plum ☐

Use of the Dictionary

The adventure of discovering new words in the dictionary should be a source of interest to language learners at all levels. As Emerson once said, "Neither is the dictionary a bad book to read!" There are several kinds of dictionaries that should serve the various needs of students. In the early grades, a blackboard dictionary provides an introduction to alphabetical order. The teacher may put both upper and lower case letters on the board, write a word, and draw an illustration:

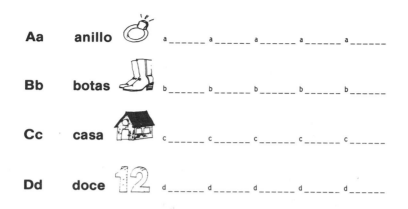

Aa   **anillo**   a_____ a_____ a_____ a_____ a_____

Bb   **botas**   b_____ b_____ b_____ b_____ b_____

Cc   **casa**   c_____ c_____ c_____ c_____ c_____

Dd   **doce**   d_____ d_____ d_____ d_____ d_____

Students may be invited to write additional words in appropriate boxes. Words can be selected from the daily lessons and grouped according to their first letters in the proper sequence. A few letters at a time may be introduced, and the students may be reminded to look at the initial letter of a word first to determine the place in which it belongs. If the words can be illustrated to suggest the meanings, then vocabulary items are added with relative ease.

Another kind of class dictionary that serves a most valuable purpose is one developed on large paper and put together with fasteners or rings so that the pages turn. Sections may be indicated by alphabet tabs or notations. When words are discovered in the daily work, the teacher discusses the word, helps the students find meanings for the words and, finally, places words, meanings, and illustrations on the suitable pages. When students need to look up a word or check its spelling, they may turn to the correct page for their help. If the class dictionary is available in a convenient corner of the room, the students may use it at any time in their reading, spelling, and handwriting lessons. The loose-leaf organization allows the dictionary to expand as students' vocabularies grow.

EL DICCIONARIO

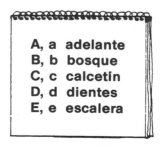

A, a   **adelante**
B, b   **bosque**
C, c   **calcetín**
D, d   **dientes**
E, e   **escalera**

Labeled pictures of important words that may be difficult to illustrate are especially helpful when the students prepare the labels. For words such as **después, al lado de, durante, arriba,** and other expressions of space and time, the word may be placed in a box, and a sentence composed by the students may explain the meaning.

 las señales de humo

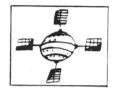 la vía satélite

The significance of the word is in the context that has been presented and discussed by the students.

Another kind of dictionary that is very interesting and useful for students is their own personal dictionaries. These may be developed in notebooks arranged with alphabetical tabs. If the notebook is the loose-leaf variety, it may be expanded as space may require. Students may be encouraged to write words from their lessons and other words that interest them. The title **Mi diccionario personal** suggests that the words contained in the notebook have relevance and importance to each student.

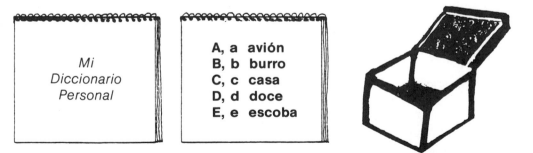

A variation on the private notebook is a personal file box. An old shoe box arranged with tagnboard alphabetical sections is an expandable dictionary for 3 X 5 inch or 5 X 8 inch cards. If the teachers' budget does not allow for stationer's quality index cards, heavy paper or other durable materials can be cut to the right size for filing. Then, when students need to look up a word or check the spelling, their dictionaries are right on their desks.

There are many commercially available dictionaries for use in the reading class-rooms. For students who are caught in the press of two languages in their developmental stages, it is wise to select dictionaries that are in **one** language only. Hispanic students need to have the experience of using **el diccionario** for the purpose of practicing a number of essential skills needed in their reading program as follows:

- alphabetizing — a study skill needed for reference work. First, students will need first letter skills and later, they need to know how to alphabetize according to a sequence of letters.
- guide words — the words that are needed to locate words. Students learn that first and last words on the page represent a certain alphabetic sequence. They may then search for words that fall within the guide words as given.
- pronunciation aides — cues to direct students' use of the words in oral form. Among the aides may be found respellings, syllables, diacritical marks, alternate spellings, inflected forms, or derived forms.
- definitions — the meanings of the words. Students may discover the common meanings and the additional meanings of words in various contexts.
- synonyms — words that mean the same thing. Students have practical opportunities to extend their word knowledge by acquiring other words and expressions for the same ideas.
- antonyms — words that mean the opposite of words given. Practice in finding antonyms is another way in which vocabulary development occurs.
- multi-semantic words — words that change meanings depending upon context. Students' facility with language is increased through the recognition of the many, varied meanings available in the same word. To some extent, the activities are like those in finding word definitions, but they enlarge the students' understanding of the many ways in which a word may be used.
- idiomatic usage — expressions carrying a meaning different from the literal or usual sense. These must be learned in specific context.

A very helpful dictionary for beginners is **El diccionario del lenguaje usual,** which may be offered to students beginning as early as the third grade. The various uses for this dictionary are given in the introductory pages as follows:

- to find word meanings
- to make meanings clearer by offering examples of usage
- to discover multiple meanings of words
- to identify synonyms and antonyms
- to learn the part of speech of a given word.

- to determine meanings and functions of words in specific contexts.
- to recognize verb forms of both regular and irregular verbs.

El uso del diccionario is described in detail to let the students know what they may expect from this book. A brief excerpt should be useful in providing students with the special terminology of the dictionary:

EL USO
DEL DICCIONARIO

Se puede hacer uso de este diccionario en muy distintas ocasiones:

1.º Cuando se desea saber *el significado* de una palabra. Por ejemplo, la palabra *bandada*. En el diccionario encontramos:

Grupo numeroso de aves que vuelan juntas.
A veces puede referirse a peces e incluso a personas que van en grupos numerosos.

A continuación, para aclarar esta definición, figuran dos ejemplos:

*Las aves migratorias vuelan en **bandadas.***

*En el año 409, **bandadas** de bárbaros invadieron España.*

2.º Cuando se desea saber la diferencia que hay entre los distintos significados de una palabra:

índice

1. Designa cualquier cosa o señal que indica la importancia de algo.
   *La abundancia de coches en un país es un **índice** del aumento del nivel de vida.*
2. Lista de los temas que contiene un libro y que aparece al principio o al final de éste.
   *Busca en el **índice** en qué páginas se estudia el descubrimiento de América.*
3. Dedo de la mano que está situado entre el pulgar y el corazón.
   *El chico señalaba con el **índice** los juguetes del escaparate.*

3.º Cuando se desea conocer palabras que tengan un significado parecido a una palabra dada. Por ejemplo:

secundario: accesorio.

4.º Cuando se desea conocer palabras con significado contrario a una palabra determinada:

secundario: principal, necesario, básico, fundamental.

5.º Cuando se desea saber qué parte de la oración es una palabra determinada:

pero

Conjunción.

6.º Cuando se desea saber las distintas funciones que puede desempeñar una palabra dentro de la oración. Por ejemplo:

éste, este

◇ Puede ser pronombre, adjetivo o nombre.

Pronombre demostrativo.

Cuando sustituye a un nombre. En este caso va acentuado: *éste.*

*Me dijo **éste** que no vinieras.*

◇ Sus formas son:
  éste, ésta, esto, para el singular.
  éstos, éstas, para el plural.

Adjetivo demostrativo.

Cuando acompaña a un nombre. En este caso no va acentuado: *este.*

*Han traído **este** libro.*

◇ Sus formas son:
  este, esta, para el singular.
  estos, estas, para el plural.

◇ Observa que la forma neutra *esto* es solamente pronombre.

Nombre.

Punto cardinal por donde aparece el Sol. También recibe los nombres de Oriente y Levante.

*Los puntos cardinales son: Norte, Sur, **Este** y Oeste.*

◇ No confundir:

  éste, con acento, pronombre demostrativo.
  este, sin acento, adjetivo demostrativo.
  Este, sin acento, punto cardinal.
  esté, con acento en la última sílaba, del verbo *estar.*

7.º Cuando se quiera saber si una palabra da lugar a formas irregulares:

salir

Verbo irregular (infinitivo).

Formas irregulares:
Presente de indicativo: *salgo.*
Futuro imperfecto de indicativo: *saldré, saldrás...*
Presente de subjuntivo: *salga, salgas...*
Potencial: *saldría, saldrías...*
Imperativo: *sal, salga, salgamos, salgan.*

8.º Cuando se encuentra una forma verbal irregular y se quiere saber a qué verbo pertenece. Por ejemplo:

quepa, quepo...

Formas irregulares del verbo *caber.* (Ver CABER.)

Subject Matter Vocabulary

The content areas of the curriculum have highly specialized vocabularies that offer both opportunities and difficulties to students beyond the third grade. Terms needed in mathematics, science, literature, and social sciences are often abstract and incomprehensible. As Cummins has reminded us, these are the words used in lectures and in textbooks, but they do not provide meanings in a situational context. Rather, the language of subject matter instruction is most often outside the range of experiences of the hearer or reader. If students are to make sense of the content in these classes, they must acquire the special words and understand the context in which they are used. As teachers of any language think about the increasing complexity of the vocabulary and language structure used in the various subjects, they may wish to consider these factors:

- the shift from the concreteness of the elementary years to the abstractness of the secondary years
- the sheer weight of the increase in vocabulary size
- the variability which exists among students' vocabularies
- the **new** meanings to be found in **old** words
- the distinctive usage of words and expressions in different subjects, and
- the increasing length and complexity of the sentences in which the words are found.

Ordinarily, content area teachers assume that their students will **read** the textbooks and other written material with a fair amount of ease, and if they encounter an unknown word, they will look it up in the dictionary or seek some other clue to meanings. Some students are able to do this, and others are not. As Hispanic students come to grips with the content areas in classrooms where English is carrying that content, they find themselves at a great disadvantage if their control of English is limited.

In some programs designed for Hispanic students, mathematics, science, social science, or literature may be offered in Spanish. When opportunities exist for the use of the native language to unlock the gates to these subjects, the students add to their concepts and their vocabularies using their language strength. Classroom presentations and assigned readings in Spanish may be discussed and explored further. An explanation of measurement in which words such as **perímetro, diámetro, igual, proporción** are used may serve effectively to help students comprehend. When the concepts, ideas, applications, and computation skills have been accomplished, students may later transfer with relative ease the needed knowledge and the vocabulary to English. Even the terminology will be similar — perimeter, diameter, equal, proportion. In the social sciences, the concepts and vocabulary of government — **república, democracia, monarquía** — may be explained in meaningful language. Once these concepts of government are understood, the vocabulary of English will be comprehensible as well. As cognates, the words themselves transfer easily. In literature and in science, these same needs to grasp the full, rich meanings of words will apply, so that the ideas suggested by them can be considered thoughtfully. The extent to which schools may have the resources to offer content areas in Spanish will certainly vary from community to community. Where such curriculum adaptations are available, however, students will grow more quickly in their knowledge of subject matter, in the vocabulary that carries the subject, and in the potential for transferring both to English. Whether subjects are taught in Spanish or in English, teachers of second language learners need to think about the following content area vocabulary considerations:

- written vocabulary in textbooks will expand at a very rapid pace
- a specialized vocabulary can never be assumed
- vocabulary can be introduced and taught as a reading skill in **any** content area
- content area vocabulary demands precision of meaning
- content area vocabularies in Spanish and in English share many cognates
- vocabulary items with multiple meanings are pitfalls for students of **any** language
- specific spatial and temporal words are absolutely necessary to comprehension
- specific words perform certain functions in connected discourse
- complexities in the sentence structure in which words are used may need more careful explanation.

Content area teachers will promote expanded vocabularies if they organize subject matter instruction to ensure that concepts and referents represented by the words are clearly understood and can be used orally. Then, students will have background information to bring to the written materials available in the subject. Films, filmstrips, study prints, pictures, objects, diagrams, maps, and other non-print media may be provided for building listening comprehension and speaking vocabularies prior to the introduction of the written words or as an accompaniment to the written forms.

Transfer of Vocabulary Skills to English
Students who have been understanding words and their function in Spanish speech and print bring a storehouse of words and meanings to English. While the

pronunciation, spelling, and/or arrangement differ, the concept of a word as a label of an experience remains the same. As the students meet the words of English in their daily lessons, there will be many of them that simply **look like** words they already know. The length of the word, its general configuration and visual appearance will register as a word from Spanish. This configural transfer may occur because the words are **exactly** alike in both languages — **patio** — **vista** — **tortilla** — **drama** — **patron** — **rodeo** — **fiesta** —**adobe** — **bronco** — **sierra** — **plaza.** Other words may immediately be recognized because the appearance of the word is only slightly changed, and the visual stimulus evokes a familiar response — **maize** — **chili** — **tobacco** — **guitar.** Of course, if the words as recognized are to make sense in English, the words must have been known and comprehensible in Spanish. The teaching implication is clear. Strong vocabulary development in Spanish will offer a large number of words that transfer totally and effortlessly to English.

Cognate Transfer

Cognates are words that are related through the same origin. Because Spanish and English share common Latin roots, there are hundreds of words in both languages that carry identical or very similar meanings. At times, these words have slight spelling differences, different endings, or other variations, but they are easily recognized in speech and in print. The potential for English language vocabulary expansion is tremendous if teachers will point out the nature of cognates as a vocabulary resource and will provide some of the common comparisons to guide students as cognates are found in their lessons. Again, it should be noted that a cognate identified in English will not be of much value unless the word is known and understood in Spanish. The following hints should be helpful to students:

- Many Spanish words ending in **o** can be recognized in English simply by dropping the **o.**

instrument**o**	cuban**o**	arsénic**o**
defect**o**	infinit**o**	glob**o**
institut**o**	act**o**	

- Many Spanish words ending in **a** can be recognized in English simply by dropping the **a.**

artist**a**	expansiv**a**	remot**a**
dentist**a**	relaps**a**	telegram**a**
violinist**a**	infus**a**	secret**a**

- Many Spanish words ending in **cia** can be recognized as **ce** endings in English words.

gra**cia**	fragan**cia**	reticen**cia**
influen**cia**	distan**cia**	competen**cia**
abundan**cia**	repugnan**cia**	existen**cia**

- Many Spanish words ending in **ción** can be recognized as **tion** words in English.

educa**ción**	emo**ción**	transcrip**ción**
administra**ción**	na**ción**	articula**ción**
conversa**ción**	narra**ción**	pronuncia**ción**

- Many other Spanish words may be useful for transfer to English on the basis of their common ancestry **if** the words have been made a part of the Hispanic students' vocabularies. Great potential for transfer occurs among other very close relatives:

  a. **sión** words merely drop the diacritical mark — **confusión** — confusion
  b. **ismo** words merely drop the **o** — **capitalismo** — capitalism
  c. **tud** words merely add **e** in English — **aptitud** — aptitude
  d. **cio** words merely become **ce** in English — **prefacio** — preface
  e. **e** words merely drop the **e** in English — **residente** — resident

- Many Spanish words may be transferred to English on the basis of very minor changes in spelling patterns.

  a. **actitud** — attitude
  b. **medicina** — medicine
  c. **contrario** — contrary
  d. **futuro** — future
  e. **teatro** — theater
  f. **esencial** — essential

The building of vocabulary strength in English may be encouraged through **direct** teaching for the transfer of cognates. A few classroom strategies could include:

- keeping a cognate notebook arranged according to the potential of discovery and organizing the notebook by the comparable characteristics,

e.g., the **al** words — **canal, personal;** the **ar** words — **lunar, circular;** the **aje** words — **personaje, follaje;** the **cia, ista, ión** words.
- playing word games in which cognates may be used.
- highlighting the cognates that may be found in a particular passage.
- developing the background knowledge of the more common prefixes and suffixes shared by both Spanish and English.
- encouraging students to use the English cognate in meaningful context in English discourse once the word has been discovered through its association with Spanish.

False Cognates

As has been previously mentioned, some words in **both** languages look the same but have totally different denotations and connotations. These false friends may be confusing and may prevent comprehension, especially if they are erroneously seen as cognates. Their visual appearance and their use in the sentence may deceive the reader because their meanings often are quite unreliable. Teachers may wish to alert students to the more common of these words by providing a brief list of them for students, or they may wish to wait until one of them appears in reading and deal with the meaning at that time. For the teachers' information, the following list is provided with English meanings:

actual — present day not actual
apología — eulogy not apology
arena — sand not arena
atender — take care of not attend
bizarro — gallant not bizarre
campo — country not camp
conferencia — lecture not con-
ference
delito — crime not delight
desgracia — misfortune not
disgrace
editor — publisher not editor

embarazada — pregnant not
embarrassed
éxito — success not exit
fábrica — factory not fabric
gracioso — funny not gracious
ignorar — to not know not ignore
largo — long not large
marca — brand not mark
ordinario — vulgar not ordinary
pan — bread not pan
red — net not red
suceso — event not success
trampa — cheat not tramp

Other false friends may be found from time to time in the students' reading material. The students may be encouraged to check the sense of the word with the rest of the context and discover whether or not their original meanings for such words apply. Comprehension begins with a clear understanding of what a word means and how that word is used. When students meet words that have the visual appearance of words they might have known in Spanish, they must be encouraged to develop the habit of checking the contextual setting for sensible meaning.

At times, teachers are reluctant to make much of the obvious commonalities in Spanish and English because of pronunciation differences and accentuation discrepancies between both languages. These are very real and serious barriers to communication in oral language, but do not loom nearly so large in reading. Hispanic students who are transferring their reading skills to English should be encouraged to read silently and to gather all the meaning they can from whatever they can bring to a page of English print. Oral reading requirements for all students are fewer and fewer as they move along the grades. Hispanic students need to read silently to gain knowledge, to discover facts, and to apply their intellectual power. Unless students are having enormous difficulties learning to read English and the teacher wishes to **hear** how they are going about the task, there is little reason to expect oral production. When it is necessary, then a private reading with the teacher alone serves to spare the student embarrassment and provides diagnostic data for the teacher.

Other Transfer Activities

If the students are engaging in English language activities designed for non-native speakers while they are becoming literate in Spanish, they should have a luxurious background of expressions that have been stored in their English listening comprehension and speaking vocabularies. Many of the experiences are common to both languages. The students have learned the speech and the print forms in Spanish but have only the speech forms in English. Since meaning can be assumed and oral production is assured, the written English can be added and practiced. The activities should be selected on the basis of interest to students.

- Amenities — all the usual expressions of greetings, courtesy, and social exchange may be written as they occur. They may be put on the chalkboard to copy or may be provided on worksheets.
- Descriptions of the room environment — students may be familiar with the labels on items in the classroom. If they can say something about the clock or plant, encourage them to write it.
- Newspapers — students may find key words in news events or sports stories and copy them. They may be encouraged to use them in other similar contexts.
- crossword puzzles — teach students how to make up their own puzzles from English words they know. Have one group solve the puzzles created by another.

- Use food as a stimulus — after students have eaten something simple (peanut butter and crackers), have them write a description — put needed words on the board — **creamy, sticky, salty,** etc.
- Develop word categories — using a category from the reading material as a stimulus, ask the students to think of other words that fit the category. Help with spelling as needed.
- Encourage writing rhymes, poetry — the beginning English readers can be helped to create simple rhyming patterns and older students who have more English fluency may be encouraged to try limericks, haiku, etc.
- Suggest personal journals — the journal may serve to record small instances of success in English reading and writing. "Today I learned to _____."
- Expect simple book reports from the students covering what they have read — provide a basic format that is not too demanding for beginning readers, and add to it for more proficient ones.
- Write an ad for a popular product — cut out illustrations from magazines or illustrate the ad with a drawing.
- Recipes and other how-to-do things — ask students to write a set of directions for making something to eat or repairing an object.
- Stories — offer opportunities for students to write short stories and illustrate them. Prepare them for class use with simple, inexpensive covers and place them in the **Author's Corner** for class reading and enjoyment.

Transfer by Principles

Concepts of synonyms, antonyms, and homonyms will transfer to English as principles. Even the words the students have learned for these concepts in Spanish — **sinónimos, antónimos, homónimos** — are similar enough in written Spanish as to be recognized in English. Students have learned their definitions and have searched them out in their Spanish reading activities. They have looked for them in their own vocabularies, in the written materials given, and in the dictionary. They **know** further how to go about finding the appropriate words to fit each category. Practice in synonyms, antonyms, and homonyms in English will serve to enlarge their reading vocabularies and to improve their reading comprehension. The students' success in locating synonyms and antonyms is likely to occur with just a little reminder that this activity is exactly the same as the one they managed well in Spanish. Work with homonyms should be more carefully carried out, however, as there are so many of them in English and so few in Spanish! Native speakers and readers of English often have difficulty with homonyms so it is little wonder that they may cause problems in meaning for non-native readers. A few common ones are listed as follows:

ate — eight	flower — flour	pane — pain
be — bee	for — four	pear — pair
blue — blew	fare — fair	piece — peace
bear — bare	hare — hair	rain — rein
beet — beat	hour — our	rode — road
birth — berth	hear — here	sail — sale
bow — bough	meet — meat	see — sea
by — buy	male — mail	sun — son
break — brake	no — know	to — too — two
deer — dear	not — knot	waste — waist
flea — flee	new — knew	write — right

Developing a reading vocabulary is a process that goes on throughout the students' entire lifetime. The activities and ideas presented in this chapter are only a few of the endeavors that appear productive in classrooms. The most important element in vocabulary growth is the excitement and interest in words that may be carried beyond the school into a lifetime habit. If teachers can instill in their students a love for the wonder and power of words, they will have offered a lasting and real treasure.

Students who have retained and expanded their Spanish vocabulary while adding the vocabulary of English have the gift of two language systems through which they may interpret their experience. If in doing so, they have enjoyed the benefits of appropriate instruction, they have the good fortune listed as follows:

- They have acquired an English vocabulary without abandoning their native Spanish.
- They have had opportunities to use their Spanish skills as a launching pad to English.
- They have built new vocabulary items on concepts they have already experienced.
- They have been encouraged to transfer and apply old learnings to new language requirements.
- They have been growing in self-confidence and self-esteem as both native and second language have been made important.
- They have moved toward the richness of true bilingualism and powerful intellectual growth.

Caveat

There is always the danger in an English-speaking school setting to press for the development of the vocabulary skills in English and to relegate to a position of lesser importance the extension of the vocabulary skills in Spanish. This viewpoint is certainly an understandable one and is appreciated by educators of both English and Spanish. However, there is a great richness in the number of Spanish words that may be acquired and learned as experiences, mediated by Spanish, advance the clarity of concepts. These verbal skills promote comprehension of the students' world and foster the verbal reasoning abilities that serve intelligence well. **Concepts are the tools of thought.** Students with abundant and clear concepts labeled in Spanish can add the English vocabulary items quite readily. In contrast, students with fuzzy, unclear concepts labeled partially in pieces of Spanish and English may end up with **poor** concepts, **poor** Spanish vocabulary, and **poor** English vocabulary. The cultivation of a vocabulary takes time, patience, and good teaching. An English vocabulary will be enhanced **not** delayed by ensuring that the time, patience, and good teaching take place in Spanish. Then, students will possess the word wealth of both languages.

References

1. **Diccionario del lenguaje usual.** Madrid: Santillana S.A., 1970.

2. **Lectura en dos idiomas.** Northvale, New Jersey: Santillana Publishing Company, Inc., 1977.

3. **Lengua Nacional, Fichas de trabajo, Levels 1-5.** Madrid: Santillana S.A., 1972.

4. Stockwell, Robert P., Bowen, J. Donald and Martin, John W.. **The Grammatical Structures of English and Spanish.** Chicago: The University of Chicago Press, 1965.

CHAPTER VII

ORGANIZING INSTRUCTION FOR TRANSFER

It is reasonable to expect that students will learn to read first the language that they speak. The associations to be made between speech and print are more easily made, and the distance between what is seen visually and what is heard auditorially is not too great. If the written code is mastered and the written content is appropriate for the readers' experiences, then comprehension of written discourse is very likely to occur. Given good instruction, students will learn to read. Hispanic students will learn to read and write Spanish, when given the opportunity, at a more rapid pace than they ever could learn to read and write English. They are able to do this because the speech-print associations can be made more sensibly, and because the distance between what they see and what they hear is not too great. Once they have learned to read well and have literacy skills, they have a powerful instrument for unlocking the gates to knowledge. They can read textbooks, workbooks, and other written materials in Spanish to locate information, discover ideas, interpret data, and study any of the subject areas of the curriculum. As they interact successfully with the content and the language that carries content, their skills, knowledge, and cognitive powers unfold. While the opportunities for academic growth continue, the students are maturing intellectually as well. When they have reached the developmental level at which they can manage abstractions effectively, they can transfer their skills, knowledge, and power to second language reading and writing in English. Usually, students have the capacity to abstract and to generalize accurately between the tenth and the twelfth year. At this point, they do not have to learn to read and write English out of nothing. They are fluent; they are literate; and they learn to read only once! The key to English literacy is not in totally **new** instruction but in transfer.

The instructional program can be arranged to make the most of the fluency and literacy skills the students bring to the acquisition and learning of English. One common characteristic of the second language learners is their **variability.** Some will have strong backgrounds of information; some will have excellent reading skills; some will have limited experiences and concepts; some will have few reading skills; some will have rapid rates of learning; some will be slower. The number and kind of differences that may be identified are so many as to defy categorization of students. However, the principal variables that must be addressed for the purpose of organizing instruction for transfer are these:

- age and developmental status of students
- background of experience for grouping purposes
- pacing instruction
- monitoring student progress and proficiency
- providing practice in needed skills.

Other characteristics may be identified in particular groups of students as the situations demand.

Age and Developmental Status

Young students who are in the early childhood developmental stage from the nursery school years to the first grade should be given the richest opportunities for oral Spanish language acquisition. Transfer to English should **not** be a major concern of the pre-primary and kindergarten teacher. As has been mentioned, this period of rapid language growth is a time for encounters with a stimulating classroom environment that promotes and clarifies concepts. Listening and speaking skills in Spanish are nurtured because the sounds, structures, vocabulary, and semantics are part of the daily experiences. During the informal and natural exchange with English-speaking classmates or other children in the school, considerable second language skill will accrue to most of the students. The children are still expanding their horizons beyond their homes and neighborhoods. As they experience the new sights and sounds of this extended reality, they need to acquire the language that helps them best in the storage and retrieval of these data. They have a native language system upon which to build and by which the prereading activities may be carried. Older students who are preliterate and who have sufficient oral Spanish may be moved quickly through a readiness phase and introduced to the Spanish writing system. Age and developmental factors are important elements to examine because of the following considerations:

- the attention span improves (or should improve) as students grow older
- the interest and motivation changes as students mature
- the experiences are different for different age groups
- the sensory-motor development needed for reading and writing is greater in younger students
- the control of oral language is evident in larger vocabularies
- the more complex use of structure is seen among older students.

Grouping Practices

The manner in which language minority students should be grouped for instruction and the criteria by which they may be assigned to different groups are issues that have yet to be resolved. There are so many factors that vary from community to community in addition to the great degree of variability found among Hispanic students. For these reasons, grouping arrangements must be discussed in fairly general terms, and decision-makers must translate into specific operational schedules those practices that appear best suited to their students. Some of the principles that may serve to guide the choice of options follow:

- Grouping should be established on the basis of the purposes of instruction. If the lesson is planned to offer teaching and practice in a specific skill area, then students who need and can benefit from the skills practice should be included in the group. Those students who have insufficient enabling skills for the activity or those who already have a high degree of proficiency in the skill should be otherwise productively engaged.
- Grouping should be arranged to accommodate the English speaker and the Spanish speaker. Serious efforts to identify the language strengths of students must be made because first language acquisition and second language learning are not identical tasks.
- Students should have the opportunities to function successfully in several groups. If they are assigned to a slow group in reading, then they may be placed in a group moving at a faster pace in some other curriculum dimension. All normal students have something that they can do reasonably well. The challenge to the teacher is to discover the gifts that each student has and to appreciate them.
- Students should spend some informal part of the day in the **total** group. Regardless of language fluency or literacy, students need the sense of belonging to the class. They need the joy of the shared experience during opening amenities, music, arts, sports, or class outings.
- Some instruction daily should be arranged for the whole class. Direct teaching of relevant material may be presented to everyone, and the practice activities may be adjusted to suit the learning rates of individual students.
- Some small group opportunities should be provided for additional teaching directed by the teacher. The small group instruction is not merely a seatwork or busy work activity when students are on their own. Rather, the small group instruction is guided by the teacher who has determined the special instructional needs of the small group.
- Students may be grouped in pairs or in teams of three or more students with a common interest or shared project. These small self-directed or student-directed groups must be carefully structured and monitored by the teacher.

- The language of instruction should be consistent with the purposes and should be kept separate. If students use Spanish in the English reading group, the teacher should accept what is offered and respond in English. If students use English in the Spanish reading group, the teacher should accept it and respond in Spanish.
- Students should be encouraged to move into groups that are more advanced. No one should feel locked into a slow-moving group forever. If a group is going ahead at a pace too rapid for some students, they should have the option to be assigned to a slower group. Flexibility and fluidity of grouping practices should serve to make students comfortable about their assigned places in groups.
- There is an advantage in having fast language learners work together. They stimulate and challenge one another to stretch and to grow. Yet, the bright have much to offer other students and should not be working together all the time. Slower students, too, have talents to share with rapid learners.
- When there is an age or grade span among the language minority students, and small numbers of them in a given school community make grouping for instruction difficult, groups across age or grade levels can be effective. Often a young preliterate student and an older illiterate one need the same instructional opportunities. The focus of learning is the task. If teachers are skillful in adapting methods and materials to suit both types of students with one common need, then the younger students may enjoy the experience of the older ones, and the older students may help the younger ones and themselves to learn. Two or three grade spans may be reached through a careful plan of ungraded grouping.
- Language groups for Hispanic students should be formed for at least the following instructional objectives: to enhance oral Spanish; to teach Spanish reading; to nurture oral English; to teach English reading or reading readiness; to provide access to subject matter; and to promote self-esteem.
- Groups may also be established on an **ad hoc** basis to follow up on a specific interest of a group. If some of the students want to get together to dramatize a story or poem, they may be given the time to put the performance together, give their little drama, and then regroup.

The Sequence of Skills

The ability to read embraces a complex array of skills — perceptual, sensory-motor, intellectual, and behavioral. As teachers consider a reading curriculum in Spanish that will promote skill development, a major concern is the sequencing of skills. Where does the teacher begin? How can the teacher assure a logical and reasonable progression of skills from the simple to the complex, from the easy to the difficult? What should be done to ensure that skills are not merely acquired and applied in a fragmentary, disparate manner? Which approaches lead students to the realization that skills must be put together into a system that works for them?

In part, answers to such inquiries are to be found in the methods and materials that the teacher has selected for use in the classroom. If the approach is a synthetic one in which the students first learn the letters, syllables, and words of the written code, then the skill sequence quite sensibly proceeds from parts to the whole. If, on the other hand, the approach is an analytic one in which students first search for meanings in whole words and groups of words, then the skill sequence may logically move from the whole to the parts that make up that whole. Some teachers prefer an eclectic approach that taps skills from both synthetic and analytic approaches. The list of skills that follows can be used as a basis for selecting and ordering the activities. Teachers emphasizing the code may work through the word recognition skills to comprehension; teachers emphasizing meaning may begin with vocabulary and comprehension skills. Eclectic teachers may pick and choose according to their particular brand of eclecticism.

Destrezas del Lenguaje escrito

I. **La Lectura**
 A. **Reconocer palabras**
  1. **análisis fónico** — reconocer los sonidos y asociarlos con los símbolos
   a. **vocales**
   b. **consonantes**
    (1) iniciales
    (2) medias
    (3) finales
   c. **conexiones irregulares**
    (1) b — v
    (2) c — a, o, u c — i, e,
    (3) g — a, o, u g — i, e
    (4) g, j, h
    (5) s, z, ci, ce
    (6) h (sorda)
    (7) güi güe
    (8) r (rr)
    (9) y — ll
    (10) x — k — w

d. consonantes en combinación
      (1) con **l** — bl, cl, fl, gl, tl*, tm*
      (2) con **r** — br, cr, dr, fr, gr, pr, tr
   e. diptongos
      (1) ia, ie, io, ua, ue, ui, uo
         oi, eu, au, iu
      (2) dos formas — (ai) (ei) (oi)
              ay, ey, oy
   f. terminaciones
      (1) en vocal — a e i o u (y)
      (2) en consonante — d, l n, r, s, z
2. **análisis de la estructura**
   a. las sílabas
      (1) la división de las palabras
      (2) su formación
   b. las palabras compuestas
   c. los aumentativos — los diminutivos
   d. los prefijos — los sufijos
   e. las formas derivadas
3. **desarrollo del vocabulario**
   a. los sinónimos
   b. los antónimos
   c. los homónimos
   d. el lenguaje figurativo
   e. el lenguaje de las áreas de estudio
4. **reflexivos**
   a. los verbos
   b. los pronombres
B. **La comprensión**
   1. **comprensión literal**
      a. reconocer la idea principal
      b. identificar los detalles específicos
      c. reconocer la secuencia
      d. usar las claves del contexto
      e. identificar personajes, lugares, etcétera
   2. **comprensión interpretativa**
      a. reconocer el propósito del autor
      b. entender la relación de causa y efecto
      c. analizar los sentimientos

*La "**tl**" y la "**tm**" no aparecen en una misma sílaba. Ambas tienen un uso en limitadas palabras (atleta, atlántico, atmósfera, etc.). La "**tl**" si es usado extensamente en palabras de origen nahuatl (tlacuache, ixtle, nahuatl) o es decir en aztequismos.

    d. identificar los absurdos
    e. reconocer el humor
    f. distinguir la realidad y la fantasía
    g. hacer predicciones
    h. reconocer las comparaciones y los contrastes
    i. extraer conclusiones lógicas
    j. hacer inferencias
    k. anticipar resultados
    l. distinguir entre opinión y hecho

Study habits are skills, too. Good teaching demands that teachers assist their students in organizing their time and materials in order to get the best out of the instructional program. Learning to use the instruments of the classroom — book, reference materials, dictionaries, almanacs, atlas, maps, and other sources of information — is a very important skill. A list of study habits to be developed is as follows:

C. Los hábitos de estudiar
   1. el alfabeto
     a. el orden alfabético
   2. las partes del libro
     a. el título
     b. el autor
     c. el índice
     d. el prólogo, introducción, o prefacio
   3. el uso del diccionario
     a. las palabras guías
     b. el glosario
   4. el uso de la biblioteca
     a. el catálogo de tarjetas o fichas
     b. los sistemas de numeración o catalogación
   5. el uso de los libros de referencia
     a. enciclopedia
     b. atlas
     c. almanaque
   6. el uso de materiales gráficas
     a. los mapas
     b. las tablas
     c. los gráficos
   7. la preparación de un recorte
       un plan general

The writing system of Spanish can be presented for skill acquisition according to the age and maturity of the students. Written language demands not only the knowledge of the orthography as a system but also the sensory-motor abilities to perform. A list of writing skills follows:

II. La Escritura
   A. Reconocer y escribir el sistema escrito
      1. El alfabeto
         a. en letra manuscrita
         b. en letra de imprenta o de molde
         c. en letra cursiva
         d. las mayúsculas y las minúsculas
      2. las marcas diacríticas
         a. el acento
         b. la tilde
         c. la diéresis (la crema)
      3. los signos ortográficos
         a. el punto
         b. la coma
         c. el punto y coma
         d. los dos puntos
         e. los signos de interrogación
         f. los signos de exclamación
         g. las comillas
         h. la raya (para diálogos)
         i. el paréntesis
      4. las reglas para las mayúsculas
      5. las abreviaturas comunes
   B. Expresión
      1. el contenido
         a. las ideas
         b. la organización
         c. el vocabulario
         d. la secuencia
         e. el desarrollo del párrafo
      2. la mecánica
         a. las palabras
         b. las oraciones
         c. la sintaxis
            (1) la concordancia

        (a) de género
        (b) de número
  d. la ortografía
  e. las mayúsculas
  f. la puntuación

The individual skills as listed are described in earlier chapters and are merely grouped in the separate categories of word recognition, comprehension, study habits, and writing for the teachers to consider in their entirety. The matter of selection and order is left to the wisdom of teachers who are in the best position to decide the skill sequence for their own students. As soon as students have begun to acquire and to practice skills, they can benefit from lessons that include **appropriate** skills from all **four** categories. One final footnote on skill development appears relevant. Skills accrue only from **practice;** skills can be improved only by **doing.** Teachers do not teach skills; nor do they give them to their students. Teachers provide the knowledge, arrange the environment, model the behavior, and then offer guided practice, practice, practice.

Pacing Instruction

Ideally, instruction should be paced at a rate that is comfortable for each student. Pacing, then, would take into account the individual student's timetable of growth and learning. Although to some extent, good teachers everywhere attempt to achieve this ideal, reading programs in reality are organized on the basis of group instruction. A classroom is a group setting. In an ordinary gathering of students, approximately twenty-five percent of them will learn rapidly; twenty-five percent will learn slowly, and fifty percent of them will have an average learning rate. Teachers usually arrange their instruction to accommodate the middle fifty percent and try to provide for the rapid learners through enrichment opportunities and for the slow learners through additional practice activities. Students at either extreme may be accelerated or remediated as warranted.

Young students can be offered a sequence of skills in reading at a lively yet leisurely pace because they have time on their side. Older students who are beginning instruction or who are somewhat delayed in skill development may not have the luxury of an unhurried pace. Teachers need to keep moving along so that new learnings are constantly being added to those already introduced. There is as much danger in moving too slowly through the reading curriculum as there is in moving too quickly. Boredom, fatigue, and loss of interest can occur if the pace of instruction is monotonously and painfully labored. The same problems may exist when the teaching moves too fast for the students and leaves them bewildered and confused. Teachers need to analyze the lessons in terms of what they expect students to do. They need to specify the standard of performance. They need to monitor progress and make decisions regarding the pace of instruction. One method of making judgments about pacing comes from the observation of many excellent classroom teachers who appear to understand clearly what they expect their students to accomplish. More than this, however, they manage to get that message across clearly to students. Their teaching is characterized by the following qualities:

- The teacher knows what is to be taught and says to the students —
  En esta lección, vamos a aprender _____.
- The teacher tells the students what they are expected to do —
  Ustedes tienen que leer, escribir, deletrear, contestar, pensar o _____.
- The teacher helps the students get organized for the task —
  Ustedes necesitarán _____.
- The teacher explains **exactly** what the task is by giving information, direction, models, illustrations, etc. —
  Me hacen el favor de mirar el pizarrón y escucharme bien _____.
- The teacher offers examples and develops them while giving explanations —
  Noten ustedes bien ésta página, éste modelo, éste ejemplo, etc.
- The teacher checks up on the students to see how the instructions are being followed —
  Voy a observar el trabajo en progreso. Quizas voy a pararme al lado de su escritorio y repasar sus tareas.
- The teacher tells the students how they are to be evaluated —
  Después de la lección, nos vamos a discutir o voy a darles a ustedes un examen corto.
- The teacher asks the students to restate what has been covered and learned in the lesson —
  ¿Quién puede decirme lo que hemos aprendido hoy día?
- The teacher gives social reinforcement for tasks well done and skills well practiced —
  ¡Bueno! ¡Bravo! ¡Formidable! ¡Que grupo bien dispuesto! ¡Tú eres trabajador! ¡Supersaliente!
- The teacher notes carefully the fast pacers, the moderate pacers, and the slow pacers and may make suggestions for further practice, remediation, or enrichment —
  Tú puedes mejorar tus destrezas en _____.
  Tú puedes enriquecer tus destrezas en _____.
  Tú puedes repasar éstas destrezas en _____.

When teachers organize the reading instruction well and know **exactly** what they want to teach, they can make it much clearer to the students what they are expected to learn. In this manner, the pace of instruction can be picked up or slowed down according to the monitored progress of the students.

Monitoring Achievement

Successful decisions can be made about grouping, skill sequence, and pacing when teachers have sound information about their students' learning. There are many ways, both formal and informal, that teachers may assess students' progress. Among these are teacher observations, criterion-reference tests, norm-referenced tests, daily work and homework. Each time that a teacher enters the classroom and interacts with students, that teacher is gathering information about the progress of the class in general and of the students as individuals. The best instrument for appraising student achievement is the practiced eye and ear of a competent, caring teacher. As Hispanic students have gained fluency and literacy in Spanish and are moving toward excellence in English, teachers have monitored progress in countless ways. Observations may have provided impressions regarding the students' progress relative to (1) the level of vocabulary; (2) the quality of speech; (3) the use of language structures; (4) the relationships with peers; (5) the control of emotions; (6) the reaction to frustration, and (7) the interest in learning. This background information is useful when teachers are considering the conditions that promote or interfere with success in reading. Observation of these behaviors may occur in classroom recitations, during individual conferences with students, in small group discussions, and in unstructured activities.

The teachers may supplement the information obtained informally with test data. There are two kinds of measures that may be useful for this intent: (1) criterion-referenced tests and (2) norm-referenced tests. They differ greatly in their purposes and content. A criterion-referenced test is one that is designed narrowly to measure performance on specific skill areas that have been included in daily instruction. Ordinarily, the test has been developed by the teacher or by the publisher of the materials used. An expected standard of performance has been established, and the students' performances are compared to the standard. Such assessment is very helpful in making decisions about the instructional plan. Students may then be offered review of earlier skills, additional practice, or new skill opportunities based on the test scores. Norm-referenced tests generally cover a broad content area. The individual student's performance is compared to the performance of the referent group, the group upon which the **norms** were obtained. Data obtained on norm-referenced measures allow for comparisons among students, classes, schools, and regions. General decisions about promotion, retention, or assignment to an accelerated class may be made on the basis of the students' test scores.

There are many problems inherent in assessment at best, and despite the existence of many carefully researched tests, there are always serious questions about the uses and abuses of test data. Issues of validity, reliability, freedom from bias, and measurement error continue to be pivotal points of debate in the traditional testing programs for English speakers and readers. The controversy that surrounds the testing of Hispanic students enrolled in schools where English is the language of the curriculum is without end or limits. There are relatively few instruments available to accommodate the special testing requirements of second language learners. There are judgments that must be made by teachers who will develop or select tests for use in their classrooms. Some of the basic principles of good testing to be considered are these:

- The test must be clearly related to the purpose for which it is used. What information does the teacher want to obtain? Reading tests may give the teacher data on vocabulary, word study skills, comprehension, or all three.
- The test items must be representative of the instructional content that has been offered and practiced. Has the teacher addressed this content in class work?
- The testing schedule should be consistent with the teaching schedule so that the expectations are reasonable. Have students had opportunites to review the material provided earlier? Are there new concepts or skills in the test that may be planned for later instruction?
- The test selected must be an instrument that has been put together according to the rules for sound test construction. Is the language of the test appropriate for the language level of students who take the test? Are the items to be truly representative of the skills or knowledge? There are other questions that may be raised about reading tests. Teacher-made tests and criterion-referenced tests developed for use in specific reading programs are likely to be more helpful in monitoring student achievement. They may be applied as a means of assessing progress as the instructional program goes along. A few of the specific instruments that may be used are described and given as illustrations for the teachers to consider. If, for example, the teacher has introduced the students to reading in Spanish by way of a synthetic approach and has depended heavily on sound-symbol connections, the teacher may determine the success or failure of the approach by very simple tests of the speech-print connections as follows:

El dictado — los sonidos y los símbolos en la posición inicial — las vocales

Note: Give words in a **natural** speech manner of delivery, neither stressing unduly nor distorting the beginning sound. Be certain that the room is quiet and that pupils are listening carefully. Allow **five** seconds after you have presented each word twice. Give practice item and show your response on the blackboard.

avión	oreja	ojalá	invierno
escoba	indio	andando	energía
anillo	escalera	imagen	adelante
uña	uniforme	ule	oro
ocho	imán	entender	uno

Escribe la letra que representa el sonido inicial de la palabra.

1. _____   6. _____   11. _____   16. _____

2. _____   7. _____   12. _____   17. _____

3. _____   8. _____   13. _____   18. _____

4. _____   9. _____   14. _____   19. _____

5. _____   10. _____   15. _____   20. _____

Las conexiones entre los dibujos y los símbolos — T, D, F en la posición inicial

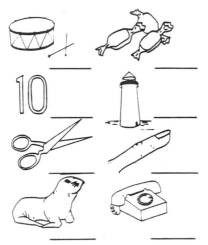

See Appendix E for additional examples of sound-symbol testing.

El dictado de las sílabas— escribir las letras que representen la sílaba inicial

1. **la**   4. **ra**   7. **la**
2. **ru**   5. **li**   8. **ri**
3. **lo**   6. **re**   9. **lu**
                            10. **ro**

Las consonantes en combinaciones

dromedario   _____   **r**e**g**la   _____
primer   _____   **cr**ucigrama   _____
fresas   _____   a**br**igo   _____
clavo   _____   **tr**en   _____

Los diptongos

nueve   ruina   aire   bueno
familia   seis   agua   siete
causa   ciudad   Europa   antiguo
diez   hoy   radio

1. _____   5. _____   9. _____   13. _____
2. _____   6. _____   10. _____   14. _____
3. _____   7. _____   11. _____   15. _____
4. _____   8. _____   12. _____

Las terminaciones

gato   león
leche   madre
flor   pared
miel   silla

1. _____   5. _____
2. _____   6. _____
3. _____   7. _____
4. _____   8. _____

If students are able to respond to these test items at a level that meets the teacher's expectations and standards, then decisions about the pacing and review of materials may be made more thoughtfully. If there are some students for whom this synthetic approach is not working, they will be identified early in the instructional program, and some alternative methods and materials may be offered.

Other assessment strategies at the early levels may include the following matching of upper and lower case forms, the visual identification of the same letters, the position of objects and letters, the recognition of syllables in words, the matching of words, the identification of pictorial sequence, the selection of the correct vocabulary item, the recognition of main ideas, details, sequence, and other comprehension skills. Examples of these test items are taken from **Las pruebas de lectura** published by Santillana.

Asociar letras mayúsculas con minúsculas correspondientes —

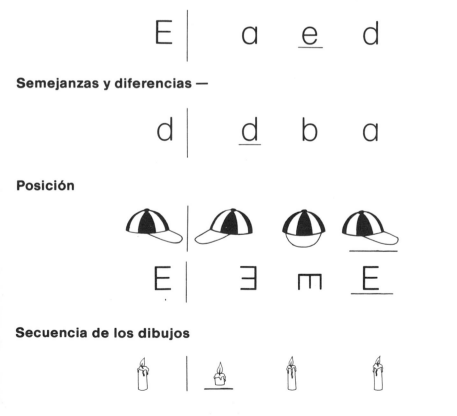

Semejanzas y diferencias —

Posición

Secuencia de los dibujos

Reconocer las sílabas

mu	mula	pesa	mata
la	lobo	tosa	lala

ha he
hi
ho hu

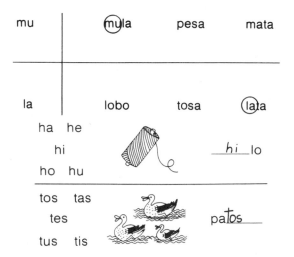

_hi_ lo

tos tas
tes
tus tis

pa*tos*

Asociar las sílabas con los dibujos

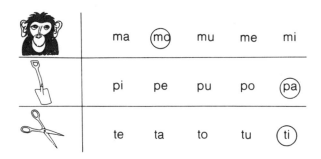

	ma	mo	mu	me	mi
	pi	pe	pu	po	pa
	te	ta	to	tu	ti

Identificar palabras

tose
sale
nada

come
toma
pone

Identificar detalles

La _____ de Polo.

| pala | | lupa | | sopa |

Es _____ paloma.

| mi | | tu |

Es _____ paloma.

| mi | | tu |

Identificar idea principal

Elsa sale de su casa para el mercado.
Su mamá la mandó por chocolates y café.
—¿Me da chocolates? —pide Elsa.
Elsa lleva los chocolates en la mano.
—¡Mira tus manos! —dice su mamá.

Elsa compra café.
Elsa sale a la calle.
Elsa y los chocolates.

Identificar secuencia

Pasean por toda
la ciudad.

La familia llega
a la casa.

La familia sale
de paseo.

Identificar relación de causa y efecto. Analizar sentimientos.

¡Alegría, Alegría! ¿Dónde estás? Busca que te busca por aquí, busca que te busca por allá, Alegría no aparecía por ninguna parte. Su mamá estaba muy asustada.

Voló por todos los nidos, se asomó por todos los huequitos, buscó cerca de la laguna... Pero nada... ¡No estaba!

—¿Qué voy a hacer ahora? —preguntó su mamá. Debemos partir enseguida. Pronto empezará a soplar el viento helado. ¡Nos moriremos de frío!

Mientras tanto, Alegría estaba entretenida mirando los gusanitos, las nubes, los árboles, las ardillitas...

"Qué extraño —se dijo Alegría—. No veo ningún pájaro por aquí. ¿Qué habrá pasado? Quizás algún zorro ande cerca. Mamá me dijo que hay que tener mucho cuidado."

De pronto, todo se puso muy oscuro. Comenzaron a caer unos copos muy blancos.

Alegría se cobijó debajo de un hongo extraño. "Brr, brr" —salió de su piquito, en vez de "pío, pío". Hacía tanto frío, que ya no podía mover sus alitas. Se acurrucó muy asustada y cerró los ojitos.

"No debí alejarme del nido", pensó.

Busca diminutivos en el cuento y escríbelos aquí :

huequitos - gusanitos - ardillitas - piquito

alitas   ojitos

¿Qué decidió hacer la mamá de Alegría?

a. Seguir soplando.
b. Seguir buscando.
c. Cobijarse debajo de un hongo.
d. Comer gusanitos.

Distinguir entre realidad y fantasía. Usar claves de contexto.

La vaca Tolona quiere ir a la luna. Se pone su blusa de seda de muchos colores.
Luego se pone sus zapatos de tacón. Lleva un bolso grande con muchas cosas.
—¿Me da un billete para ir a la luna? —pide Tolona.

Subraya la respuesta correcta:

¿Puede ser verdad este cuento?

a. Sí.
b. No.

¿Por qué?

a. Las vacas hablan.
b. Las vacas no hablan.
c. Las vacas se ponen zapatos de tacón.

¿Qué pide Tolona?

a. Un bolso grande.
b. Muchas cosas.
c. Un billete.

¿Qué se puso primero Tolona?

a. Sus zapatos de tacón.
b. Su blusa de seda.
c. Su bolso grande.

In addition to teacher-made tests and publishers' tests that are intended to monitor students' progress in specified skills, there are a few norm-referenced tests adapted in Spanish or developed in Spanish for a particular Hispanic population. Measures such as the Inter-American Tests, the Comprehensive Test of Basic Skills-Español, and the Moreno Reading Comprehension Tests have to be evaluated carefully. Their titles and Spanish language should not give teachers a total sense of security that such tests are appropriate for use with all Hispanic students. Norm-referenced tests in any language are tests and are subject to the same potential hazards that exist among all tests. To be useful, norm-referenced tests must meet these three basic requirements upon which the validity and reliability of such instruments depend. They are (1) that there has been equality of opportunity for the students to have been exposed to the test content in an instructional program; (2) that the language of the test directions and the language anticipated in the test responses are understood by the students; and (3) that students just like those who are taking the test have been included in the standardization samples upon which the norms have been established. If these basic assumptions have not been met, then the inferences made about any individual's performance may be erroneous or even dangerous. Measures designed and standardized on Puerto Rican students may not be suitable for use with Mexican students. Tests developed and normed on Venezuelan illiterate adults are not appropriate for a Cuban population of secondary students. Instruments very carefully constructed and researched in Spain are of very limited usefulness in classrooms in the United States. For these reasons, as well as many others, teachers and administrators are wise to look beyond test titles and catalogue descriptions to the number of other variables demanded by responsible testing.

Providing Practice

Teachers will immediately notice that not all of their students require the same amount of practice. The rapid learners seem to become skillful after a few practice sessions while others need more time and more practice. Differences in learning rate, previous educational experiences, and motivation account for these variations in progress even when the quality of instruction remains constant. Practice is best defined as the student's response. For reading skills at any level to grow, students must have many opportunities to make responses. One of the major concerns that teachers have is the question of how to use students' (as well as teachers') time wisely. Classroom hours spent on meaningless repetitive practice and drill may not result in effective learning. Most of the learning theorists agree that practice distributed over time is preferable to long periods of practice. Small skill segments presented for practice in an orderly sequence may serve to keep interest alive and may prevent fatigue or boredom. Practice needed by learners functioning at different levels may be accomplished through grouping and subgrouping as the need arises.

A few principles to guide the teacher in arranging for reading practice are these:

- Practice activities should make sense to the learner.
- Short periods of practice are generally more effective than long, drawn-out periods.
- Students differ in their need for practice.
- Practice should be monitored to ensure that only correct responses are being repeated.

- Practice is vital for the overlearning necessary to develop speedy, accurate, and automatic responses to print as a medium.

The organization of reading instruction for Spanish to English transfer will vary according to the philosophy of reading and the resources available in the community. In any school, there is the possibility of at least forty legitimate organizational plans for providing instruction. When these patterns are further modified or combined into other models, the potential for local creativity can be readily appreciated. Local legislation and policy may influence decisions regarding the manner in which the reading program may be organized. Teachers and administrators would be wise to examine the accepted methods of organizing reading instruction and to consider the factors that appear best suited to their own students. Among the important views are these:

- there is not **one** plan of organizing instruction that is clearly superior to all others.
- what the teacher does in the organizational pattern has a greater impact on learning than the pattern itself.
- there is generally a need to reorganize and revitalize plans after a period of time because they appear to become stale or outmoded.
- the better the plan of organizing instruction identifies the needs of individual students, the more demands are made on teachers.
- there are elements of the good and the bad in all organizational plans.

To guide teachers whose goals are excellence in English for Hispanic students, there are a few other guideposts to follow. Instruction should be organized

- to accommodate Hispanic students at the preliterate, literate, and illiterate levels.
- to offer readiness to read Spanish if it has been established that Spanish is the native language.
- to nurture concepts and oral language in Spanish first.
- to provide instruction in Spanish reading vocabulary, comprehension, and study skills.
- to promote access to the content areas by way of oral and written Spanish to the extent resources are available.
- to provide comprehensible lessons in English that will develop not only the informal communication skills but the academic language skills as well.
- to transfer to English reading the applicable Spanish reading skills and to use those transferred skills in content areas in English.

- to allow students to enter the reading curriculum at a level appropriate for their skill development in Spanish or in English.
- to foster self-confidence and self-esteem in every activity in both languages.
- to expect excellence of performance to the best of each student's potential for learning to read Spanish and English.

Caveat

It is extremely hazardous for anyone to write about grouping practices, skill sequences, instructional pace, and other dimensions of a curriculum. At best, the information can serve only as a guidepost. At worst, the suggestions may be construed as prescriptions for teaching. Teachers and administrators who know their students are in the only position to decide what may be appropriate and beneficial for **their** students. There are numerous variations that stem from the numbers of Hispanic students in any school or grade level. There are differences in staffing patterns, resources, and curriculum organization. Therefore, the choices about planning instruction must be left in the capable hands of the educators who have thoughtfully considered the greatest good for the greatest number and who have carefully made decisions in the best interests of all.

References

1. Garry, Ralph and Kingley, Howard. **The Nature and Conditions of Learning.** New York: Prentice-Hall, Inc., 1957.

2. **Las Pruebas de Lectura.** Northvale: New Jersey: Santillana Publishing Company, Inc., 1979.

3. Strang, Ruth. **Diagnostic Teaching of Reading.** New York: McGraw Hill, Inc., 1964.

4. Thorndike, Robert and Hagen, Elizabeth. **Measurement and Evaluation in Psychology and Education.** New York: John Wiley and Sons, 1977.

CHAPTER VIII

OTHER INSTRUCTIONAL VARIABLES

The resources needed to attain high-quality language goals vary as much as the students for whom the instruction is intended. Significant among these variables are the kinds of teachers, the amount of time, the quality of materials, the choice of the methods, the support of administration, the cooperation of parents, the advocacy of community, and the nature of students. No two school communities will have exactly the same elements arrayed in precisely the same manner. Yet, all of them will share a common objective — excellence in English for language minority students. When the school is one in which there are relatively large numbers of Hispanic students enrolled, the most reasonable and promising road to excellence appears to be the one that begins with the Spanish of the home. Educators for centuries have held to the time-honored maxim of beginning with students' strengths. Despite the conventional wisdom that has led schools to abandon Spanish and begin with English, logic from learning theory and evidence from empirical research suggest that better results will accrue from a program of instruction beginning in Spanish. Transfer of native language and literacy skills can be predicted to improve language and literacy skills in English.

The Teachers
The reading teachers for Hispanic students should be fluent, literate persons in Spanish. As individuals, the teachers should have the same personal qualities of all individuals who are working with youth. They should enjoy the energy and extravagance of the young. They should appreciate the responsibility and challenge residing in the art and science of teaching them. As professionals, teachers need to **know** what reading is all about; they need to **know how** to teach reading; and they need to **believe** that reading is **one** school subject that no normal child may be permitted to fail.

The teachers should have a solid academic preparation in human growth and development, first and second language acquisition and learning, and the subject matter required by the teaching assignment. Knowledge of linguistic principles as they apply to the phonology, morphology, and semantics of Spanish and English should be part of the teachers' professional education. The methodologies for teaching reading should be well known and the advantages and disadvantages of the various approaches to literacy should be clearly understood. Teachers should know about the materials that are available to use with students. They need to be able to judge their effectiveness with different kinds of students and to recognize the strengths and weaknesses of print and non-print media. Teachers should know about the social and cultural settings from which their students come and should have opportunities to study the literature, history, art, and music of the Hispanic people.

It is insufficient only **to know;** teachers also have to **know how** to do certain things in a classroom in order to be successful professionals. They need to **know how** to arrange a classroom to create an orderly, well-organized setting in which learning can take place. They need skills in managing students in several groups, as well as skills in determining which students could best benefit from placement in which group. They need to know **how to** interest and motivate students. Teachers also have to **know how to** present a lesson; **how to** guide practice; **how to** monitor progress; and **how to** vary teaching strategies and techniques.

The most knowledgeable and clever teachers may not succeed in a reading program if they do not also know how to bring their knowledge to the students in a variety of ways for a diverse group of students.

Teachers' beliefs make a significant impact upon their effectiveness in the classroom. In addition to knowledge and know-how, teachers must believe that sensitivity and courtesy are essential to the creation of a supportive classroom climate in which learning can take place. Teachers must have a sense of fairness and justice that applies to **all** students. They should believe in themselves and in the joy and excitement of teaching. They should above all have a sense of humor and not take themselves too seriously. The personal and professional qualities of teachers will vary as teachers bring to teaching the temperament and training so unique to each one of them. Yet, all effective teachers will bring to their students these three dimensions as teachers: a substantial background of knowledge; good skills in delivering that knowledge; and a strong belief in themselves and in their students.

Beyond the general and professional education requirements of teaching, reading teachers for Hispanic students ideally should have enjoyed opportunities during their pre-service years to acquire the **knowledge** of both Spanish and English. Specifically such languages competencies may be listed as these:

- acquisition of the **two** languages leading to proficiency in understanding speaking, reading and writing.
- awareness of the most commonly recognized differences in dialects.
- background of information from linguistics, including contrastive analysis of the two languages.

- knowledge of the cultural differences and similarities between both communities.
- recognition of the impact the cultural variables have on learning.
- identification of significant historical and cultural contributions of the Hispanic world.
- knowledge of learning theory including transfer principles and motivation.
- understanding of the varied methods and techniques of teaching reading as well as the advantages and disadvantages of each.
- recognition of a logical scope and sequence of reading skills.

Teacher preparation programs would serve the reading teachers well if they were to include opportunities to develop the **skills of knowing how** to manage the following challenges in a classroom:

- the provision of rich oral language development in Spanish, including

    (a) storytelling
    (b) poetry, rhymes, songs, puppetry
    (c) conversation, dialogue
    (d) sharing

- the preparation of students for reading, through

    (a) the visual-perceptual activities
    (b) the auditory-perceptual activities
    (c) the spatial activities

- the introduction of the beginning reading and writing, using varied methodologies, as

    (a) onomatopoeic
    (b) phonic
    (c) syllabic
    (d) language experience
    (e) global
    (f) basal
    (g) eclectic

- the awareness of varied approaches to accommodate learners' modalities of strength recognizing

(a) visual needs
(b) auditory needs
(c) kinesthetic needs
(d) multi-sensory needs

- the refinement of the many techniques for word recognition, including

    (a) phonic analysis
    (b) visual configuration clues
    (c) structural analysis
    (d) context clues

- the development of students' excellence in the comprehension skills of written material, particularly

    (a) precision of literal comprehension
    (b) breadth of interpretive comprehension
    (c) range of creative comprehension

- the provision for encouraging strong study habits, as

    (a) using reference materials
    (b) organizing time
    (c) planning for practice

- the evaluation of student progress, including

    (a) administering tests
    (b) interpreting data
    (c) using obtained data wisely

- the delivery of instruction to groups of students in order to adjust

    (a) scope and sequence of skills
    (b) pacing and practice
    (c) levels of skill difficulty

- the management of the classroom routine, especially

    (a) grouping
    (b) identifying students' needs
    (c) record keeping

Along with **knowing** and **knowing how,** teachers need to develop their personal values and beliefs about teaching. As reading teachers are preparing for their responsibilities in classrooms where Hispanic students are taught, they need to believe in the following:

- the normal student can learn to read and write.
- it is reasonable to expect that students will read first the language for which they have oral referents.
- well-developed speech is required for success in reading.
- first language literacy in Spanish has great potential for transfer to English.
- the nation's youth — all of them — are the greatest natural resource.
- the international world of this century needs to preserve all its citizens' language skills.
- the strength in Spanish is the best predictor of strength in English.
- the road to excellence in English fluency and literacy is best traveled in Spanish with transfer at appropriate places along the way.

There are, of course, many additional competencies that reading teachers could possess. There are fields of knowledge, skills in knowing how, and beliefs that may be given high priorities on anyone's list. These few have been listed to suggest the kinds of teachers who may best teach Hispanic students in an English setting. Some teachers have all of the competencies and more! Others have some of them and are still working to gain additional knowledge and skills. In a few schools, teachers work cooperatively in pairs, or in teams to combine the best skills of everyone and apply them in the best interest of students. No matter in what combination of persons — one or several — these teaching attributes are found, **the teacher** in the reading class is the most important element in the instructional program.

Materials
Materials for a reading program that will promote skills in Spanish and, ultimately, in English may be difficult to identify. In countries where English is the language of the curriculum there usually is an abundance of attractive and appropriate material for the English dimension of the reading plan. These materials are designed, however, for native speakers of English and must be used differently for non-native students. The materials to support reading instruction in Spanish, however, are likely to be in short supply. Two immediate concerns are the availability of readers and other books and the criteria for selecting them. If teachers expect Hispanic students to practice and enjoy their reading skills, there should be books of high literary quality for them to use. Reading in Spanish for

enjoyment and for information has the effect of improving the language skills and the reading proficiencies of students. In order for practice to occur, books and other print media must be found and placed at the students' disposal. The selection must be made on the basis of reasonable criteria that meet the standards of the school and the community.

The criteria may reflect the local concerns for quality and may minimally include these factors: the attractiveness of the books, the authenticity of language, the relevance to instructional goals, the content, the illustrations, and the cost. One of the most critical considerations is the suitability of materials imported from Hispanic countries for use in an English school setting. Such books may contain social, political, or religious themes that may be unacceptable to a particular school board or community. A selection committee should be sensitive to such issues. Materials generally are found to be available from these sources: (1) commercial publishers and bookstores abroad; (2) commercial publishers in English-speaking countries; and (3) local development agencies and centers. Materials from Hispanic countries abroad may be original versions or translated ones; those found in the English-speaking countries are likely to be translations of English content into Spanish; and those created by local curriculum groups are usually the home-grown efforts of teachers whose work reflects local interests and regional language. The checklist, which is in the appendix, is intended merely as a guide and does not presume to address all the concerns that are raised in the selection of reading materials.

Materials in Spanish should be sought for at least four specific purposes:

- for the introduction and development of reading and writing Spanish
- for the introduction and development of the study of the Spanish language
- for the introduction and development of the content areas, including science, literature, social sciences, and mathematics
- for the development of lifelong reading habits for pleasure and enhancement of self.

An additional concern about print media is its level of reading difficulty. This issue is discussed in the next section.

Readability of Content Area Print
A reasonable assumption is one that expects most of the Hispanic students to move rather rapidly into the print of English in the content areas. These are realistic expectations because of the following reasons:

- there are few textbooks in content areas available in Spanish in schools where the majority language is English.
- imported print media in Spanish may be inappropriate for a number of reasons, including

    a. too difficult vocabulary
    b. too complex language structures
    c. incompatible philosophy
    d. religious content.

- there are fewer secondary content area teachers who are fluent and literate in Spanish.
- the higher cost of content area textbooks in two languages at the secondary level.
- the logical demand to meet graduation requirements in English in countries where English is the language of the economy.

Whether Hispanic students use Spanish or English materials as educational sources in their subject matter classrooms, there are many factors that influence the readability of the textbooks. One element to consider is the organization of the book, itself. The size and kind of the type may make the material easier or more difficult to read. The length of a line of print may influence the comprehensibility of the message. The quality of the paper and ink may enhance or may detract from the appeal of the content. The kind of illustrations, their number, and their size may contribute to the attractiveness of the chapters. The presence or absence of white space in margins on the sides, top, and bottom may invite the readers or discourage them. These are physical features of printed material that impact immediately on the readers. Readability, however, depends upon other factors: the readers themselves; their interests, the nature of the content; the vocabulary and concept burden; and the language complexity.

A number of readability formulas have been developed by reading specialists in an attempt to quantify levels of reading difficulty. Most of the formulas developed for English print take into consideration these features: (1) the average length of the sentence; (2) the number of polysyllabic words; (3) the presence of abstract words; and (4) the sentence structure, complexity, and the vocabulary difficulty. A very popular formula has been prepared by Edward Fry,* whose formula for estimating readability is based on two factors; sentence length and number of syllables. Three passages of one hundred words are selected and are used for this purpose. Fry's assumption is that longer sentences are generally more complex in structure. The average sentence length and average number of syllables in the samples form the basis for judging reading difficulty.

*Fry, **Graph for Estimating Readability-Extended** is in the appendix.

The readability index of Spanish print has been more difficult to establish because the several suggestions for making estimates of reading levels have come from the attempts to assist second language readers of Spanish rather than Hispanic students reading in their own language. The Spaulding index, which represents an attempt to determine readability of Spanish as a second language for English speakers, is such an example. Spanish linguists have pointed out that native speakers of Spanish are accustomed to multisyllabic words because of their propensity for the enclitic and the derivational processes. Simple affirmative and negative statements can be conveyed in a number of syntactical patterns. These are only two reasons why the traditional readability formula cannot be applied across the two languages. There are no doubt many others. An adaptation of the Fry formula for the purpose of applying it to Spanish print has been suggested by Gilliam, Peña and Mountain.* The syllable count is modified to adjust for the expected number of syllables in Spanish words. The researchers suggest that this modification is useful for determining the reading levels of primary materials. The Fry adaptation for connected written discourse in Spanish suggests that the number sixty-seven (67) be subtracted from the total syllable count and then the formula be applied as usual.

When subject matter teachers have not been successful in obtaining materials suitable for reading levels of their students, they may consider simplifying the existing resources. Teachers who have the skill and the stamina to adapt difficult materials in order to make them more comprehensible may wish to consider some of these possibilities.

- Review the textbook chapters for key concepts and identify them.
- Present the concept and allow time for questions, explanations, and discussions.
- Examine the vocabulary. Introduce new words or new meanings for them.
- Provide study sheets with essential ideas written in shorter sentences.
- Rewrite complex syntax patterns into simpler ones.
- Avoid translation from one language to another.
- Add diagrams, sketches, or other simple visuals as aids to meaning.
- Whenever available, supplement printed material with non-print media film, filmstrips, study prints, real objects, and pictures.
- Adjust reading assignments to a reasonable number of pages when students are on their own.
- Read the material to the students in short sessions and follow up the reading with questions, discussions, and explanations.
- Remember that the textbook is only a tool and as such will be effective only to the extent that it is a comprehensible, useful tool.

*Gilliam, Bettye, Peña, Sylvia C., and Mountain, Lee, **The Reading Teacher, January 1980, pp.426-430.**

Time
The development of literacy skills takes time for **any** student in **any** language. Ordinarily, monolingual students have five years of oral language practice at home before entering the reading classroom. After a period of readiness for reading, students are offered reading instruction for the next five or six years. Usually, the students who leave the fifth or sixth grade have the necessary fluency and literacy skills to use in their junior and senior high school years. From this point on, there is little attention given to the teaching of reading as a subject. The curriculum emphasis shifts to subject matter, and students are expected to acquire content, knowledge, and skills. In terms of chronological age, students have enjoyed approximately eleven or twelve years to acquire the fluency and literacy skills that will serve them well the rest of their lives. Teachers recognize that skill acquisition takes appropriate instruction, guided practice, and time.

For students who spend the first five years of their lives in a Spanish environment, their oral language in Spanish may be adequate for supporting a program of reading readiness in Spanish but Is most inadequate for an English reading readiness program. When the next few years of schooling provide opportunities for instruction in Spanish reading and writing, these students at the end of their fifth or sixth grades should have literacy skills comparable to their English-speaking peers. During the oral English lessons and the opportunities to acquire English through the many informal contacts with English-speaking classmates, comprehension of speech should be coming right along. As students **add** the literacy skills of English, they are building **balanced** skills in both languages and are moving toward the oral **and** written control of English as well as Spanish. These valuable proficiencies take time and patience. The organization of a curriculum to adjust the time needed and to accommodate the students is provided on the chart in the appendix. It should be noted that ultimately the school time is no greater in terms of total time than a regular kindergarten through high school program.

The Administrator
The school site administrator contributes greatly to the success of **any** reading program in **any** language. The leadership of a fluent, literate person who engenders a love of language and reading in the school creates a climate of excitement and support for the efforts of teachers. Decisions regarding personnel, materials, reports, community meetings, and budgets reside in the office of the administrator who is in a position to help create an effective reading program. Even when the administrators have few or no skills in Spanish, they have a powerful impact if they review the research and understand the rationale of a dual language viewpoint. Administrators can be great ambassadors in the community.

They can explain the philosophy of excellence in English through the development of fluency and literacy in Spanish. They can help guide policies and decisions that are made by superintendents and school boards. They can keep parents abreast of new curriculum developments. Good leaders recognize that one of their major responsibilities is to support the efforts of teachers. The reading program needs administrators who will offer wise leadership by doing these things:

- informing the parents of the nature and goals of the instructional plan.
- developing the roles and responsibilities of staff members.
- arranging for the ongoing opportunities for staff to improve teaching skills.
- ensuring the availability of needed materials, equipment, and other resources.
- monitoring total program direction through reasonable evaluation.
- establishing the credibility of the program in the community.
- supervising the instruction in the reading classrooms.
- reporting program needs and strengths to the superintendent and school board.
- using the resources of the program efficiently and wisely.
- encouraging parents, teachers, and students to seek the goal of excellence.
- searching always for better ways to serve teachers and youth.

The Parents
Parents are their children's first teachers. Fluency and literacy begin, like charity, at home. Students whose parents have used oral and written language in positive ways clearly develop in their children values and attitudes that contribute to success in school. The literature is filled with studies regarding the importance of parents' support 'for the schools' reading efforts. For **all** children who have opportunities to talk and to read with their parents in **any** language, learning to read is likely to be viewed as an expected and significant requirement of growing up. Parents of Hispanic students, like the children themselves, cannot be considered as fitting one set of descriptions. Some are fluent and literate in Spanish, but not in English; some are fluent and literate in Spanish **and** English; some are fluent but not literate in one language or the other. In many homes, there may be one Spanish-speaking parent and an English-speaking one. Some of the children may come from single parent homes. There is as much variability among the parents as there is among the students. For this reason, the teachers will have to work cooperatively with parents according to the kinds of parents that they have in their schools. All parents of Hispanic children should be encouraged to use their native Spanish in the home. Fluent, literate parents whose resources allow the time and leisure for reading, for volunteering in the classroom, for serving on school committees, and other traditional activities can offer their children and others a very rich experience in the Spanish language. Parents who are not literate

236

also have many wonderful talents to bring to the students in art, handwork, music, cooking, and other beautiful and practical skills. Parents from all groups should be most welcome to share in the development of their children's talents as they grow toward literacy.

The school has a serious responsibility to make crystal clear to parents the intent of the instructional program in reading. Particularly, teachers must stress the philosophy, rationale, and strategy for promoting literacy through the first language as a means to literacy in English. Hispanic parents have many anxieties over the English language skill development of their children. They need to understand that excellence in English is the instructional goal. They need to realize that **immediate** instruction in the writing system of English is not necessarily a guarantee of success in learning to read English. Parents need straightforward, plain reasons why the use of Spanish serves to strengthen the acquisition and learning of English. They need to appreciate how important parents are in the process. Above all, they should **not be told to speak English** at home if English is not a comfortable, useful language that is meaningful in the family context. The suggestions for parent involvement with their children's educational program should be practical and realistic. A young mother with preschool age children and an infant may not have time to volunteer in a classroom. A very poor family may not have the transportation nor the money to take their children to visit historic sites or museums. Parents with few or no English language skills may not feel comfortable about participating actively in committee work where the business is conducted entirely in English. Yet, all parents can be appreciated for whatever time and resources they may have to offer their children both at home and at school. All parents may be made to feel welcome in the classroom and should be appreciated for their support of the reading program. A few suggestions for Hispanic parents are offered below:

- recommend that parents use Spanish in talking and listening to their children.
- suggest that parents read to their children the traditional **cuentos, poesía, rimas** that represent their literary heritage.
- urge parents to share their history and traditions in proverbs, games, recipes, songs, and other memories of their own childhood.
- point out the need to be consistent in the use of language in the home by keeping English and Spanish separate to the extent possible.
- explain that concept acquisition and vocabulary development are promoted in a home where children and parents communicate.
- remind parents to send their children to school every day unless there is a serious reason not to do so.

There are many other kinds of suggestions that teachers may make as they work cooperatively with Hispanic parents. The recommendations depend on the nature of the students' language needs and the realities of the parents. The essential characteristic of the parent-school relationship is one of mutual trust. Teachers must have respect for the parents' concerns for their children, and parents must have confidence in the teachers' plans for educating them. The need for good school-home communication is great for **any** reading program. For a plan that proposes the gift of biliteracy, effective communication with parents is the bedrock foundation upon which a successful program rests.*

The Community
The school is an institution created by society and becomes a reflection of the community that it serves. The reading program receives careful scrutiny by members of any community. Professional groups want the reading program to produce college-bound students with strong literacy skills for academic work. Leaders in business and industry want the reading program to train students as literate future employees. Community groups of many kinds want the best reading program for their tax dollars. The total community has a reasonable concern for high quality reading instruction. When a reading plan is organized on the basis of transferability of skills from Spanish to English, there are likely to be many serious questions raised by members of the community concerning its legitimacy.

The school has a grave responsibility to provide jargon-free explanations to various community groups. The best and most successful activities at school can be completely cancelled by negative response from the community. A reading program that begins with the students' Spanish and develops fluency and literacy in Spanish as a launching pad to English must be understood by the community. **Administrators and teachers have to speak out clearly and say that excellence in English is the anticipated outcome.** They need to describe the reading framework; they must show the relationships between speech, print, and thought; they should point out the Spanish transfer power for English. **In addition, the community can be encouraged to value the preservation of the native language and literacy as needed in a Spanish-English community.** The economic usefulness of the two languages in the stores, the banks, the theatres, and the public agencies in the home community can be highlighted. The need is very real for Spanish language and literacy skills in government, teaching, and business in the international world of today.

Schools may reach out to the community to offer information, as well as to answer the questions coming from community sources through a variety of strategies:

*See Dorothy Legaretta's article in **Schooling and Language Minority Students** for many valuable suggestions in working with parents.

(1) school programs to which the community is invited; (2) newspaper articles covering essential characteristics of the reading plan; (3) distribution of pamphlets describing the scope, sequence, and objectives of the program; (4) speakers' presentations at community activities; (5) celebration of special days and events in which the community participates; (6) parent groups serving as school ambassadors; and (7) radio and television coverage. The best reading plan in the world will not be effective if the school is isolated from the community it serves. The responsibility for good information exchange resides in the school.

The Students
Students from Hispanic families have **all** the needs of **all** students learning to read **any** language. They need rich language opportunities, good teaching, appropriate materials, varied methodologies, and warm support in the classroom. They need to develop good study habits and positive attitudes about themselves and about reading. They arrive at the classroom with the same range of variability in development, maturity, intelligence, experience and motivation as may be found in any group of students. There is no one typical Hispanic student any more than there is **one** typical English-speaking student. Each student is unique and brings to the task of learning to read the personal background of characteristics that belongs solely to him or to her. Often, categories and labels have been assigned to students who come from a language group different from the language of the curriculum. Criteria for assigning labels or categories have been notoriously imprecise and have been very unsatisfactory for making decisions about the kind of reading programs from which the students could derive the most benefit.

A high priority in any consideration of Hispanic students is the necessity of identifying the language proficiencies in listening, speaking, reading, and writing. Another important concern is the previous opportunity for schooling that the students may have enjoyed. The kind of reading instruction in prior settings should be addressed, not only from the point of view of language of instruction (Spanish or English?), but also from an inquiry regarding methodology (synthetic, analytic, eclectic?). The identification of students' strengths and the placement of students in reading instruction to accommodate their functioning levels is readily accomplished in communities where there is a degree of population stability. In schools where the students experience a high rate of school transfer, however, the identification of language and literacy strengths and the placement in appropriate programs are far more difficult. The chart in the appendix (Design for Decision/The Royal Road to Reading) is an attempt to trace the process of identification and placement. The major questions to address include: the determination of the language of the students; the reading or readiness to read status; the use of the two languages; the relative strength or weakness of each language, and the preparation for second language reading.

Students have only **one** given characteristic and that is: they are different from one another. Yet, the provision of appropriate reading instruction for each student will depend upon grouping them for teaching so that their commonalities of instructional needs can be well met despite their differences.

Caveat
The nature of the multiple instructional variables has been mentioned only to encourage teachers everywhere to consider how many critical factors have an impact on reading instruction. These many elements should be explored in much greater depth in the specific settings in which students and teachers are negotiating the serious business of learning how to read. It would be impractical if not impossible to describe all the influences in accurate detail for all school communities. Furthermore, it would be foolish, even dangerous, to attempt to be highly prescriptive in recommending strategies for dealing with these variables. Thoughtful teachers and wise administrators know the importance of identifying these dynamics and of searching creatively to make them work together in the best interests of their students.

References
1. Fishman, Joshua A. and Keller, Gary D. (Editors). **Bilingual Education for Hispanic Students in the United States.** New York: Teachers College, Columbia University, 1982.

2. Fry, Edward. "Graph for Estimating Readability-Extended." **Journal of Reading,** December, 1977.

3. Gilliam, Bettye, Peña, Sylivia C., and Mountain, Lee. **The Reading Teacher.** January, 1980, pp.426-430.

4. **Schooling and Language Minority Students: A Theoretical Framework.** Sacramento, California: California State Department of Education, Office of Bilingual Bicultural Education, 1981.

5. Thonis, Eleanor W. **Teaching Reading to Non-English Speakers.** New York: Collier Macmillan International, 1970.

CHAPTER IX

TEACHING FOR TRANSFER

Transfer of one set of skills to a new situation that may require the same or similar skills is a key construct in teaching and in learning. Transfer of learning means that the students' experiences or their performance on one task exerts some significant influence on future tasks. Such influence may make the subsequent work easier or more skillfully performed; it may make the new task more difficult or more clumsily carried out; or it may have no impact at all. Learning theorists refer to these variations in influence as **positive, negative** or **zero** transfer. Furthermore, psychologists recognize that almost all learning that occurs after the very early years must be influenced to a great extent by previous learnings. Within the context of learning to read two languages, the issue of transfer will raise the questions of

- the principles of skill transfer
- the nature of general and specific transfer
- the variables that influence positive transfer
- the circumstances that ensure avoidance of negative transfer
- provisions for the optimum curriculum design to ensure efficient and effective transfer from Spanish to English.

Principles of Skill Transfer

Transfer of learning, according to theorists, is one of the most important considerations in the educational process. Although there are many indicators to suggest that individuals do apply previously learned skills to new situations, the wonderful way in which transfer occurs is not entirely clear. There are, however, several basic principles that may be examined as a guide to transfer. The doctrine of identical elements, first formulated by Thorndike in 1901, advanced the notion that skills from one activity would transfer to another as long as the critical features of the second task were like those in the first task. Later theorists criticized this view of transfer, and stated that the idea of transfer taking place due to the identical features of two functions or two parts was much too narrow and restricted. Yet, the identical elements theory of transfer does still enjoy considerable respectability and appears very relevant in a comparison of the task similarities and differences of learning to read English after having learned to read Spanish. There are certainly a number of features of both written languages that may be described as identical elements or substantially similar features.

Judd, as early as 1908, had recognized that people appear to generalize from their experiences and to apply such generalizations to new situations. His view of transfer and the views of others who later studied transfer by generalization and principles felt that experiences must be structured in thinking. They noted that **comprehension** of the rule and the **realization** of its **applicability** to the new task were necessary if transfer were to occur. As students see with greater clarity that the reading and writing skills they have acquired in Spanish are governed by certain rules, they begin to understand the rules and their applicability in their native language. When they are faced with generalizing from their experiences in the Spanish reading activities, they may be helped to see the principles that may also apply to the second language. Transfer by generalization and principle involves more than a search for identical elements common to both learnings. This kind of transfer is reasoned, thoughtful transfer.

The Gestalt theorists deny that similarity of content in the two tasks accounts for transfer. Rather, transfer possibilities lie within a pattern of relationships. For example, a competitive, aggressive athlete could be expected to transfer his skills successfully as a businessman because both endeavors require teamwork, coordination of efforts, and aggressiveness in order to succeed. Relationship transfer from Spanish reading to English reading may be observed in the students' perceptions of the role of the teacher as the provider of instruction, and of the responsibility of the student as a learner and as a follower of instructions. The patterns of peer relationships, the status of various school personnel, the textbook as an informational source, and countless other relationships emerge as patterns that apply to both reading programs.

The transfer of attitudes and ideals may be the most essential of all types of transfer. Research in 1910 by Ruediger documented in his studies that neatness training (an ideal) does transfer. Students who have been encouraged to be orderly, organized, and neat in one school subject appear to develop an attitude toward these qualities and this attitude carries over positively to other school subjects. Learning to read requires a reasonably orderly sequence of learning. Developing an organized approach to the reading of Spanish will transfer to the reading of English. The positive feelings toward reading and a confident sense of self represent attitudes that will transfer as a result of good supportive experiences in the classroom. Teachers may be assured that English print will be encountered with enthusiastic efforts and expectations of success if students have felt good about their Spanish language skills.

Sensory-motor transfer takes place on the basis of response similarity. Tasks that require the same response from a learner increase the potential for transfer.

Students who respond in reading and writing through the integration of visual, auditory, and kinesthetic channels have the network of nerves, muscles, and glands working smoothly together to produce the required response. This same sensory-motor integration is needed for the reading and writing acts of both English and Spanish.

These major theories of transfer have been investigated since the turn of the century. They have appeared to stand today as reasonable assumptions advanced to explain the phenomenon of transfer. Transfer by identical elements, by generalization, by Gestalt, by attitude, and by sensory-motor ability provide a strong basis for suggesting guidelines for educational practice. Transfer is best when

- there is similarity in the learning conditions
- there is similarity in the learning task
- there is similarity in the expected student response
- there is opportunity for practice in the first learning
- there are comprehensible connections between first and second learning tasks
- there is clear understanding of the rules or generalizations that can apply to the second learning task.

The manner in which these fundamental principles of transfer are exemplified in the transferability of fluency and literacy skills in Spanish to English are outlined in the next section on the nature of transfer.

The Nature of Skill Transfer

There is good reason to expect that skills in reading will transfer in the general and in the specific sense. The visual stimuli in the print of any language represent the speech of that language community. The expectation that the written symbols stand for the spoken symbols is an understanding basic to learning to read in Spanish and in English. At a very early stage in their development, most students have this knowledge. Transfer theorists have noted that there is potential for transfer when there are identical or similar elements present in both tasks. These language-specific features are present in the shared alphabet, the common directionality, and the sensory-motor skills in both languages. The names of the letters are pronounced differently, but their formation in Spanish is identical to the writing system of English and will need no extended teaching for effective transfer. The conventions of the written Spanish require that the symbols be placed across the page in a left-to-right direction. As print proceeds, the writing flows from the top to the bottom of the page. This same directional movement is the order of the English writing system. In terms of the neurological organization of eye and hand, no accommodation or change is needed as students move from Spanish to English. The tracking of the eye from left to right, from top to bottom, the coordination of eye and hand, and the control of fine muscle movement are identical requirements of both Spanish and English. Unlike Asian languages, which are read from top to bottom, or some Mideastern languages, which may be read from right to left, there is no new sensory-motor requirement for the students to learn and to practice. The figure-ground skills, too, transfer as students will have had ample opportunity to perceive background and figure in their Spanish reading. The figure may come out of the ground in a different arrangement in English, but the general awareness of what constitutes figure and ground is already part of the students' perceptions. The need to pay careful attention to visual detail will have been an important teaching in Spanish. Students should have had abundant exposure to the letters that may cause reversals; the b's, d's, p's, q's or inversions; n's, u's, m's, w's. They will have had to note the details of **marcas diacriticas** in **lleno, llenó; cayo, cayó.** Words that look very much like one another — **conmigo, contigo; ello, ella** — will have been carefully differentiated. These skills of observing letters and words carefully in their particular environments will transfer as a general skill in attention to visual detail. The visual perception and visual discrimination skills follow ordinarily when students have been trained to notice the fine differences in letter and word formation. The sequencing of visual forms is transferable in the sense of a general awareness of the need for consistency in order. However, the specific ordering of letters in spelling and of words in syntactical patterns will become easier as the specific order of English becomes more familiar through specific practice in English.

Auditory skills, too, have good potential for transfer. The skill of screening out competing stimuli in the auditory ground and of attending to the speech sounds as the figure has been mastered by students. The sharpness of auditory perception, auditory discrimination, and auditory sequencing, of course, increases with the comprehensibility of the stimuli. If Hispanic students have been enjoying oral English in comfortable, comprehensible lessons, then they are well on their way to effective processing of the English sound system.

The spatial organization needed for both languages, as has been mentioned previously, should have been very well developed and very well practiced by the time that the students are coming to grips with formal instruction in the English writing system. The limitations of space on a page, margins, lines, and other spatial constraints of writing are the same for both Spanish and English. No new skills are needed to manage spatial integration, orientation, or sensory-motor organization.

The sensory-motor transfer from Spanish to English may be summarized in the following chart:

POTENTIAL FOR TRANSFER FROM SPANISH TO ENGLISH
SENSORY-MOTOR TRANSFER

Visual Skills	Language Specific Skill Transfer	Language General Skill Transfer
Figure-ground		X
Attention to detail		X
*Perception	X	X
*Discrimination	X	X
Memory	X	
Sequencing		X
Eye-hand coordination		X
Fine muscle control		X
Auditory Skills		
Figure-ground		X
*Perception	X	X
*Discrimination	X	X
Memory	X	
Sequencing		X
Spatial Skills		
Left-to-right orientation		X
Top-to-bottom organization		X
Spatial integration		X

*These visual and auditory skills have elements of **general** transferability from Spanish to English but improve with additional practice in the English forms. Discrimination and perception in English are **refined** with **specific** teaching for skill transfer.

The common features of both writing systems promote skill transfer consistent with the learning principle of transfer by identical elements. English and Spanish use an alphabetic system of writing, and both use the same letters from the Roman alphabet. There are a few minor variations, but essentially, the alphabet of Spanish has great applicability to written English. There are a number of sound-symbol associations shared, and many of these connections transfer, but the phonics skills of each language are very different. The sound-symbol relationships do require specific ear training and guided practice in recognizing the auditory-visual associations. There are several generalizable skills from the punctuation and capitalization requirements of Spanish that transfer easily to English. There is common logic in the organization of beginning and ending thoughts as signaled by the marks of punctuation at the end of sentences. The new thought is cued by the capital letter. The differences in specific rules of capitalization and/or punctuation are necessary to learn for English, but the logic is universal and transfers readily. The general and specific transfer potential from the features of written Spanish are listed in the chart that follows:

WRITING SYSTEM TRANSFER

	Language Specific Skill Transfer	Language General Skill Transfer
Alphabet		X
*Sound-symbol connections	X	X
*Capitalization	X	X
*Punctuation	X	X
Spatial Conventions		X

*Both general and specific language transfer may be expected, but the differences will need to be addressed and practiced in phonics, capitalization, and punctuation. The general understanding of relationships and functions will transfer as an intellectual skill.

Multiple skills in reading can be carried to English by principle and generalization transfer. Reading as a process of gaining meaning from written material has enormously rich potential for transfer from Spanish to English. The understanding that speech can be represented by print; that concepts of words, phrases, sentences and paragraphs are the same; and that reading comprehension is thinking in any language are all general language transfers. The rule-governed aspect of reading and the speech-print connections have elements of both general and specific transfer possibilities. These transfer elements are given in the chart that follows:

PRINCIPLE AND GENERALIZATION TRANSFER

	Language Specific Skill Transfer	Language General Skill Transfer
Understanding that print represents speech		X
Concepts of words, phrases, sentences, paragraphs		X
Comprehension as thinking		X
main idea		X
sequence of ideas		X
supportive details		X
inferencing		X
predicting outcomes		X
drawing conclusions		X
seeing cause and effect		X
distinguishing fact from fantasy		X
recognizing propaganda		X
Rule-governed aspects (morphology, grammar, syntax)	X	X
Speech-print connections	X	X

The intellectual skills developed as students have learned to read Spanish transfer completely because the same mental activity is involved in reading both languages. Rules governing English morphology, syntax, and grammar must be taught specifically. However, the understanding that written language operates according to rules and that the rules share commonalities as well as differences will transfer. The written code as a representation of the spoken one, too, has its share of common and different features. Teachers will need to introduce and offer practice in these contrasts from Spanish and English.

There is an affective dimension of learning to read that should be considered along with the cognitive and sensory-motor skills. Students' characteristic behavior in the classroom influences greatly their achievement. Their sense of self-worth, also, may have a significant impact on their success or failure as readers. Good habits, positive attitudes, and self-confidence contribute immensely to fluency and literacy in school and in life. The appropriate classroom behavior, good study habits, and organized approaches to learning tasks are non-cognitive skills that transfer. The sense of competence as a reader and writer of Spanish will certainly transfer as students undertake the reading and writing in English, their second language. Transfer of habits and attitudes are summarized in the chart below:

TRANSFER OF HABITS AND ATTITUDES

	Language Specific Skill Transfer	Language General Skill Transfer
Non-cognitive skills		
attention		X
listening		X
concentration		X
persistence		X
task completion		X
possessing specific study skills		X
Self-esteem skills		
being literate		X
feeling capable		X
achieving		X
believing in one's ability		X
having specific competencies		X

The reminder to students that they are competent, organized learners with literacy skills in Spanish is appreciated. Students like to hear that they are capable and successful. Attitudes and habits transfer as general language skills.

Negative Transfer From Spanish to English

Negative transfer occurs when the performance on the first task inhibits or detracts from performance on the second. Negative transfer may result when students are expected to make a new response to the same stimulus. For example, Hispanic students may pronounce the ten-cent coin, **dime,** in two syllables — **dee-may** — the word they have learned to associate with the command form of the verb **decir** — to say. If the error is merely a pronunciation one, the negative transfer is using the sound-symbol connection of Spanish as a response to the same stimulus in English. However, if they also transfer the meaning of **dime** from Spanish, they may further confuse themselves. The concept of negative transfer has greater application to interference that may occur between the two languages as spoken because of differences in the patterns of intonation and stress and in the contrastive sound and structural systems. English interrogative sentences do not carry a rising inflection as high as Spanish questions. The Hispanic student may, therefore, not recognize that a question is being asked. The double negative permitted (even required) in statements in Spanish may carry over into speech and create errors in English. These, and many more of the oral features of Spanish, may act in an interfering way when the students are generating English spontaneously. Negative transfer to the reading of English, however, is not so great a problem. Teachers must remember that reading is a receptive act like listening. Just as students are capable of listening to English and are able to understand most of what is said long before they are productive talkers themselves, students often can read passages in English and gain the essential meaning.

There are, of course, some stumbling blocks that may be strewn in the path as a matter of negative transfer, but if teachers will observe certain safeguards, these difficulties may be avoided. A few guidelines to assist teachers are listed below:

- Offer practice in **silent** reading in English.
- Check comprehension at reasonable intervals through a variety of students' short responses, picture selections, checklists.
- Introduce idiomatic words or expressions ahead of time and explain their non-literal or unusual meanings in the context of the written material.
- Tell the students before they read about any particularly convoluted structure or syntactical pattern that could obscure meaning.
- Alert the students to false cognates and warn them that although they look like Spanish words, they carry different meanings.
- Avoid the over-emphasis on sound-symbol connections. They are not a high priority in silent reading. Help the students avoid comprehension errors that may be caused by using Spanish responses closest to English — e.g., **tin** for **thin; bean** for **beam.** These sounds cannot appear in Spanish. There

is no **th** and **m** will never be found at the **end** of a word.* If these are read silently as **bean** for **beam** or **tin** for **thin,** then the students will not understand the passage.

- Deal immediately with occasions of negative transfer. Be straightforward in telling students that the response was a logical one based on their previous learnings **but,** unfortunately, it did not apply in this instance. Then, explain the correct response.
- Collect in the teacher's log examples of negative transfer as these errors occur, and review the more serious ones from time to time.

Conditions for Best Transfer from Spanish to English
There are several conditions that clearly suggest the best possibilities for transfer of literacy skills. Among the most significant considerations are these:

- the strength of the original learning
- the role of meaning
- the importance of generalizations
- the establishment of effective habits
- the nature of emotional responses
- the sense of self-confidence.

The creation of a classrooom climate in which optimum transfer may take place is the challenge for teachers at any level. They can consciously and purposefully teach for transfer.

Research on transfer of learning has been very consistent in sustaining the view that only strong learning transfers. The strength of the skills in the original task determines in large measure the extent of transfer to the second task. Special efforts should be made in the initial learning period to ensure skill mastery. When teachers are planning to introduce new concepts, unfamiliar language, or unknown skills, they must be crystal clear in their instructions, and must offer very thorough practice. The potential for positive transfer is increased by opportunities for in-depth learning at the beginning. After students have moved well into their reading program and have developed a good sense of what reading is all about, such emphasis on thoroughness may not be needed. If teachers plan the instructional program so that skills are sequenced from the simple to the complex, from the easy to the difficult, from the known to the unknown, then students will be able to build on the earlier strengths and will probably need fewer practice sessions. The lower, enabling skills at earlier levels are reinforced along with the practice opportunities of higher level skills. Teachers should keep in mind that

*Except **álbum**

250

weak learning does **not** transfer, and may even cause negative transfer effects. The critical concept for positive transfer is this: **Only strong skills transfer.**

Meaningful material has much greater promise of transfer. There is better retention of information if it makes sense than if it is lacking in comprehensibility. In initial reading, the written code is often meaningless for many students. The learning of isolated letters, syllables, words, and other fragments of written language is unlikely to be put together into a comprehensible whole. Teachers who use a synthetic approach should be very careful that the pieces are put together to make sense to the students as they are acquiring the skills of how the writing system works. Teachers should continually check for understanding of material as the hoped-for transfer is occurring. The likelihood of transfer is always greater when students understand how the two tasks are related and what characteristics or attributes of the first task are held in common by both tasks.

If expected transfer is anticipated on the basis of the students' finding relationships and recognizing principles or generalizations, students will need many opportunities to clear up any lack of clarity that may occur. Learning theorists suggest that a variety of examples, in contrast to many non-examples, is helpful for students in discovering and understanding an applicable rule. When students are encouraged to find the rule that applies, after sufficient encounters with material representing common concepts, they grow in their abilities to learn. Opportunities and practice in making generalizations lead students to what has been often referred to as **learning how to learn.**

Habits transfer, as teachers so well know. Unfortunately, bad habits will transfer as readily as will good ones. If students are fortunate enough to be encouraged early in their Spanish reading instruction to pay attention, to listen, to organize the time, to take care of their materials, to take pride in a task completed well, then the practice in these good habits for learning will make them strong enough to transfer. Good habits accrue to students as they find satisfaction and pleasure in what they are doing. Teachers promote good habits through social rewards and appreciation of students' efforts. Students who may need help in improving study habits may benefit from a redirection of their energies, appropriate models, and occasionally, consequences suitable for the situation.

Emotional responses, too, transfer. If pleasure and joy have been engendered in the Spanish reading program, these positive feelings will transfer to the English reading program. If, on the other hand, students have become angry and frustrated in their attempts to read Spanish, these same negative emotional responses will transfer to English reading attempts. It is so very important for students to feel good about themselves and their accomplishments. The negative impact of anxiety and failure is noted by many researchers. Teachers are wise to create a learning environment that is safe and secure for all students. The reading program that does not assault the ego of students and does not demand skills that have not yet been acquired is a program planned carefully to take students' feelings into account. Feeling successful and competent about reading in Spanish will transfer fully to feeling competent and successful in reading English.

When teachers think about the development of self-esteem and self-confidence as a powerful motivating force in learning, they need to appreciate that the students' native language is a part of their sense of identity. The language of their families is part of their heritage and has been acquired in the warmth and intimacy of their homes. The sounds of Spanish are part of their reality and are essential to knowing who they are. A reading curriculum can be designed to recognize the importance of these influences on the character formation of students. Then, the **self** is enhanced, sustained, and valued. **Self-esteem transfers totally.** If students can read, they can read! They know they are literate in Spanish and appreciate themselves for this accomplishment.

Teachers can maximize their students' transfer of skills from Spanish to English reading by arranging instruction in accordance with the established principles of transfer of learning. Strong introductory skills will be guaranteed if the teacher will do the following:

- Spend adequate time in the initial stages of Spanish reading by
  - (a) developing clarity of concepts mediated by Spanish
  - (b) promoting strong listening comprehension skills in Spanish
  - (c) expanding the vocabulary and the control of structure of Spanish
  - (d) providing visual, auditory, kinesthetic, and spatial opportunities.
- Teach the basic decoding skills of Spanish and give sufficient practice in
  - (a) associating speech and print relationships
  - (b) acquiring the names of the letters of the alphabet
  - (c) learning the regular and irregular sound-symbol connections
  - (d) knowing the system of diphthongs
  - (e) recognizing the form and function of consonant clusters
  - (f) perceiving the limited ways in which words can end.
- Avoid language confusion at the early levels by
  - (a) offering only informal oral English opportunites
  - (b) keeping the acquisition of English natural and consistent with students' developmental level

(c) using the languages in separate contexts

(d) making careful provision for second language comprehension in English during all activities.

When students have acquired the word recognition, comprehension, and study skills of the Spanish reading program, strong reading skills from Spanish to these same skills in English will be possible if the teacher will do the following:

- Give thorough practice in using the many strategies for unlocking new words in reading Spanish by
  (a) acquiring the phonics clues to be found in speech-print connections
  (b) learning the structural signals of words and word patterns
  (c) interpreting the information provided in pictures
  (d) using the system of syllabication
  (e) watching for the placement of diacritical marks.
- Teach the techniques and guide the practice through which the students may make sense of what they read in Spanish by
  (a) developing skills in **literal** comprehension
  (b) learning to read between the lines for **interpretive** comprehension
  (c) reading creatively for expansion of ideas
  (d) using reading as a means to improved thinking skills.
- Prevent premature introduction to the second language word recognition, comprehension, and study skills in English by
  (a) keeping clear of **simultaneous** reading programs in Spanish and English
  (b) developing sound criteria for timing transfer opportunities and teaching in the reading of English
  (c) reassuring students and their parents that they are building a strong background for English
  (d) using native language reading skills for content areas as resources permit
  (e) encouraging encounters with the English writing system on the basis of what students hear, and understand in speech, and what they can see and read in print
  (f) maintaining the **two** writing systems in separate contexts.

Transfer of learning is a very exciting prospect for reading teachers and may provide highly satisfactory outcomes for both the teachers and the students who are on their way to excellence in English. The English reading program will be abundantly successful if the teacher will stress these qualities in the classroom:

1. effective habits — for non-cognitive transfer
2. positive feeling — for emotional transfer

3. rich meanings — for cognitive transfer
4. inductive discoveries — for principle transfer
5. optimistic attitudes — for attitude transfer

The teacher improves greatly all transfer potentiality by pointing out the specific points of transfer and by reminding the students of how much skill they bring to English reading.

Criteria for Transfer from Spanish to English Reading
Teachers are interested in the nature and conditions of skill transfer. They certainly need to have a clear understanding of transfer principles. Yet, the most pressing concern that the teachers have is not a theoretical one. They want to ask the questions: **When** should transfer be promoted and **how** can teachers be sure that students are ready to transfer skills. Teachers want to establish firm guidelines for transfer and wish to construct reasonable criteria upon which decisions relative to transfer may be made. Often, the timing of transfer may be dictated by conditions and criteria that have been shaped by circumstances outside the classroom and may be beyond the teachers' control. Legislation may define the time allowed for native language literacy instruction. Resources available in specific instructional settings may restrict or expand time frames. Constraints of local policy or philosophies may determine the timing of language transfer. The shift from Spanish to English may take place as a result of numerous elements to be found both inside and outside of the school. The development of the yardstick, the criteria, by which students are placed in **formal** second language instruction in English must consider these many factors sensitively and cautiously. Since the success of the reading program depends on the several influences, none can be ignored or set aside.

Ideally, criteria for transfer from Spanish to English reading instruction should minimally include these considerations of first language skill:

- the oral fluency in Spanish
- literacy skills in Spanish
- the level of achievement in subject matter
- the age and/or grade placement of the students.

Students who have learned to read in Spanish should be able to demonstrate reading, writing, and spelling skills commensurate with their grade placement. These students should also be handling the content areas according to the basic requirements of students who are their English-speaking peers in comparable content classes. Students should be able to demonstrate that they have the concepts, the knowledge, and the skills to achieve at the same level expected of all students in the assigned grades. Listening comprehension and oral expression in Spanish should be developed well. Their vocabulary, control of structure, functional grammar, and storehouse of meanings should document the students' verbal abilities as fluent speakers of their native language when compared to students of the same chronological ages and educational opportunities. Because transfer of skill does demand ability to abstract in many instances, the timing of transfer should include a concern for the stage of development of the students' thinking skills.

The criteria must consider, in addition to the native language proficiencies, the second language competence that has been developing as a result of formal oral English instruction, informal English language classrooms, and English language contacts in play at school and in the neighborhood. Teachers need to evaluate the extent to which Spanish speakers are approaching accuracy in using the new sounds of English. They will want to note the control of English structures and will be concerned about the size of the basic English vocabulary that students have acquired.

The specific readiness to read English, in the formal sense, is yet another variable to be examined. Teachers will wish to look at the kinds of readiness activities that have been offered to train auditory skills in English, for improving visual and spatial skills generally, and for building the background of classroom language needed to follow instruction in English. Teachers will also want to check up on interest, motivation, and attitude toward reading in English. The several dimensions of the criteria to be applied as the standards for transfer include native language competence, second language skills, and readiness factors. Because these criteria will be constructed differently as diverse school and community requirements shape a reading curriculum, the criteria for transfer can be stated only in general terms. Consider these essentials:

- the oral proficiency in Spanish.
- the literacy level in Spanish.
- the achievement in content areas.
- the ability to use logical thought.
- the production of the sounds of English.
- the receptive and expressive vocabularies of English.
- the control of simple English structures.
- the specific readiness and preparation for English print.
- the interest and motivation to make the transfer from Spanish to English.

As teachers weigh these factors that comprise the criteria, they will have to decide the **specific** measures by which fluency, literacy, and achievement levels may be best evaluated. The school staff will have to agree on the standards and will need to cooperate fully in establishing and in following through on meeting the criteria.

Caveat

As powerful as the principle of transfer of learning is, transfer cannot ever be assumed to occur without proper teaching and guidance. A few students seem to make what Jerome Bruner has called "an intuitive leap" and appear to see the relationships that exist between Spanish and English on their own. Most of them, however, need to have transfer possibilities pointed out to them at critical stages in the English reading program. Enthusiasm and confidence in transfer principles are important qualities for teachers, but they are not enough to ensure that students will make the best of transferability of skills. Teachers must know how to make transfer happen by assisting students to recognize transfer possibilities and by consciously working transfer teaching into the curriculum whenever it seems appropriate and wise. Teachers are the best resource for the transferability of skills as they arrange instruction for transfer to take place and **tell** the students about skill transfer whenever a possibility exists.

References

1. Deese, James. **The Psychology of Learning.** New York: McGraw Hill Book Company, 1958.

2. Kingsley, Toward L. and Garry, Ralph. **The Nature and Conditions of Learning.** Englewood Cliffs, N.J: Prentice-Hall, Inc., 1957.

3. Morse, William C. and Wingo, G. Max. **Psicología aplicada a la enseñanza.** Mexico: Editorial Pax-Mexico, Librería Carlos Cesarman, S.A., 1967.

4. Smith, Henry P. and Dechant Emerald V. **Psychology in Teaching Reading.** Englewood Cliffs, N.J: Prentice-Hall, Inc., 1961.

CHAPTER X

EXCELLENCE IN ENGLISH

¡No cabe duda! There is no doubt about the need for the very best language and literacy skills for all students. The Hispanic student in the United States or in other countries where English is the majority language must become fluent and literate in English. The educational objectives of reading instruction must place competence in English at the very top of the list. The students' instruction in reading must be planned to take into account the variables of age, experience, first language level, previous schooling, and English language proficiency. The transfer potential of reading skills along the way must be identified and made the most of whenever appropriate for the students. While students are learning to read and write in Spanish, they must be given the chance to use their literacy skills in the content areas of mathematics, science, social sciences, and other school subjects. Academic achievement can be advanced through the stronger language in both oral and written activities. Concept formation, reasoning skills, and problem-solving abilities are fostered through the improvement of language as a precision instrument of thought. Culturally relevant material, positive communication with parents, and suitably paced teaching combine to make the reading classroom a more comfortable, interesting learning environment. Reading instruction moves from the known to the unknown according to sound learning principles. Success rather than failure and discouragement can be realized by the majority of the students.

The English-Spanish Connection
Within the context of reading, writing, and spelling, teachers should ask: What has been learned in Spanish? This question can be answered for students at each phase of the reading program. During the readiness period the students have been growing rapidly in their understanding of the world around them. They have practiced the essential perceptual, motor, and spatial skills. They have expanded their listening and speaking vocabularies. They have been introduced to the school behaviors necessary for learning to read. They are beginning to build good work habits of paying attention, concentrating on specific skills, completing assigned tasks, and discovering the routine of the school. At this point in their readiness development, English language instruction is oral, natural, and relatively informal. Structured readiness materials and activities in English are **not** recommended during the period of preparation for Spanish print. A far more effective use of both student and teacher time is the time spent in Spanish. At this level, students need the thoughtful teaching of concepts and the careful arrangements

of pre-reading skill practice, without facing the possible problems present in the intrusion of readiness activities in another language.

When students are introduced to the Spanish writing system, the letter names, the sounds presented by the letters, and the connection between visual and auditory symbols represent useful knowledge and skills. This understanding of the code has provided students with an alphabet, an awareness of writing based on an alphabetic principle, and the letter formation practice. Depending upon the methodology applied to introduce speech-print correspondences, the students will acquire useful information regarding the function and form of a symbolic code. A key question that the teacher will ask is: What can be used in English? There are both rich promises and unexpected pitfalls in the transfer of decoding skills. Students may be expected to use the abilities to form letters, the knowledge of the Spanish alphabet, and **some** of the sound-symbol associations in their English decoding activities, if these are part of the reading approach in English. The comprehension of phonic principles and the knowledge of how to apply a phonic generalization may also be very helpful. The transfer to English should be cautious and slow at this juncture because the students may not have had sufficient practice in connected written discourse to make the most of transferability of skills.

When the students are well into their reading program and are learning a variety of strategies to assist them in recognizing words, they can bring every skill practiced in the recognition of Spanish words to the word recognition lessons of English. Sight vocabulary activities demand the same response of remembering the visual appearance of words. Phonic analysis as a word recognition strategy has several applications to English, but is one skill that has to be cautiously applied and carefully monitored. Transfer that is **too** indiscriminate may lead non-native speakers into error. The same visual symbols may have differences in sound-symbol correspondence. Also, though the phonics clues may help students **call** the word, its meaning may not be understood. The use of phonics in English reading may be very effective for Hispanic students who are auditory learners and for those who have strong phonic skills in Spanish and **oral** control of the sounds of English.

Other word recognition skills have good potential for transfer to English reading. Spanish and English morphology have much in common. The two systems of root words and affixes share many identical prefixes and suffixes. Other words are formed with variations that are very close and readily recognized from language to language. The skill of analyzing the structure of words is a most useful one that can be applied to discover new words in English. The recognition of two words that make up a single compound word will have been practiced in Spanish. Compound words are much more numerous in English than they are in Spanish, but the skill of recognizing the single words that go together to create a new word is exactly the same. As in Spanish, the teacher has to be certain that the students have meanings stored for the single English words before they put them together in a new word with a new meaning. The division of words into syllables in order to find out what the word is can also be transferred with some limitations to English. The concept of a syllable, the awareness of a syllable as a component part of a word, and the role of a vowel sound in a syllable are examples of good transfer by principle. However, the syllable systems of English and Spanish differ in many ways, and teachers should take care to point out the similarities and differences so that students may make the best of their knowledge and skills in syllabication as they come to English.

Yet another excellent means of recognizing words that has great power of transfer to English is the habit of searching the context of written discourse for the identity and meaning of specific words. Good habits are formed during the Spanish reading lessons in which students are encouraged to look at the unknown word in its surroundings of other words. The practice of finding meaning and of making sense through context clues is the very same process in English.

Reading comprehension is thinking. All of the mental activity the students will have enjoyed in discovering the main idea, the details, the sequences, and other explicitly stated information in a written passage will be precisely the same in English. The interpretive skills of reading in inferencing, drawing conclusions, seeing relationships, and recognizing emotions involve the identical thought processes. Students who are able to think and to use their thinking skills in comprehending Spanish need only to learn the written code and to develop meaningful oral referents in English. Then, their thinking strategies for both literal and interpretive comprehension may be transferred totally. Transfer of skills in the comprehension of English depends on strong thinking skills **in** Spanish, well-developed **oral** English, and good word recognition skills in written English.

Students have been learning about speech-print connections as they have been reading, writing, and spelling in Spanish. They have been growing in their sensitivity to how oral forms are presented as written ones. They have acquired a certain degree of comprehension of the grammatical system. Even if their teachers have not considered grammar rules important, the students will have developed an intuitive grasp of many features of the oral-written forms. They will be confident in recognizing and using plurals. They will have a clear concept of agreement. They will have learned to manage a highly complex verb system. The understanding of possessive forms, pronouns, and shortened words will have become a part of their knowledge of how these elements of language are organized in both speech and print. The rule-governed aspect of language has been internalized and may operate on a functional, automatic level. The orthographic features of punctuation and capitalization, too, have become part of their skills in seeing how oral forms look in writing. These oral-written connections have strong generalizability to English. The concept of number, the formation of plurals, the agreement requirements, the pronoun system, and the mechanics of written form have much in common with English. Of course, there are many differences as well. There is powerful transfer to be gained from a Spanish language program that has taken the time to build some analysis of the language, if such activities have been considered appropriate for the students. In classrooms where students have been encouraged to abstract and to generalize from language, these students have been learning to reason inductively. The speech-print connections and the oral-written forms of English may be approached in a very similar manner as students transfer their reasoning skills to the new writing system.

The development of a reading vocabulary in Spanish will have provided an excellent foundation for the acquisition of a strong reading vocabulary in English. Many of the words will look like words the students already know. There will be **thousands** of cognates, words that have the same or almost the same spelling. There will be **hundreds** of words formed by the very same or almost the same prefixes and suffixes. Students will have learned about homonyms, synonyms, and antonyms and can be encouraged to apply these concepts in the expansion of their vocabulary skills in English. The transfer of vocabulary to English is **in part** a function of the richness of experiences available and encoded in Spanish; transfer is also dependent upon the importance given vocabulary development in **both** languages. Effective transfer of word knowledge takes place when strong, well-stocked vocabularies in Spanish are perceived as being just as valuable as the growing vocabulary in English.

In summary, reading in any language is thinking. An educated person who is fluent and literate in **any** language **is** an educated person. The most powerful transferability of skills takes place when a fluent, literate, educated individual brings abundant knowledge, strong skills, and positive attitudes to a second language. For Hispanic students, effective transfer to English is commensurate with their knowledge, skills, and attitudes.

The Best of Biliteracy
The central message of the nine previous chapters has been that Hispanic students may be best brought to excellence in English reading by way of their fluency and literacy in Spanish. As a bonus for having traveled this route, students will have **added** English, the second language, and literacy at **no loss** to their Spanish. The preservation of the home language makes it possible for the students to continue securely in the circle of family and friends, which is essential to their emotional growth and well-being. The addition of strong English language skills ensures that the students will deal effectively with the demands of the world beyond their homes and neighborhood. The second language competence is greater because of the first language proficiency. Though this book has addressed a reading plan designed to develop reading skills in two languages, it is not suggesting that teachers offer the two plans of reading instruction as simultaneous programs or as duplicate ones. Rather, it is recommending that the reading plan for Hispanic students be organized to develop **first** the fluency and literacy skills in Spanish. Then, learning to read English becomes a matter of **transferability** of these skills. Mastery of the writing system of English by literate Hispanic students **is not** learning to read **again**. It **is learning** to apply those skills already acquired to a new written code that shares many commonalities and differences with the known one. To accomplish this reasonable goal of biliteracy, the schools may need to re-examine the traditional English reading instruction as ordinarily provided for Hispanic students. Schools may wish to consider a revision of the scope and sequence of skills and the language used as the medium of initial instruction. Research clearly indicates that stronger English language skills can be built on a foundation of solid Spanish language development. A very brief summary of the applicable research findings follows. Readers who would like to pursue these issues in greater depth should consult the references listed at the end of this chapter.

The Research
Researchers who have investigated the several models of schooling for language minority students conclude that academic success is dependent upon language proficiency. High-level skills in the first language and in English predict the maximum benefits from instruction. (Cummins, 1979, 1981; Lambert, 1978; Swain, 1979; Skutnabb-Kangas and Toukomaa, 1976; Legaretta-Marcaida, 1981).

The informal acquisition of language in the ordinary activities of living outside of the school may not be sufficient for the demands of formal instruction in a classroom. Language that is understandable in the context of personal exchange is normally acquired by everyone. Language skills, however, that are learned through formal instruction in the school represent a different dimension of language. (Genesee, 1979; Cummins, 1980; Dulay and Burt, 1978).

First language skills provide comprehensible access to the content areas and promote academic growth at a normal rate. The language minority students do not fall behind their English-speaking peers because the concepts, ideas, and information necessary to academic achievement are available to them. School adjustment and sense of self-worth are positive. (Kaminsky, 1977; Downing, 1978; Cummins, 1979, 1980, 1981). Second language skills in English grow as a result of activities that make sense to students and the motivation to learn. (Krashen, 1976, 1978, 1981; Legaretta, 1979; Terrell, 1977; Saville-Troike, 1978).

Learning to read in the first language is influenced by a number of factors that have been studied. The findings suggest that normal children by the age of five or six years bring to the school a background of basic first language oral skills. There are many elements in the school and in the home that have an impact for better or for worse on the attitudes of students toward learning. Language stimulation in the family and in the classroom by teachers who know the students' language is a very strong force in determining first language development and second language acquisition. Personal variables of age, maturity, values, attitudes, intelligence, and motivation may be expected to vary the results of instruction. (Lapkin, 1979, Garcia, 1979; Wells, 1979; Merino, 1979; Ramirez and Politzer, 1975).

The major implications for teaching reading that may be drawn from the research on first and second language learning follow.

- Reading instruction for Hispanic students should be provided in Spanish.
- Sufficient time should be given to the development of excellent literacy skills in Spanish.
- Teachers who are proficient in Spanish should guide the reading instruction.
- Culturally authentic materials to support reading for information and for pleasure should be available in the school.
- Literacy programs in English and in Spanish should be separate plans.
- Comprehension of written material at all levels and in both languages should be the essential objectives of instruction.
- The written symbol system must be made sensible to students through the provision of referents from the students' reality.
- Grouping practices must be consistent with the goals of reading instruction.
- Parents should be encouraged to use Spanish in the home for high-quality parent-child relationships.

- Community and parents need to understand the rationale for the reading program and appreciate the ultimate outcome of biliteracy.
- Teachers, administrators and other school personnel must have the information and training necessary for the reading program as modified.
- Transfer to English reading should follow the principles of transfer of learning.

The Learning Triangle
Reading instruction for **all** students must promote the language and literacy skills that will ensure the highest achievement in school subjects. Access to the many content areas throughout the grades is made possible when students can listen to the teacher and comprehend the substance of the teacher's classroom presentation. The assigned tasks in textbooks must be read and understood. Students' responses to instruction are expected to be oral and/or written. Both language modalities demand a high degree of competence in expressive language. Teachers at all levels of instruction agree that well-developed skills in speech and in print are necessary for success in school. To comprehend oral or written language, students must be engaged in thinking. This mental activity involves remembering, associating, judging, generalizing, and any number of other cognitive processes. Students, then, must **receive** oral and written language as they listen and read; they must also **express** oral and written language as they speak and write. Supporting all language and literacy activities is thought. The essential triangle for learning can be represented as follows:

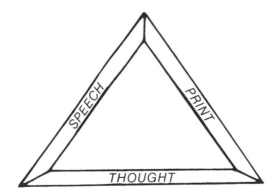

Hispanic students who have been provided with reading instruction in Spanish and in English have two linguistic codes by which their thoughts may be processed. Their learning triangle may be represented in this manner:

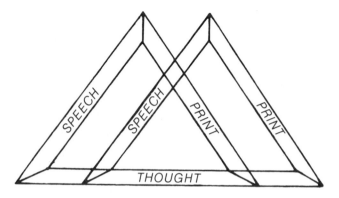

Thus, fluency and literacy in the two different languages are bonded to the same base of the learning triangle. The strength of the linkage among three essentials — speech, print, and thought — is determined in large measure by the quality of the educational program. If students have few opportunities to receive instruction that will enhance their first language skills, that language remains a very poor organizer of thought. If students are rushed prematurely into the print of the second language before the oral referents have been established, the tenuous connection between English speech and English print will **not** serve thinking well. The challenge for teachers is to arrange instruction that will promote the improvement of speech, the acquisition of print, and the development of thought. Strong and lasting bonds must be forged among these mutually dependent relationships.

The Student Differences
As has been stated frequently in this book, excellence in English must be the ultimate goal for students who are living, growing, and learning in a country where English is the majority language. For Hispanic students, this excellence is more likely to accrue to those students who have Spanish fluency and literacy to bring to the acquisition and learning of English, the second language. The road to speaking, reading, and writing English can be best traveled in the vehicle of Spanish, which has opened the gates to the field of knowledge. The indispensable ingredient in the teaching-learning transaction is the transferability of knowledge, skills, and attitudes.

Reading instruction for the Hispanic student who is enrolled in an educational setting where English is the language of the curriculum, like reading instruction in **any** language, in **any** classroom, must be of high quality. Success for these students depends upon a competent, caring teacher who knows how to use appropriate materials and suitable methods. Opportunities for fluency and literacy will vary greatly according to the kind of reading program available to the students at different developmental stages. Preliterate, literate, or illiterate Spanish-speaking students obviously will need reading programs that are organized, paced, and presented differently.

Preliterate students who are young must have a reading program that cooperates with their growth and development. Reading and writing are neurological tasks of middle childhood, and students cannot be rushed regardless of the language of instruction.

Teachers will need **time** and **patience** in building the background of skills during the readiness period. Although the end in view is also fluency and literacy in English, teachers will find that more concepts made meaningful through Spanish and larger vocabularies in Spanish ultimately enhance the readiness to read English. The young students are engaging in thinking and are improving their native language skills as an instrument of their thought. Furthermore, because so much of the early learning during the preparation for print period has potential for transfer, there is little to be gained by a casual treatment of these developmental tasks in Spanish and a rush to English reading readiness. During pre-reading activities, students have the chance to explore the magic of written symbols and to discover the connections between the auditory and visual symbol system. All teachers expect that normal students **will learn to read** and to **write.** The expectation from the students' point of view is that they will read and write the language that they speak. Both teachers and students have a better chance of meeting their expectations when the instructional program is arranged in that logical sequence. For many preliterate students who are older, there is the same requirement for readiness activities designed to prepare them for formal instruction. Some of the visual, motor, and perceptual preparation may not be necessary, but many of the tasks will be the same. For these students, a major concern will be the suitability of content to accommodate more mature interests and experiences.

At times, students enter an English language curriculum with partially developed literacy skills in Spanish. These students may have had rich opportunities to learn to read and write in a Hispanic country, or in some other setting where Spanish has been used as the medium of instruction. It will be important for the teachers to determine the level of reading achievement in Spanish and to assess the readiness to read English. The criteria for transfer from Spanish to English are the same as those applied to all students. The students should be encouraged to continue strengthening their native fluency and literacy while adding English.

Unfortunately, many Hispanic students who enroll in school are functionally illiterate. Some have inadequate reading skills because they have had inappropriate instruction or limited opportunities for schooling. There are many such students whose reading programs have sadly consisted of bits and pieces of the Spanish and English writing systems. Other students may have experienced a high rate of school transfer, and many have lost out on a proper sequence of skill development. A few students may be intellectually slow and may have had serious problems in learning. Whatever the reason for the students' failure to learn to read, the reading teacher must take an inventory of oral and written skills in both Spanish and English and use the obtained data to organize a suitable program. The timing of transfer will be different for Hispanics in the diverse groups — the preliterate, the literate, and the functionally illiterate.

Schools in today's society are often confronted with negative attitudes toward the use of Spanish in the classroom. The misunderstandings regarding its value, not only to the students' personal development, but also to the strength of second language fluency and literacy, are everywhere. To add to this difficulty is the criticism that non-standard Spanish or barrio Spanish is not acceptable. The arguments relative to the standard forms of Spanish or of English will continue to be heard and will generate more heat than light on the issues. In the discussion of the literacy needs of Spanish-speaking students in these pages, the term Hispanic students has been used to describe in a general way the students for whom a program of first language fluency and literacy in Spanish has been recommended. There has been no intention to suggest that all Spanish speakers using the many variations of Spanish as spoken by particular groups can be placed in a single category. The specific language usage of the students enrolled in school should be thoughtfully analyzed for its system of sounds, structures, vocabulary, and meaning. Wherever the students begin in Spanish that may be considered standard or not, ultimately the instructional program must lead them to competence in standard written English. The political, economic, or social controversies have not been considered. The focus has been limited to **learning to read** and has promoted the notion that Hispanic students will learn to read more efficiently if they are taught the written symbols of their native Spanish first. Then, the skills of reading English become more readily and economically available to them. The viewpoint comes from learning theory, educational principles, and developmental psychology.

Opportunities to learn in a school where biliteracy and bilinguality are encouraged offer students the gift of two languages. They grow, develop, and learn in an environment that does not denigrate themselves or their families. They keep intact their cultural heritage and their sense of identity. They acquire English fluency and learn to use written English. These abilities to understand, speak, read, and write in Spanish and in English enhance their relationships at home, in the community, and at school. They have the potential for becoming, as adults, productive workers in government, business, education, or industry. They will have the resources to care for their families and to contribute to their communities. They are social and political assets to the nation. Contrast this outcome with present-day data that reveal the highest rates of illiteracy in English-speaking countries where Hispanic students are stripped of their written language and maimed by an illogical instructional program.

Excellence in English is made possible for Hispanic students in a program of instruction that recognizes the value of Spanish in the unfolding of the students' intellectual power. Learning how to read is perceived as a developmental task, one part of the total growth of human beings everywhere. The task involves non-cognitive skills, thinking skills, sensory-motor processes, and transfer of learning. The symbiotic relationships between oral and written language in the receptive and expressive dimensions of language are appreciated and followed in arranging the instructional sequence. Students acquire and learn the linguistic code that opens the doors to knowledge in subject matter and continue to achieve academically. While the Spanish fluency and literacy skills are expanded and practiced, the students are receiving strong, appropriate teaching in **oral** English until the criteria for transfer to written English are met. These ingredients — fluent Spanish, good Spanish reading skills, knowledge of content areas, and **oral** English — are the essentials for successful transfer.

The Apparently English-Dominant Students

In many schools where English is the language of instruction, there are students of Hispanic heritage who appear to use more English than Spanish and who are generally described by their teachers as fluent English speakers. These students are rarely viewed as students in need of an adjusted reading curriculum. Ordinarily, they are thrust into the English materials and activities along with their native English-speaking classmates. A few of them make good progress, but many of them are found in the low reading groups, in the remedial programs, or in the classes for underachievers. Planning an appropriate program of reading instruction is especially difficult because they appear overtly to be English speakers. A number of these students need the opportunity to develop the language of the home, just as the more obviously Spanish-speaking student does. Some of the questions regarding these students are: Who are they? How can they be identified? What are their strengths? What are their needs? How can their language and literacy skills be improved?

The discovery of the language background is of utmost importance because although these students use English and appear to fit comfortably in the school environment, they may still be using Spanish as their inner language as they process information. Such students may be identified by careful observation by the teacher, by language dominance tests, and by an examination of the family life variables in the home. Teachers may be relatively certain that students whose **mothers** speak Spanish in the family are organizing their reality in Spanish. Their strengths may be noted in the fact that they have acquired sufficient English to get by socially. They usually have a good understanding of the dominant English culture and are very aware of the essential roles and expectations of the school personnel. They are generally able to establish positive peer relationships and to participate fully in play, in sports, and in many of the activities that are not demanding academically.

The needs of these students are in many respects like the needs of all students. They need extended opportunities in all dimensions of language. They must improve their literacy skills through appropriate instruction in reading, writing, and spelling. They are desperately in need of more reasonable access to the content areas in order to raise their achievement levels. These students need a great deal of encouragement for their efforts and aspirations. Their surface control of English may have misled teachers and may have caused an overestimation of their English language competence.

English-dominant students of Spanish heritage may not be truly proficient at a depth required to manage the traditional reading program in English. Suitable instruction for these students may need to include opportunities for the stimulation of their native Spanish, activities for the appreciation of their cultural legacy, and direct lessons in reading Spanish. They also will need a strong oral English language program and systematic teaching in written English. They could benefit from modified materials, both oral and written, in subject matter. Above all, they need time and patience to develop the fluency and literacy demanded by the school. Additionally, career options and vocational choices for older students should be left open. Reading instruction for students of Hispanic families who are not doing well in the usual reading program and who are **apparently** English dominant should be considered with great caution. Some of them may indeed speak **only** English or may have far better abilities in English than they have in Spanish; but many of them, upon more careful scrutiny may have neither language adequately developed or may be found to have stronger receptivity to Spanish. The school failure rate of these students makes it critical for teachers to look very closely at the language they bring to class.

The characteristics of a plan of action for **apparently** English-dominant students are offered for consideration:

1. Identify the students and determine who are
   (a) students with two languages of importance in their daily lives
   (b) students with low levels of school achievement
   (c) students with problems in reading the English textbooks.

2. Assess the students for language functioning by
   (a) thoughtful observation of their language proficiencies
   (b) informal assessment of **both** receptive and expressive language in English and in Spanish
   (c) formal testing on measures of bilingual competence.

3. Discover their strengths by looking at the extent to which
   (a) students have sufficient oral English acquisition to get along socially and academically
   (b) students have adequate knowledge of the dominant culture
   (c) students have formed friendships and positive peer relationships with English-speaking peers.

4. Determine their instructional needs by making certain that the teachers have considered
   (a) curriculum adaptations to ensure improved oral language development generally
   (b) reading and writing assignments that promote better literacy skills
   (c) access to subject matter course content through reasonable modifications
   (d) encouragement for their personal goals and aspirations.

5. Plan the language and literacy instruction to the extent possible and to the fullest as resources permit to accomplish
   (a) the enhancement of oral Spanish
   (b) the knowledge of Hispanic culture

(c) the acquisition of written skills in Spanish
(d) the teaching of oral English, possibly as a second language
(e) the development of stronger skills in reading and writing English
(f) the highest achievement in content areas
(g) the encouragement of many vocational and career options
(h) the support for self-confidence and self-esteem.

Some of the students who **seem** to be English dominant may benefit from these modifications of their language and literacy instruction. Since their success rate has been poor in a program designed for native speakers of English, the changes are not likely to make things worse for them and may ultimately result in significant improvement.

The Last Word

This book has been written for teachers who are charged with the awesome responsibility of teaching Hispanic students to read English. The case has been made for an introduction to English print through fluency and literacy in Spanish. No attempt has been made to address **all** the complex issues involved in such a proposal. This book is **not** a thorough review of the research on second language learning. It is **not** a comprehensive study on the comparative phonologies or structures of English and Spanish. Neither has it been a book on English-as-a-second-language methodology and materials. The socio-cultural elements of reading have only been mentioned, but **not** considered in depth. **Not all** Spanish language transfers — positive, negative, and zero — have been included. To have written about these very significant areas would have created a work too lengthy and one of doubtful usefulness to classroom teachers. The intent has been to present the major constructs relative to second language reading in English and to identify the reading skills of Spanish that can be transferred to English reading. For teachers who are teaching reading in Spanish, there have been included some practical considerations of the scope and sequence of skills in Spanish. For their English-speaking colleagues, the transferability of language general and language specific skills has been identified. For **all** teachers in **any** reading program designed to bring Hispanic students to literacy, the purpose for writing this book has been to create a deeper awareness of the language and reading needs of these students, and to wish teachers well in their valiant efforts.

References

1. Cummins, James. "Linguistic Interdependence and the Educational Development of Bilingual Children." **Bilingual Education Paper Series.** Vol. 3, No.2. Los Angeles, California: National Dissemination and Assessment Center, California State University, September, 1979.

2. Cummins, James. "The Exit and Entry Fallacy in Bilingual Education." **NABE Journal, IV.** 1980, 25-60.

3. Cummins James. "The Role of Primary Language Development in Promoting Educational Success for Language Minority Students," **Schooling and Language Minority Students: A Theoretical Framework.** Los Angeles, California: Evaluation, Dissemination and Assessment Center, California State University, 1981.

4. Downing, John. "Strategies of Bilingual Teaching," **International Review of Education, XXIV.** No.3., 1978, 329-346.

5. Dulay, Heidi C., and Marina K. Burt. "From Research to Method in Bilingual Education," **International Dimensions of Bilingual Education.** Ed., James E. Alatis. Washington, D.C: Georgetown University Press, 1978.

6. Garcia, E. "Bilingualism and Schooling Environments," **NABE Journal, IV.** Fall, 1979.

7. Genesse, Fred. "Acquisition of Reading Skills in Immersion Programs," **Foreign Language Annals, XII.** No. 1, February, 1979, 71-77.

8. Kaminsky, S. "Predicting Oral Language Sequences and Acquisition: A Study of First Grade Bilingual Children," Paper presented at the **Annual Meeting of the American Education Research Association.** New York, 1977.

9. Krashen, Stephen D. "Bilingual Education and Second Language Acquisition Theory," **Schooling and Language Minority Students: A Theoretical Framework.** Los Angeles, California: Evaluation, Dissemination and Assessment Center, California State University, Los Angeles, 1981.

10. Krashen, Stephen D. "Formal and Informal Linguistic Environments in Language Acquisition and Language Learning," **TESOL Quarterly, X.** No. 2, June, 1976, 157-168.

11. Krashen, Stephen D. "The Monitor Model for Second Language Acquisition," **Second Language Acquisition & Foreign Language Teaching,** Ed., Rosario C. Gringas. Arlington, Virginia: Center for Applied Linguistics, 1978, 1-26.

12. Lambert, Wallace E. "Some Cognitive and Sociocultural Consequences of Being Bilingual," **International Dimensions of Bilingual Education.** Ed., James E. Alatis. Washington, D.C: Georgetown University Press, 1978.

13. Lapkin, Sharon, Christine M. Andrew, Brigit Harley, and Jill Kamid. "A Study of the Relationship Between School Environment and Achievement in a French Immersion Program," **Immersion Centre and the Dual-Track School.** Ontario, Canada: Ontario Institute of Studies in Education, 1979.

14. Legarreta, Dorothy. "The Effects of Program Models on Language Acquisition by Spanish Speaking Children," **TESOL Quarterly.** XIII, No. 4, December, 1979.

15. Merino, Barbara, Robert L. Politzer, and Arnulfo G. Ramirez. "The Relationship of Teachers' Spanish Proficiency to Pupils' Achievement," **NABE Journal, III** Winter, 1979.

16. Ramirez, Arnulfo G., and Robert L. Politzer. "The Acquisition of English and the the Maintenance of Spanish in a Bilingual Education Program," **TESOL Quarterly, IX.** No. 2, June, 1975, 113-124.

17. Saville-Troike, Muriel. "Implications of Research on Adult Second-Language Acquisition for Teaching Foreign Languages to Children," **Second Language Acquisition & Foreign Language Teaching.** Ed., Rosario C. Gringas. Arlington, Virginia: Center for Applied Linguistics, 1978, 68-77.

18. Skutnabb-Kangas, Tove, and Pertti Toukomaa. **Teaching Migrant Children's Mother Tongue and Learning the Language of the Host Country in the Context of the Socio-Cultural Situation of the Migrant Family.** Helsinki, Finland: The Finnish National Commission for UNESCO, 1976.

19. Swain, Merril. "Bilingual Education: Research and Its Implications," **On TESOL 1979: The Learner in Focus.** Eds., C. Yorio, K. Perkins, and J. Schacter. Washington, D.C: Teachers of English to Speakers of Other Languages, 1979.

20. Terrell, Tracy D. "A Natural Approach to Second Language Acquisition and Learning," **The Modern Language Journal.** LXI, No. 7. November, 1977, 325-337.

21. Wells, Gordon. "Describing Children's Linguistic Development at Home and at School," **British Educational Research Journal.** V., 1979, 75-89.

OTHER RECOMMENDED REFERENCES

Materials for Students

A Guide to Young People's Books in Spanish. New York:: Behe Bilingual Publications Company, 1982.
Annotated bibliography of books in Spanish for children and young adults.

Diccionario Santillana. Madrid: Santillana S.A., 1975.
A comprehensive dictionary useful for students in the middle grades through high school.

El informador escolar. San Diego, CA: Fiesta Publishing Company, Inc., 1983.
Student newspapers in two reading levels for English and four reading levels for Spanish.

Las claves del kinder. Oklahoma City: The Economy Company, 1983.
A program of prereading activities and oral language development in Spanish.

Lectura en dos idiomas. Northvale, NJ: Santillana Publishing Company, Inc.
Reading in two languages, Spanish and English, designed for kindergarten through fifth grade.

Lenguaje. Madrid: Santillana S.A., 1976.
A series of five books in Spanish that comprise a complete language arts program covering grammar, oral and written expression, and reading. **Guías didacticas** provide information and direction for the teachers.

Mexico, visto por sus niños. Washington, DC: The National Foundation for the Improvement of Education, 1981.
Two volumes, one in English and one in Spanish, presenting the children's perspectives of their experiences.

Mi casa, tu casa. Hollywood, CA: Cameron McKay Productions, 1982.
A program of sound-symbol association, listening skills, and oral language in Spanish.

Santa Cruz Reading In Spanish. South Pasadena, CA: Bilingual Educational Services, Inc., 1981.
A program in reading in Spanish for kindergarten through grade three complete with teacher training systems.

274

Senda libro de lectura. Madrid: Santillana S.A., 1971.
A series of five books in Spanish containing selections in prose and poetry from the universal literature of childhood.

Spanish Roll. Dallas: Melton Peninsula, Inc.
A system of teaching reading and writing in Spanish for K-3 pupils.

Additional Readings for Teachers

Brown, Roger. **A First Language: The Early Stages.** Cambridge, Massachusetts: Harvard University Press, 1973.

Cazden, Courtney B. **Child Language and Education.** New York: Holt, Rinehart and Winston, Inc., 1972.

Diller, Karl Conrad. **The Language Teaching Controversy.** Rowley, Massachusetts: Newbury House Publishers, 1978.

Mackey, William F. and Theodore Anderson (eds.). **Bilingualism in Early Childhood,** Rowley, Massachusetts: Newbury House Publishers, 1977.

Northwest Regional Education Laboratory. **Assessment Instruments in Bilingual Education.** Los Angeles: National Dissemination and Assessment Center. California State University, 1978.

Ramirez, Manuel and Alfredo Castañeda. **Cultural Democracy, Bicognitive Development and Education.** New York: Academic Press, 1974.

APPENDIX

APPROPRIATE INSTRUCTION FOR HISPANIC STUDENTS
CURRICULUM FRAMEWORK AND TIME LINE

	Pre-School	Kinder-Garten	Grade 1	Grade 2	Grade 3	Grade 4	Grade 5	Junior High 6-7-8	High School Yrs. 1-2-3-4
1. Experiences:	Encounters with the environment through first-hand and vicarious experiences mediated by Spanish		Mediated by Spanish and/or English						
2. Oral Spanish	Sound system								
	Structural complexities								
	Vocabulary development								
	Semantics								
3. Written Spanish	Pre-Readiness	Readiness	Introductory Program		Basic Skills Developed	Specialized Skills		Critical Reading / Literary Appreciation	
4. Oral English	Sounds Structures								
	Vocabulary Semantics								
	English								
5. Written English	Readiness	Readiness	Readiness		Introductory Basic Skills	Specialized Reading Skills		Critical Reading / Literary Appreciation	
			Mediated by Oral English						
			Mediated by written English modified as needed						
6. Fields of Knowledge	Mediated by Oral Spanish		Written Spanish						
	Varies with individual students to the extent resources and community resources are available.								

Time Line (Continued)

1. Experiences
Encounters with one's environment continue throughout the school years from preschool through high school. The language which accompanies such encounters and helps to make them comprehensible may be gradually expanded from Spanish to English until full use of both languages is accomplished.

2. Oral Spanish
The sounds of Spanish should be well controlled by the end of the second grade or earlier for normal children.

The simple structures are generally internalized during the primary years. More complex use of language structures continues through the grades.

Vocabulary and meaning systems are lifetime learnings and remain part of the curriculum.

3. Written Spanish
Skills in reading, writing, and spelling proceed as improved abilities and increased maturity permit.

4. Oral English
The sound system of English may need informal and formal teaching and practice through the middle grades. Teachers would be wise to avoid over-emphasis on **"perfect"** reproduction of English sounds. Structures in English will continue to receive attention in the curriculum as more English language opportunities are provided.

Vocabulary and Semantics in English continue for life.

5. Written English
The readiness period should be a time for informal oral language growth.

Basic reading skills in English are introduced when criteria for **formal** reading are met. The specialized reading skills, critical reading, and literary appreciation become a matter of skill transfer.

6. Field of Knowledge
Subject area content is made available and comprehensible by means of stronger language and best modality (listening, speaking, reading, writing). As students develop in age and maturity, their increased abilities and skills allow them more varied access to the fields of knowledge.

DESIGN FOR DECISION: **THE ROYAL ROAD TO READING**

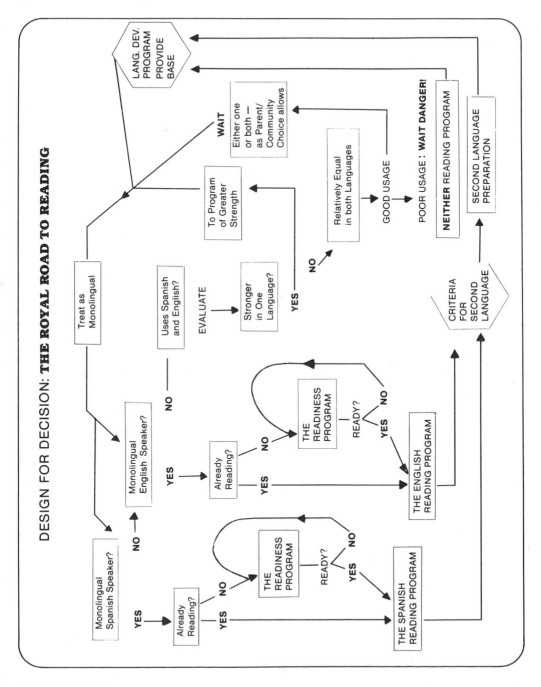

APPENDIX C

*CRITERIA FOR SELECTING MATERIALS

Name _____ Publisher _____

Type of Material
(Workbook, Textbook, Library Book, Other) _____

Grade Level _____ Evaluator _____

	Yes	No	Non-related
1. Teacher competencies			
a. Do the materials demand a high degree of teacher competency?	_____	_____	_____
b. Do the materials require language proficiency in the language of the learner?	_____	_____	_____
c. Do the materials lend themselves to good use by inexperienced as well as experienced teachers?	_____	_____	_____
d. Are the materials suitable for use by teachers who have varied teaching styles and temperaments?	_____	_____	_____
2. Objectives of the instructional program			
a. Are the materials consistent with the natural order of language learning?	_____	_____	_____
b. Do activities proceed from listening comprehension and speaking fluency to reading and writing?	_____	_____	_____
c. Are the materials organized in a speech- to- print direction that provides for oral language development sufficient to support written language?	_____	_____	_____

*Adaptation from **Teaching Reading to Non-English Speakers.** Eleanor Thonis. Page 209-210, New York: Collier Macmillan International, 1970.

	Yes	No	Non-Related
d. Do the materials respect the language of the pupils, appreciate the sound and structural conflicts, and provide for the use of the native language strengths of the learner?	_____	_____	_____

3. Age of the pupils
   a. Are the materials appropriate for the age at which reading English as a second language is begun? _____ _____ _____
   b. Are the content, situation, and language suitable for the maturity of the pupils? _____ _____ _____
   c. Are the situations and stories of interest to the pupils? _____ _____ _____
   d. Are the motivational possibilities of the materials realistic? _____ _____ _____

4. Time available for use
   a. Are the classroom realities of time considered in the skills development? _____ _____ _____
   b. Is use of teacher time efficient and economical? _____ _____ _____
   c. Is pupil time demanded on a uniform or individual basis? _____ _____ _____
   d. May pupils adjust time allowances without too much difficulty in managing the materials? _____ _____ _____

5. Provision for individual learners
   a. Do materials provide for differential aptitudes of pupils, (intelligence, experience, maturity, health, resistance to fatigue, etc.)? _____ _____ _____
   b. Are there materials that will interest both boys and girls? _____ _____ _____

	Yes	No	Non-related

c. Do the materials offer practice as needed for slow and fast learners?

d. Can the materials accommodate visual, auditory, and kinesthetic styles of learning?

e. Are special strengths and weaknesses in reading skills provided for?

6. Articulation status
   a. Do the materials offer sequential and orderly progression through the grades within an individual school program?
   b. Do the materials provide background for reading at higher levels of instruction?
   c. Do the skills build the basic and specialized abilities necessary to deal with subject matter in the content areas?
   d. Are the materials generally consistent with those used in other programs within the geographic region or nation?

7. Services available to assist teachers
   a. Does the school or district provide consultants to help teachers use materials well?
   b. Are there resource teachers and supervisors inthe schools for immediate services when needed?
   c. Do the commercial publishing houses offer assistance jn implementing programs with the materials?

	Yes	No	Non-Related
d. Are there workshops, institutes, and continuing education programs in which teachers may receive additional training in the use of the materials?	_____	_____	_____
e. Are college and university resources available to assist in research and evaluation of programs in which the materials are to be used?	_____	_____	_____
8. Ease of handling and attractiveness	_____	_____	_____
a. Are there relevant and effective charts, filmstrips, flashcards, pictures and other instructional materials available to support the basic program?			
b. Are the aids readily accessible, easy to use, and interesting to the pupils?	_____	_____	_____
9. Cultural content			
a. Is the content of these materials culturally authentic?	_____	_____	_____
b. Are the people, events, and situations portrayed in a fair, factual manner free from stereotyping?	_____	_____	_____
c. Do the materials promote an appreciation of the richness of cultural diversity?	_____	_____	_____

APPENDIX D: GRAPH FOR ESTIMATING READABILITY — EXTENDED

by Edward Fry, Rutgers University Reading Center, New Brunswick, N.J. 08904

Average number of syllables per 100 words

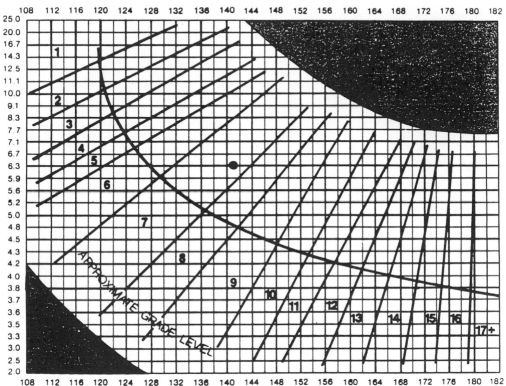

DIRECTIONS: Randomly select 3 one hundred word passages from a book or an article. Plot average number of syllables and average number of sentences per 100 words on graph to determine the grade level of the material. Choose more passages per book if great variability is observed and conclude that the book has uneven readability. Few books will fall in gray area but when they do grade level scores are invalid.

Count proper nouns, numerals and initializations as words. Count a syllable for each symbol. For example, "1945" is 1 word and 4 syllables and "IRA" is 1 word and 3 syllables.

EXAMPLE:		SYLLABLES	SENTENCES
	1st Hundred Words	124	6.6
	2nd Hundred Words	141	5.5
	3rd Hundred Words	158	6.8
	AVERAGE	141	6.3

READABILITY 7th GRADE (see dot plotted on graph)

For further information and validity data see the Journal of Reading, December 1977.

REPRODUCTION PERMITTED — NO COPYRIGHT

APPENDIX E: TEST OF SOUND-SYMBOL CONNECTIONS

In order for the teacher to be certain that pupils have achieved mastery of the sound-symbol relationships, it is prudent to check pupil progress at appropriate intervals. It is important to provide extra practice and additional review for pupils who do not meet acceptable standards of performance at any given check point. Sample activities for evaluating progress follow:

General directions:
The **pruebas** consist of dictation, matching capital and lower case forms, writing letters to represent sounds, recognizing sounds, and the formation of syllables. Teachers should give the directions carefully and offer a sample item or two so that the students understand fully what is expected of them. Words given for dictation should be pronounced naturally and presented twice. Five seconds may be allowed for students to respond after each item.

For **el dictado,** it is helpful for the teacher to explain as follows:
> Niños, me hacen el favor de escucharme bién — **aguja** la palabra **aguja** empieza con **el sonido /a/.** ¿Quién puede decirme **la letra** que representa este sonido **/a/?**

Elicit the responses from students and then **write** the letter on the blackboard **A, a.** Say the word again, stress the beginning sound, and point to the letter as it is stressed — **a - gu - ja.** Give other examples as needed. Check for questions and explain that the students are to write the **letter** that represents the beginning sound in each of the words given.
¿Listos?

Sample word lists for each dictation exercise are given below.

Vowels	M, P, B, V	T, D, G	C, Qu, G, Gu	L, R
avión	manzana	toro	casa	luna
escoba	pato	dulce	queso	reloj
iglesia	boca	fuego	gallo	lápiz
ocho	vela	dedo	gusano	regalo
uña	papel	tomate	cama	rey
anillo	mano	falda	gallina	libro
energía	burro	tambor	quijada	rama
imán	vaca	dientes	carne	limón
oro	montaña	fiesta	gorro	rosa
uniforme		taza	cabeza	lunes

S, Z, Ce, Ci	CH	N, J, Ge, Gi	Ll, Y	H, Hie, Hue
seis	chocolate	nueve	llave	hierba
zapato	chimenea	jarra	yema	huerta
cerco	chaleco	gemelos	llanta	hueso
cinco	chicle	girasol	yarda	hielo
zarpa	chuleta	nubes	lluvia	huellas
sol	chile	jabón	yunque	hiena
cesta	chal	geranio	llamas	hiedra
cine	chaqueta	gigante	yugo	huevo
zorro		nariz	llave	hombre
seis		jamón	yegua	

Juntar la forma mayúscula con la forma minúscula.

Explain that the forms should be matched by drawing a line to connect upper and lower case forms. For example:

Dibujen una línea entre las formas correctas.

A	e
E	u
I	a
O	o
U	i

As the letters are learned, the matching of capital and lower case forms may be presented.

Matching pictures and the letters representing the initial sounds.

Escriban las letras que representen los sonidos iniciales.

Note: If the students are not certain what the drawings represent, tell them about them.

El dictado y las sílabas.

Initial syllables may be explained and written from dictation in the same manner as consonant and/or vowel sounds were presented. They may first be tested in isolation and then by pictures representing whole words.

Escriban la sílaba inicial.

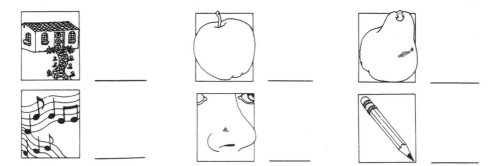

Las consonantes en combinación

Give the word for the picture and have the students write the blend.

Los diptongos
Give the word for the picture and have the students write the diphthong.

canar___

inv__rno

palac___

__r__na

d__z

ab__la

lluv___

Glor___

p__rco

rad___

igles___

ag__

h__vos

b__lar

Las terminaciones
The **word endings** may be tested when the students have had sufficient experience in hearing and seeing these sound-symbol connections.

Give the word for the picture and have the students write in the word ending.

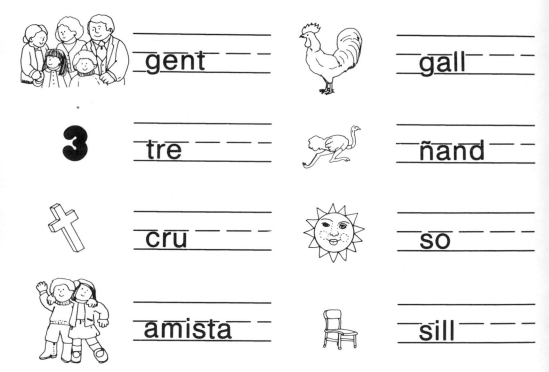

gent _____

gall _____

3 tre _____

ñand _____

cru _____

so _____

amista _____

sill _____

A dictation exercise.

1. rifle
2. abrigo
3. diploma
4. atrás
5. chicle
6. aprobado
7. regla
8. decreto
9. tabla
10. padre

11. iglesia
12. febrero
13. pueblo
14. refrigerador
15. sastre
16. cumpleaños
17. siempre
18. mezcla
19. Mazatlán
20. Alfredo

INDEX

Eleanor Wall Thonis was educated in Boston, Massachusetts. She holds an Ed.M. from Boston University and a Ph.D. from Stanford University. Her major areas of study were in childhood education, Spanish language and educational psychology. Presently Dr. Thonis serves as District Psychologist in the Wheatland, California Schools, Consultant in bilingual education for the Marysville, California Schools, and part-time lecturer for the University of California, Davis.

Among her previously published works are *Teaching Reading to Non-English Speakers, Literacy for America's Spanish Speaking Children,* and *Aprendamos a Leer.* Dr. Thonis is one of the contributors to the State of California document entitled *Schooling for Language Minority Students: A Theoretical Framework.*

REMOVED FROM THE
MANKATO COLLEGE LIBRARY

REMOVED FROM THE
MANKATO COLLEGE LIBRARY

REMOVED FROM THE
MANKATO COLLEGE LIBRARY